The Importance of Work in
an Age of Uncertainty

The Importance of Work in an Age of Uncertainty

The Eroding Work Experience in America

DAVID L. BLUSTEIN

OXFORD
UNIVERSITY PRESS

OXFORD
UNIVERSITY PRESS

Oxford University Press is a department of the University of Oxford. It furthers
the University's objective of excellence in research, scholarship, and education
by publishing worldwide. Oxford is a registered trade mark of Oxford University
Press in the UK and certain other countries.

Published in the United States of America by Oxford University Press
198 Madison Avenue, New York, NY 10016, United States of America.

Library of Congress Cataloging-in-Publication Data
Names: Blustein, David Larry, author.
Title: The importance of work in an age of uncertainty : the eroding work
experience in America / by David L. Blustein.
Description: New York : Oxford University Press, [2019]
Identifiers: LCCN 2018061146 | ISBN 9780190213701 (hardcover : alk. paper)
Subjects: LCSH: Work—Psychological aspects. | Uncertainty.
Classification: LCC BF481 .B567 2019 | DDC 158.7—dc23
LC record available at https://lccn.loc.gov/2018061146

1 3 5 7 9 8 6 4 2

Printed by Sheridan Books, Inc., United States of America

Contents

Preface

The story of work in people's lives is invariably complex and very personal. To frame this book, which has consumed so much of my life in the past 5 years, I begin with a personal story of how I found myself again in my own work—completing a significant portion of the first draft of this book during the summer and fall of 2017. The summer of 2017 will be noted for many events and transitions in the United States, and indeed the world, as political winds shifted in ways that could not have been predicted even a year or two ago. To complement my experience of the darkness of the political situation in the United States, I also faced a major personal crisis during this period. My brother, Richard (known as Rich) Blustein, passed away at the age of 66 after a courageous 8-year battle with multiple myeloma, a very insidious blood cancer. I was very close to my brother: We shared a room throughout our childhood in a small apartment in Queens, New York; more than that, we shared many aspects of our lives. We were very different in all of the ways that siblings differ, but something visceral drew us together. This loss threw me into a period of grief that I had never experienced before, even after losing my parents in 2008, eight months apart. Interestingly, this context sets the stage perfectly for this book that has consumed so much of my life in the past few years.

During this particular summer, I decided to heed one of my brother's deathbed wishes for me: to reduce my stress and to cut back on work. I took this advice seriously, especially as he recounted how quick the endgame of life was for him. As a result, during the summer of 2017, I had more time to reflect, introspect, walk, and write. In a sense, the death of my brother resulted in me losing my direction and purpose as well as a bit of my confidence. It is hard to describe this sort of grief; indeed, other authors (some of whose work I read during the summer of 2017, including the masterpiece on grief by Joan Didion, *The Year of Magical Thinking*)[1] have done a wonderful job in describing this feeling of being so untethered to oneself and to the world. In this process of exploring myself so deeply, from such a dark place, I found myself gravitating to two particular places in my life: one a physical location and the other a more experiential space that was inhabited by meaningful work.

The physical place for healing is a small reservoir in Lexington, Massachusetts (where I live), which I pass in my nearly daily walks every morning, often with my wife and at times by myself. At this reservoir, which currently appears as a pond in a heavily wooded area, I would sit at the lone bench and reflect on loss and of life and on the nature of work for people, which has been a passion throughout my adult life. I was aware of my privilege in life, having an opportunity to stare at a body of water that was walking distance from our house; to live near water was a goal that my parents had in their lives, one that they could never afford. Indeed, the fact that I am able to live in such a lovely place struck me as a strange counterpoint to this book, which is about work and how hard it is for so many in our society. That I had the time and space to explore this magical spot certainly underscored how far I had come, starting out as the youngest son of a sheet metal mechanic and department store clerk, loving parents who did not have more than a few hundred dollars in the bank for the first few decades of their marriage.

Staring at this pond and thinking about my brother evoked in me vivid memories of growing up in the various small apartments and homes that we lived in during the 1950s and 1960s (including a house without air conditioning in southern Florida in the late 1950s) as my father struggled to find his foothold in the world of work. My parents were hard-working people who were thankful for any opportunity they had to make a living in a decent and dignified way. They rarely complained about their circumstances and always looked forward to advancing the lives of their two sons. Watching their family and friends struggle so much in making a living shaped me profoundly and inspired me to devote my life to understanding work and to advocating for opportunity for all. This book is one of the outcomes of my lifelong hope to improve the work lives of people.

The pond in Lexington provided me with healing and with a return to my more hopeful and forward-looking self. Walking from the pond to my home was more challenging. How could I go back to my traditional work life of preparing lectures, answering emails, and reviewing students' research papers while immersed in so much grief? How could I honor my brother's memory and the legacy of my parents and their working-class peers? Somehow, the answer seemed clear to me: I felt a calling to immerse myself in writing this book, with sense of purpose and direction that reconnected me to my more hopeful and optimistic self.

By reducing my traditional obligations as a professor (which was also a function of the summer) and by responding to my brother's wishes for me to slow down, I now had space to really think and be with this book. What felt comforting to me during this period was writing, not just writing in general, but writing something meaningful that I hope will help to transform how work is understood in our society. I therefore made a deep dive into this book, writing more than 100 pages in less than 2 months, completing nearly one third of the text. Connecting to the stories shared by the 58 people we interviewed left me humbled, moved, and inspired to do something for them and for all of those that they represent. Their stories were filled with pain, pathos, and poignant insights into the nature of work during this period of uncertainty. The writing space actually ended up as one of the key ways that I journeyed back from a dark and frightening experience of overwhelming grief.

I realized as well during this particular summer that having a project that felt important and that captured my passion was healing in a way that few other activities could be. Having an opportunity to give voice to my own passion about work and psychology was deeply purposeful. More than that, the act of writing took me back to my own personal roots and connected me to the memory of my brother, whose work life was hard in ways that I was able to avoid.* However, the contrast in my opportunity to immerse myself in this book and the more fragmented work lives that have consumed so many others in our nation (and indeed around the world) is striking and worrisome.

As I propose in this book, working, at its best, is integral to helping us to feel alive in the world. Writing and editing this book energized me much as the Lexington Reservoir soothed me. The fact that I had an opportunity to do what I wanted with the support of my employer and the buy-in of my publisher is clearly not the norm; the vast majority of people are struggling, often to sustain themselves in survival mode. My transition from a family whose work life was governed by the need for survival to my current life in which my work provides not only financial stability and meaning but also solace in the face of unspeakable grief is a powerful story. It is the move that so many in the United States hope to make, ranging from immigrants crossing the border to escape poverty and violence to American citizens whose families have been wracked by intergenerational poverty. That I made this transition, with enormous help from my family, teachers, mentors, and community, certainly is a privilege that never eludes me.

However, I am very much aware, through my work as a therapist and researcher in this field for over three decades, that working for far too many people is a struggle, often becoming one of the most challenging parts of life. In this book, I explore a full range of psychological experiences of working, encompassing the pain that many experience in sustaining themselves in a harsh labor market as well as the sense of purpose, and even comfort, that I experienced during the summer and fall of 2017. The vast continuum between these poles of experience is the terrain that I seek to bring to life in the pages that follow.

---

* My brother had a challenging life at work for much of his life. In fact, he graciously agreed to be interviewed for this book, and his very moving impressions about work are sprinkled throughout this book. At my brother's request, I have used his actual first name throughout the book.

Why This Book, and Why Now?

Working is the thread that connects many of our social ties, our economic relationships, and our shared commitment to a just and caring community. Working provides access to the social and economic worlds, offering opportunities for satisfaction and success as well as despair and frustration. At its best, working can provide a firm foundation for people to connect to their better selves, find meaning in their lives, and create a life of purpose, contribution, and accomplishment. However, work does not always go well for many people. While there have always been people who have struggled on the margins of the labor market, the proportion of people in the United States who feel insecure about work and who are working in jobs that are temporary, unstable, or lacking in the core components of decency and dignity is growing.[2]

To explore this vast terrain, I review some of the latest findings from psychology and related social sciences in conjunction with the voices of people from the diverse narratives culled from the Boston College Working Project. The vignettes, which are derived from interviews that my research team and I conducted with people around the United States, were coded into major themes, consistent with the focus of each particular chapter.** The structure of the book takes shape around the core needs and dreams that working can optimally fulfill, which reflect our inherent striving to engage in the world and to be productive, creative, and connected to others. By exploring the inner experiences of people at work, people seeking work, and people transitioning in and out of work in both the marketplace and caregiving contexts, I hope to create a compelling argument about the importance of dignified and accessible work opportunities for everyone.

Working is unquestionably a central part of life. Yet, with work becoming increasingly unsteady, the moorings on which our communities stand have created worry and insecurity. On the surface, the changes naturally encompass the loss of long-term jobs and rising unemployment and underemployment. At the same time, the underpinnings of working are being transformed: Working is no longer the stable part of life that offers people a sense of grounding. Many people facing grief as I have in the final phases of writing this book or other life

---

** The scope of this book, while I hope it is relevant to many contexts across the globe, is rooted in the American context. In every aspect of my life, I seek to broaden my horizons and actively eschew a US-centric perspective. However, in the case of this book, I felt that making the focus too broad would make it difficult to develop coherent ideas and connect these ideas to broad policy implications that optimally will make a difference in a given context. I very much encourage readers from non-American contexts to read this book and reflect on the extent to which the insights and implications are relevant in their own locations. I look forward to learning about how readers across the world may adapt the insights and inferences from this book to their own lives and their work-related practices.

challenges do not have the opportunity to find themselves again in their work. Increasingly, people are less attached to organizations and work settings and are now engaged in portfolio careers or precarious work. Moreover, millions of others are locked out of the workplace by unemployment, disabilities, and lack of opportunities. In addition, the two unequal worlds of "haves" and "have-nots" are becoming far more entrenched, with significant and daunting implications for the quality of life for those without access to education, privilege, and other resources. Furthermore, the boundaries between work and family life are increasingly porous. In short, the working world of the twentieth century is long gone, and the new world of work is just beginning to take shape.[3] As these amorphous changes settle into a period of great uncertainty, people are struggling to sort out this critical aspect of life. This book provides a psychologically informed road map for readers. My hope is that hoped the stories that are told in each chapter resonate deeply, and readers will learn important new insights about how our society can support people and communities in creating fair and equitable access to work.

Audience for This Book

I have written this book with the intention of connecting with a broad readership. Optimally, this book will be of interest to readers who want to learn more about work in America from the perspective of individuals and their lived experiences; one does not need to be a scholar or policy expert to relate to this book. The infusion of a psychological perspective serves to enrich the in-depth description of how people are managing their work lives. As such, this book should be relevant to readers who are interested in the psychology of their own work lives as well as the work lives of their communities. Readers who are thinking about the broad challenges that our nation and globe face with respect to growing inequality and the challenges of rapidly evolving changes in the world of work will connect deeply to this book.

I also wrote the book in a way that will be relevant to social scientists, psychologists, economists, organizational psychologists and consultants, policy analysts, and other scholars and leaders who are interested in learning about the complex and nuanced ways that people are managing their work lives. In addition, students and academics may find the book useful for undergraduate and graduate classes on work, vocational psychology, career development, organizational studies, management, and occupational sociology. I am hoping that this book will be a resource that clearly makes a case for including all of those who work and who want to work in the deliberations about work. I have cast a broad net in this effort, and I hope that the inclusiveness of my mission foreshadows a diverse readership who will join in creating decent and dignified work in our nation.

My Vantage Point

This book is about work, but unlike other books about work, it takes a different stance and makes a stand. The stance that I adopt here reflects an openness to knowledge that does not overly privilege either the voices of scholars or the voices of individuals experiencing a given situation or crisis; both perspectives are treated as viable sources of knowledge. I view different streams of knowledge as complementary, creating a whole that is greater than the sum of its parts. In this book, I take the stand that working is essential for life and essential for the welfare of our society. Employment, unemployment, work stress, harassment at work—these are all ultimately human experiences that are deeply felt. I argue in this book that any debates about labor and employment policies need to incorporate the insights of those who work and who are striving to work as well as relevant literature on the psychological impact of work in people's lives. Throughout this contribution, I seek to create a picture of working that conveys its complexity, richness, and capacity for both joy and despair.

Working, at its core, has been and continues to be about ensuring our survival: sustaining our existence. Moreover, working is one of the strongest threads connecting us across the eons and connecting us across cultures. With all of the differences among communities and people, threads of continuity are important to note. Working is ubiquitous; it is part of what keeps us alive and connected to each other. Yet, the actual experience of working is not well understood, leaving people without the language and foundation to fully grasp what working means. Much of the research that informs public policies about work and labor issues comes from economics, which tends to view people in aggregate. Of course, this is important, but it is not sufficient, especially during this era of such radical changes in the world of work.

A psychological perspective has the potential to enrich discussions about working in a number of important ways. In contrast to the "managerial" focus of much of the recent literature, which has primarily emphasized the lives of professionals and managers, I have sought input from an inclusive array of people in the United States who have volunteered to be part of this project, including many people who were unemployed and underemployed as well as those who were working in trades and service occupations. In addition, we have interviewed a few people at the top of the career ladder. The questions that comprised the interview protocol included such issues as the participants' stories of their work histories, their relationships and family lives, their hopes and dreams, their perspectives on the American dream, their sources of frustration and joy in relation to their work lives, and their recommendations for the creation and sustenance of dignified work in the United States.*** The contrasts conveyed in the narratives of those with a relative degree of choice in how they choose to work in comparison to those who are struggling in their working lives speak volumes about the impact of growing inequity. Indeed, as shown in the chapters that follow, the story of working in the United States is really multiple stories, with very different trajectories and outcomes.

At the conclusion of this book, readers will have gained a powerful and emotionally evocative connection to the rich tapestry of life that revolves around and within work. The emotional insights complement the conclusions of the best science and policy analyses on working, culminating in a powerful call for policies that attend to the real lives of individuals in twenty-first century America: In short, the book's underlying message is a clarion call for work as a human birthright.

Approaching the Psychological Experience of Working: Methods and Assumptions

This book seeks to introduce new ideas and concepts to our psychological understanding of working in the United States as well as to present some of the most notable findings that have been obtained over the past century of research on work and psychology. The structure of the book is organized via my initial impressions of the various ways that work can function to enhance our sense of being fully alive in the world. The notion of aliveness, for me, reflects the sense of being engaged and meaningfully connected to tasks, people, communities, and the overall social fabric of life. Taken as a whole, this book fleshes out the notion of being fully alive by exploring the various ways in which we derive satisfaction, joy, meaning, and sustenance at work. (Naturally, many other aspects of life also furnish us with a sense of being alive, such as loving relationships, family, leisure activities, sports, the arts, as well as many other life spaces and opportunities.) The dimensions in which work can foster a feeling of aliveness form the chapters for the book. These dimensions have been suggested by previous research and theory in the psychological study of working as well as my own experiences as a therapist, researcher, and professor.[4]

The qualitative methods that we used in this project are based on an adaptation of narrative inquiry with a strong infusion of content analysis to guide

---

*** Readers who are interested in reviewing the interview questions can request them by writing to me directly at the following email address: David.Blustein@bc.edu.

the analysis of the interviews.[5] In brief, the narrative aspect of this approach was based on the use of an interpretive stance in deriving meaning from the participants' interviews and on the notion that people's interviews provided a map of their life histories, current experience, and future aspirations. The interpretative stance and the focus on life stories fit well with the narrative inquiry methodology, which provides an opportunity not only to report what people have shared but also to embed their impressions into a meaning-making framework. The meaning-making framework is reflected by integrating observations among the participants and exploring the broader themes that emerge in light of existing research and theory. Moreover, the interpretive framework involves interactions between the researchers and the narrative material. In this context, the research team and I worked diligently to discuss our own biases and to understand how our positions and stances may be shaping our interpretations.

The holistic narrative inquiry approach was complemented by a content analysis, which focused on analyzing specific segments of the participants' interviews and then integrating the observations.[6] In order to identify the subthemes within each chapter, my graduate students and I devoted extensive efforts to qualitatively analyze the interviews that we obtained from the participants. First, we read each interview to get a sense of what the participants were sharing with us. Second, I instructed my research team in qualitative research methods so that they could create codes for each chapter. The result of this process was the development of passages from the participants that were categorized by each of the chapter themes, which were then coded into subthemes. A frequency count of each subtheme was also used in order to identify the prevalence of the themes. The most common themes then became the subsections for the central third of each individual chapter, which was devoted to the exploration of the narrative interviews. The use of frequencies ensured that the prevailing themes were the ones that were examined in depth, thereby reducing the potential for bias in the data analysis.

The participants were obtained via an intentional process of seeking people who would represent a broad range of people who were engaged in either seeking work or working. Members of my research team each identified people we knew or were connected to in our social networks; we then discussed each potential candidate in our team meetings to consider how their involvement might add to the richness of the interviews. As we progressed in our work, we then sought participants who represented communities that we felt were not well represented in our sample or were marginalized in the world of work as a whole. To enrich the sample with people who we were not likely to know, we interviewed people at a local One-Stop Career Center in downtown Boston, which allowed us to connect with people who were living in shelters and very much on the margins of our labor market. I also posted a notice on my LinkedIn site, which resulted in more geographic diversity as well as participants who were not well represented in our sample.

We clearly oversampled in this project in order to ensure that we would have a rich body of text to work with and to provide a broad and diverse range of narratives. One of the most common indices of the comprehensiveness of a sample in qualitative research is the notion of data saturation, which refers to the point at which the interview data no longer produce new categories and subthemes.[7] We reached data saturation in the qualitative analyses of each chapter theme and in the subthemes, which underscores our confidence in the meaningfulness of these interviews. Although we cannot state that the sample represents the broader American public, the diversity of our participants coupled with the data saturation within each of the chapter themes and subthemes affirm the richness and coherence of the interview data.

The outset of each chapter seeks to frame the content within what I call an introductory journey that provides some historical or personal frame for the material that follows. The middle third of each chapter is devoted to the presentation of vignettes and interpretive comments about the individual participants and the broader themes that emerged. The final third of each chapter is designed to introduce some cutting-edge research that complements and deepens the discussion, culminating in a conclusion that identifies concerns and ideas for our collective consideration.

I would like to highlight a few other points that I believe will respond to questions that may emerge as readers engage with this book. This book is designed to be unique and is constructed to introduce new ideas and important policy implications for work in the United States. The main goal of this project is not to tell the full story of work within psychology; that overarching literature review approach is well represented in our field by handbooks and textbooks.[8] The objective of this book is to inform a public that is hungry to know about how work is impacting people during this era of massive uncertainty and anxiety. As such, some readers who are immersed in psychology as their hobby or profession may notice that I did not include a particularly compelling line of work or set of ideas that may have relevance. This is true; this book is not designed to be exhaustive in its coverage or comprehensive. My decision about the literature to include has been based on my intention to provide readers with the necessary knowledge to evaluate and connect to the ideas that I am advancing and to join in the public debates about the future of work. I am hoping that this book will culminate in a critically educated body of citizens who will demand human rights in all aspects of their lives, including their working lives.

I also want to comment on some decisions that I made in presenting the narratives. First, I asked the participants for permission to share their stories, and I indicated that I would provide them with pseudonyms or would use their first name if they concurred with that particular option. Most of the participants elected to have me select a pseudonym. I did not guarantee that their confidentiality would be protected; as such, each participant who consented to this project knew that some aspects of their life story might be discernible by readers. That said, I have sought to ensure that any public disclosures would not unintentionally harm any of the participants.

Also, I elected to provide the racial and ethnic identity of each participant the first time that I introduce them to readers. After the first introduction, I no longer refer to the participants' background unless it is related to the issue that is being discussed. Throughout this process, I have sought to dignify each of the participants who have given so much of themselves in the hopes that their input would help to create a more just context for work.

Acknowledgments

Writing this book has been a labor of love that, as I noted at the outset of the Preface, has involved many of the best attributes of meaningful and purposeful work. As I discuss in depth further in the book, relationships form the essence of our lives—and of our work lives. This book project is a wonderful exemplar of this observation as people were the fabric and the stitches of this contribution.

I begin by thanking all of the participants who agreed to be part of this project. These individuals gave their time and wisdom and spoke from their hearts in detailed and informative interviews. These interviews individually and collectively helped me to tell this particular story and to develop the conclusions that I believe help us to find a better way to live and work in the twenty-first century. Most of the participants were strangers to me and to most members of my team. However, some were people we knew from our personal and work lives. In each case, the participants shared their honest experiences with us, helping us to understand the depth and nuance of contemporary working in America. We all owe a debt of gratitude to these wonderful spokespersons who have shared their individual experiences with us so that we can learn from their insights and life stories.

I also want to thank the many members of my research team during the past 6 years. Throughout the 6 years of research and planning on this project, the doctoral students who have elected to work with me have provided more than assistance; they contributed critical thinking and ideas during our weekly team meetings and individual conversations about this project. This group included the following Boston College students from the PhD program in counseling psychology: Ellie Gutowksi, AJ Diamonti, Chad Olle, Whitney

Erby, Lily Konowitz, Tera Meerkins, Alek Davila, Saliha Kozan, and Alice Connors-Kellgren.

I also was fortunate to have a number of master's and undergraduate students in counseling and education volunteer to work on the team. Included in this group are the following individuals, who also contributed extensively in developing the sample for the project, fine-tuning the interviews, conducting and transcribing interviews, and coding: Rachel Paciorek, Erin Kilbury, Isaac Soldz, Gabriel Nnamdi Ezema, Ava Floyd, Danielle Berado, Adam Cushner, Kristen Carnavale, Deborah Wan, Yun Lu, Talitha Collins, Tyler Delaney, Amber Morley, Julia St. Jean, Alexandria Kinder, Scott Matthews, Nai Saetern, Benjamin Tan, Patrick McMahon, Xiaozhen Lu, Ashley Kaippallil, Juan Martinez, Seth Nable, Roberto Garcia, Jae Kim, and Michele Mastropieri.

I would like to thank Oxford University Press, and particularly Abby Gross, for believing in this project and for giving me the space and time to delve deeply into the issues that have inspired me so much. I also would like thank my colleagues and friends who I have worked with and consulted with over the years about work; this list will invariably miss some important influencers, and for this omission, I apologize. Within my community of colleagues at Boston College, I very much appreciate the input and advice from Maureen Kenny, Dennis Shirley, Janet Helms, Jim Mahalik, Paul Poteat, Belle Liang, David Scanlon, Mike Barnett, Lisa Goodman, Usha Tummala-Narra, AJ Franklin, Eric Dearing, Mary Beth Medvide, Andy Hargreaves, Stanton Wortham, Jim Slotta, Henry Braun, and many others who have shared their wisdom with me over the years. Outside Boston College, I am honored to have so many colleagues and friends from across the globe who have offered their creative perspective on the role of work in people's lives, including (in no particular order) Mary Sue Richardson, Ryan Duffy, Saba Rasheed Ali, Lisa Flores, Peter McIlveen, Blake Allan, Kelsey Autin, Matt Diemer, Uma Millner, Justin Perry, Mark Savickas, Hanoch Flum, Gali Cinamon, Chris Briddick, Bob Lent, Steve Brown, Terry Tracey, Nadya Fouad, Ruth Fassinger, Sue Whiston, Rich Feller, Skip Niles, Brian Hutchinson, Paul Hartung, Annamaria Di Fabio, Jean Guichard, Violetta Podgórna, Marek Podgórny, Lori Foster, Alexander Glösenberg, Tara Behrend, Joaquim Ferreira, Eduardo Santos, Valerie Cohen-Scali, Fred Vondracek, Graham Stead, Jerome Rossier, Jonas Masdonati, and so many others who have shaped my thinking over the years.

I also would like to thank my daughters (Larissa and Michelle) and stepdaughters (Miranda, Lila, Rachel, and Zoe) for their kindness, advice, and reminders about what is important in life. In addition, we now have four grandsons who are further reminders that work includes caregiving: Ben, Milo, Shimmy, and Yitzy. I also want to affirm the wisdom of my parents, Harry and Janet Blustein, who continue to appear in my books, classes, and therapy sessions (sometimes as words of wisdom or silently as internalized caring). Thanks Mom and Dad: Even though you are no longer with us, your memory is indeed an abiding blessing to me every day.

I want to dedicate this book to two incredibly important people who have nurtured my intellect, soul, and capacity to feel for those who are struggling. My wife, Lisa Thayer, has been a gift from the angels to me—a beautiful reward, to quote Bruce Springsteen. We have had the unique luck to meet in midlife and to begin a relationship that has been transformative and inspiring. Lisa has consistently provided support and an uplifting comment when I felt discouraged and affirmed my dreams of making a difference. Observing Lisa make a difference in her pediatric practice every day, with patients and their families, many of whom have been struggling for decades to gain a foothold on the American dream, has underscored the power and beauty of work that is truly alive in every sense. Thank for you making space for me to work so hard on this project and for believing in me. Your presences is felt throughout this book.

Finally, I want to offer a second dedication to my brother, Richard Blustein, who appeared at the outset of the Preface. My brother was a participant in this project; in fact, he agreed to have his actual first name used in the book prior to his death. My brother and I had a fascinating and wonderful relationship. He found my lifelong fascination with work to be amusing because he claimed that I only had four jobs since I was 22 and he had about 100. He felt that he should have been writing books about work, which would have been a great idea, as indicated by what he shared here. My brother also believed in me in a way that was humbling and moving. As I mentioned, he struggled in his work life, whereas I was able to navigate a clear way out of a working-class life into the middle class. My brother also navigated that journey, but with more unexpected turns and twists. I dedicate this book to my brother, Rich, whose courage, heartfelt love for his family and for his community, and his unwavering commitment to a better life are evident in his family and in the broad reach of his presence.

Closing Comments

As I stated at the outset of the Preface, I have had a very wonderful opportunity to write this book; indeed, from a personal perspective, this process has served as a resource for me during a very difficult period of mourning. However, the driving motivation for this project has been to transform how we understand the nature of working from a deeply psychological perspective. In my view, the existing debates about work are almost completely devoid of any mention of individual experience: identity, purpose, meaning, joy, despair, anxiety, and the like. By telling the story of working at this point in our country's life, I am hoping to shape future conversations and debates so that people are not left out of the brainstorming or solutions. I also hope that readers will join with my students, colleagues, and me to form a community of activists who will shape the public debates about the current dilemmas at work and the future of work. The stakes are clearly very high now; optimally, this book is viewed as part of the solution in creating a more just, inclusive, and dignified working life for all.

David L. Blustein
Lexington, Massachusetts
December 2018

1

Being Alive

Work as a Central Role in Life

David, you don't look well.

It was the end of a cold, gloomy January day spent interviewing people about their work lives for this book at a One-Stop Career Center in downtown Boston, one of the many government-funded agencies across the United States for job hunters. I was a bit surprised that my face gave away my feelings so vividly. My final participant for the day had picked up on the fact that I was drained, sad, angry, and overwhelmed after listening to how people's lives had fallen apart in the shadows of the Great Recession. Even for someone like me, who helps people navigate their working lives for a living, I felt heart-broken when hearing how people's lives had fallen apart as their work options diminished or disappeared.

More than a decade after the start of the Great Recession, the news headlines have moved on, but work issues continue to dominate. For so many Americans, the nature and essence of work have changed inexorably. As a professor of counseling psychology who studies the psychology of working and who has worked as a psychotherapist and career counselor for over three decades, I have a unique perspective—and a rare glimpse into the lives of people on the front lines of the American economy. Through the Boston College Working Project, my research team and I have interviewed 58 people from all walks of life, including homeless people looking for work; people stuck in tedious jobs; people who have experienced great joy and accomplishment in their work, such as a four-star general and a member of Congress; as well as countless others who are toiling away in relative obscurity.

This is the story of work in America, as conveyed in intensive interviews that included diverse people from across the United States. The narratives from the research participants are interpreted and embedded in the rich literature on work from psychology and related fields. The goal of this book is not simply to tell the stories about the lived experience of people at work (or struggling to find work). The overarching objective is to inform public policy about work in the United States and to inform readers about how they can best manage the challenges that face us all as work becomes increasingly unstable.

The vast majority of public policies about work are informed by economics, which is certainly helpful and essential; however, the voice of workers, for the most part, has been missing for decades. This book seeks to redress this gap by using the lens of psychology and related fields to map how work (or lack of work) is impacting the lives of individuals, their families, and their communities. In this book, I explore in depth how people are dealing with work in an age of massive and pervasive uncertainty.

On that cold January day when I felt so gloomy, I had just interviewed four very diverse adults who were using the services of the One-Stop Career Center. Interviewing these participants, which was an essential part of this project, helped to underscore the reasons why I was writing this book. The stories that I was hearing needed to be told and needed to be placed in a psychological context so that readers (and, it is hoped, leaders across the full range of institutions that comprise our nation) understand clearly and evocatively how work (or lack of work) affects our lives. The epiphany that I had on this rather dark, cold day was that the lived experience of people struggling in their work lives was profoundly missing in discussions about unemployment rates, labor market participation, and predictions about the future of work.

The final participant, who had noticed how exhausted I was, actually seemed to face better job prospects than the three individuals who I interviewed earlier that day. This particular middle-aged African American woman was about to finish her undergraduate degree from a major university in the Boston area after a hiatus from education of nearly 20 years, during which time she had worked as an administrator in a startup firm. Her position gradually became less central to the company, and when the organization was sold, she lost her job. She returned to school and was now using the services of the One-Stop Career Center to consider her options and jumpstart her job search. However, she did take notice of my emotional state after I had listened to stories of personal and financial devastation all day.

My first interviewee of that day, a 51-year-old White woman, Elizabeth, worked as a cashier for a supermarket chain that had gone out of business. The location of the store where she worked was taken over by a new and trendy organic grocery chain, which had initially hired this former deli worker only to fire her a few weeks later for reasons that were not clear to me or to the interviewee. Her story was gut wrenching. She was about to be thrown out of her apartment as her unemployment benefits had ended. She only had $30 worth of food stamps to last her for 3 weeks. After completing the interview, I provided a bit of counseling and support, suggesting some housing and job search resources for her as well as giving her some extra cash to help her get through the coming weeks. As she left the office, I felt that I had opened up a Pandora's box with these interviews, tapping into people's darkest fears about survival. I realized that given the gravity of what this woman faced, my suggestions to her were modest at best. However, something about this particular interview was profoundly illuminating.

The next two participants also faced daunting challenges as they sought work after a few years of unemployment. I felt inspired to write this book to make the case for the centrality of decent and dignified work—and to amplify the voices of those who continue to struggle. I also despaired about the toll that unemployment, underemployment, and inhumane work exact in people's lives; in effect, I was bearing witness to the erosion of work in America. Simply put, many of the participants have been shut out of the American dream and exist in a sort of twilight life, feeling neither completely excluded from society nor completely included.

In this book, I place these powerful interviews, along with the additional interviews conducted as part of the Boston College Working Project, at the center of this story about the nature of working in the United States during this age of uncertainty. The book delves into the various ways that work functions in our lives, encompassing the need for survival as well as the more transcendent aspects of work that are available to those who can find their passion in their efforts to create, collaborate, and contribute. I also describe how people who are stuck taking any job they can find manage to make meaning, often in very creative ways, as they grapple with challenging work lives. In addition to the narratives, I summarize exciting new psychological and sociological research that will further inform our understanding of work during these perilous times.

What Is Work?

Defining work is a complex endeavor, one that necessarily must be done with clear attention to the various social, economic, and historical influences that shape how we understand the multifaceted, and often extremely personal, aspects of this very human activity. One of the challenges in defining work is that this concept has links to many fields, such as economics, sociology, theology, and psychology, among others.[1] Often contrasting with these academic views are the diverse definitions that working people (and people who want to work) have crafted as they strive to adapt to their work lives.[2]

Working, at its essence, is about survival; however, working, at its best, can encompass much more than survival. Beginning with the hunting and gathering that formed the cohering framework for a major period of human evolution, people have engaged in activities that would optimize their survival.

For example, consider the essential tasks of survival early in human evolution: People needed to find shelter, seek sources of food and water, locate safe places to create homes and communities, and stay warm. Out of these tasks grew various early occupations: hunters, builders, caregivers, protectors or warriors, and people who sought to infuse meaning into the increasingly complex experience of life (such as spiritual guides and tribal leaders). These essential activities then required some sense of structure and meaning, forming the essence of the concept of working, which has been woven into the depth of our psyches and embedded into our interactions with others and our planet.[3]

I consider working as having multiple dimensions and meanings, depending on a host of factors, including culture, access to opportunity, and the meaning that individuals construct about this critical aspect of human life. For many people, working entails the expenditure of effort and initiative to perform activities that will yield the resources needed for survival. In addition, working includes efforts that we devote to caregiving, which is also central to the human enterprise.[4] Working also has the potential to provide people with opportunities to create and contribute to the social and economic order. Another key ingredient of working is engaging in activities that one finds intrinsically interesting and meaningful. When we are involved in work that is consistent with our dreams, we have a wonderful opportunity to determine the course of one's day, week, and, indeed, the overarching arc of one's life.

Work, at its core, functions to ensure our individual and collective survival; indeed, this aspect of work unites people across the eons and across cultures. As an example, in my diverse travels around the globe, I have found the observation of people at work to be a cohering theme in human life, which has made me feel less alone in foreign lands: Knowing that people everywhere get up each day to go to work has provided me with a sense of community—and a built-in conversation topic! I have found this to be soothing and inspiring. For many people, working for survival may entail activities that are inherently tedious and even painful, physically or psychologically. Indeed, the struggle to obtain work when insufficient jobs exist is one of the most demanding challenges in life, one that has defined the lives of far too many people in the past few decades and, indeed, throughout human history. As an exemplar, Mitchell, an unemployed 58-year-old White man who we interviewed for the Boston College Working Project, described the following when reflecting on his inability to survive financially: "I think it's probably one of the worst feelings. I'd say that it's worse than losing a relationship maybe, to a certain degree 'cause, it's right at the core of your being."

Often, experiences in our lives take on a deeper or transformed meaning when they are missing or lost. Within the past few decades, the growing infusion of technology into the workplace along with other forces are resulting in a loss of steady work for millions of people around the globe.[5] In this chapter (and, indeed, throughout this book), I deepen this definition to fully capture the essence of working as a core human activity that is essential to our very being.

Within psychological circles, especially within communities and nations that are fairly affluent, conversations about working are often embedded in discussions about careers. In contrast to working, *career* generally denotes a work life that one has some degree of input in selecting, which optimally provides an outlet for the expression of one's interests, values, aspirations, and dreams. Moreover, the term *career* captures a sense of forward progress in which the individual is able to move up into an organization or profession to increasingly more responsible and, ideally, more rewarding positions.[6] As discussed in the historical review further in this chapter, the notion of career is very much connected to the experience of choice and volition, which is often related to access to opportunity and to the capacity to derive meaning in one's work life. While many scholars in psychology would suggest that careers reflect greater intentionality and planning than working for survival, it is also conceivable, as we shall see throughout this book, to consider that people may be able to find meaning in jobs without much intrinsic value or interest.

Although there has been some hearty debate about the use of the terms *work* and *career* in psychology and other academic circles, the reality is that both terms are used in the general conversations that people have about their work lives.[7] In this book, I focus on *work* and *working* to provide a more inclusive perspective to describe the lives of everyone who works or would like to work. I use the term *career* to denote more intentional work lives that encompass a related array of occupations, generally reflecting positions that are consistent with, or at least somewhat related to, one's interests and values. At the same time, I am aware that people may choose to construct meaning about their work lives in ways that are not consistent with academic definitions. The janitor at my office building at Boston College may construe that she has a career that provides her with a great deal of meaning; similarly, a teacher may feel burned out by his job, yearning for a chance to do something different, even though his work life meets traditional definitions of a career. In keeping with my intention to empower the participants in our project who are giving voice to the lived experiences of people, I defer to the ways in which people define their own work lives and will seek to derive meaning in a way that is consistent with their views.

The Age of Uncertainty

Writing a book about working during this era is challenging for many reasons. Perhaps foremost among these reasons is the fact that we have entered a period of uncertainty that has significantly shaken the moorings of work. Trends from diverse influences are converging to create growing levels of unemployment and underemployment across the globe as well as anxiety and insecurity for those lucky enough to still have a stable and decent job. In addition, the Great Recession of 2007–2008 led to the worst economic collapse since the Great Depression, resulting in unemployment, underemployment, and increasing levels of job insecurity for millions of people around the world. Furthermore, growing levels of inequality in the United States and in other regions of the world are reshaping the nature of our societies, with significant implications for the future of work. In this book, I review these trends in more depth, highlighting how each of these factors is serving to undercut our sense of stability at work.

Radical Changes in Technology: The Second Machine Age

In a prescient discussion of the impact of technology on the world of work, Erik Brynjolfsson and Andrew McAfee, two professors at the MIT Center for Digital Business, have argued convincingly that we have entered the Second Machine Age.[8] Beginning with a discussion of the Industrial Revolution in the late eighteenth and nineteenth centuries, Brynjolfsson and McAfee described how the First Machine Age transformed work initially in Europe and North America and then gradually reshaped the very essence of work across most of the world. The First Machine Age led to an explosion in the number and variety of jobs and also generated the need for people to acquire more education and training to manage the demands of a machine-rich work environment. Brynjolfsson and McAfee thoughtfully described how the digital revolution is leading to a second, and potentially even more impactful, age known as the Second Machine Age.

Brynjolfsson and McAfee argued that the computer, particularly recent iterations of computer-based technology developed within the past decade, has the potential to radically transform the occupational landscape. In order to understand the nature of these changes, Brynjolfsson and McAfee suggested that we mull over the following trends:

- In 2004, driverless cars seemed impossible to imagine. Within the last decade and a half, the technology has been developed that will likely transform driving in the near future.
- A great illustration of these changes is the transition from a flip cell phone to the smartphone. The smartphone that many readers are using is probably more powerful than the average computer that was in use 10 years ago.

- We now have free phone service on our computers that allows us to see and talk to our friends and family around the world. This was a fantasy that fueled many World's Fair exhibits during the twentieth century.
- Computers that can compete in chess and that demonstrate other seemingly uniquely human skills are now being developed and ramped up for use in industry and other sectors of society.

In many sectors of life, the developmental leap forward that technology has made in the past decade is leading to positive outcomes. Medical care is improving; consumer products are becoming more attractive, reliable, and fun; transportation is safer and faster; and robots are being developed to take care of the elderly and individuals with disabling conditions. In short, the world is changing quickly. However, the advent of the Second Machine Age is not without its potential costs, particularly in relation to work. Brynjolfsson and McAfee cautioned that those without relevant and marketable skills will likely struggle considerably in sustaining a decent and stable livelihood. The consequences for individuals who are left behind in attaining viable skills are likely to be dramatic and far-reaching, especially if our society does not establish a strong safety net.

Building on the very worrisome contributions noted, additional reports and analyses of how automation will impact the world of work have been published in recent years, with important implications about the future of work.[9] In 2015, the Organization for Economic Cooperation and Development (OECD) published a groundbreaking report, *Securing Livelihoods for All*, which argued that automation will be a "game changer" in the labor market, resulting in massive losses of work, particularly among less skilled workers.[10] In contrast, a contribution by the Economic Policy Institute countered the view that automation will lead to major job losses, proposing that the predictions of major disruptions in the marketplace have been exaggerated.[11]

Perhaps the most comprehensive and balanced analysis was offered by the National Academy of Sciences in a report, *Information Technology and the US Workforce: Where Are We and Where Do We Go From Here?*[12] This report examined a wealth of data, policy analyses, and empirically based projections about the future of work and automation. The conclusions of this report were appropriately nuanced given the complexity of the issues considered, highlighting the following points:

1. Information technology, which includes both automation and artificial intelligence, will continue to result in the loss of work, particularly for individuals who do not have skills that are needed by the labor market.

2. Automation and artificial intelligence will also result in vast improvements of products and services, reducing some work tasks and enhancing the well-being of many people.
3. Many scholars and policy analysts believe that new work opportunities can be created out of the interface of human labor and automation. However, it is not clear how many new jobs will be created in this process and how accessible these positions will be for individuals who do not have the requisite education and skill set.
4. The authors concluded that automation may elevate existing problems with inequality, creating an increasingly bifurcated labor market (and society).

What I have found most compelling in this very comprehensive report is the notion that the changes that are outlined are not viewed as automatic or predetermined. The authors of this very exhaustive study of automation, artificial intelligence, and work believe that we have an opportunity to shape the future by making thoughtful decisions about how we want to engage with work in the years and decades to come. In this light, this book's publication is timely in that I believe strongly that we need to infuse a psychological perspective into our thinking about the future of work, and that we also need to include the experiences and voices of workers who are living on the front lines of these very intense and far-reaching changes.

The Great Recession

In addition to the challenges of technology, the Great Recession, which technically has been over for many years, has further transformed the world of work. On the surface, of course, the Great Recession led to record levels of unemployment and underemployment around the globe. Only a few regions of the world were insulated from the ravages of the economic downturn. Perhaps the most illustrative reflection of the impact of long-term unemployment can be found in the following statistic: The median number of weeks of unemployment at the time that this book was completed is 9; however, the mean is 22 (over 5 months), which reflects the large number of people who have been unemployed for 6 months or longer. Indeed, 21% of the unemployed have been out of work for more than 6 months.[13] (The challenges of unemployment are discussed in further detail in Chapter 8.)

Underneath the surface, the statistics and charts reflect lives that have come apart as a result of unemployment and underemployment.[14] Moreover, retirement is more complex currently, with some having to retire early due to an inability to obtain a stable job and others having to postpone retirement because of inadequate resources. In addition, wages have remained stagnant for nearly a decade, a situation that has been particularly hard on people from poor and working class backgrounds.[15] Indeed, the stagnation of wages has led to dramatic growth in inequality, as discussed in the next section, which has become one of the major issues in contemporary economic and political debates within the United States.

Rise of Inequality

Another disconcerting trend that is affecting the nature of contemporary work is the growing inequality in the United States between those with affluence and those without. As Joseph Stiglitz, the Nobel Prize–winning economist, noted in his recent book, *The Great Divide: Unequal Societies and What We Can Do About Them*, the dramatic rise in inequality is a relatively recent phenomenon, taking place over the past three decades. For example, during the past 30 years, the bottom 90% of wage earners have experienced growth of about 15% in their wages; in contrast, the top 1% has experienced an increase of 150% of earnings.[16] Another index of inequality is that much of the wealth for individuals in the bottom and middle tiers of the U.S. economy is derived from the capital embedded in their homes. As the housing crisis of the Great Recession revealed, that wealth is tenuous at best. The wealth of the top tier of income earners tends to be more diversified, offering them greater protection against the vicissitudes of economic shifts. Even more dramatically, Stiglitz reported that chief executive officers (CEOs) in the United States earn 200 times the salary of a typical worker. He also noted that this extreme difference is growing and is not typically replicated in our peer nations; for example, the ratio in Japan is 16 to 1.

Moreover, the growing nature of inequality is having a dramatic impact on the workplace. Paralleling the observations noted previously in this chapter, Stiglitz indicated that the job market is becoming increasingly polarized. Low-paying jobs that involve care work are growing, as are some highly skilled jobs, such as those in the STEM (science, technology, engineering, and math) fields, even though keen competition exists in many of these fields. In addition, the nature of working varies considerably between the haves and have-nots. The protection offered by labor unions is increasingly diminishing or disappearing for the poor and working class; this has been a long-term process that is significantly reshaping the world of work.[17] Indeed, many people are forced to work in the precarious marketplace, which is characterized by lack of stability at work; few, if any, benefits; and the prevalence of short-term work contracts. Guy Standing, a British sociologist who has written extensively about changes in the workplace, described the precariat as forming the core of what he called the "withering working class." The precariat class of workers, as Standing noted, is characterized by a notable loss of voice and agency; precarious workers tend not to be protected by labor laws or unions, and they are often in fields where the competition for work is so intense that they feel that they ought not to advocate for themselves or their colleagues. Standing described the growth of the precariat throughout many Western countries and eloquently depicted the substantial psychological and social impact of this movement.[18] (This notion is revisited throughout this book.)

The Problem of Contemporary Work: Global Responses

The challenges of work, writ large, have been addressed for many decades by important global institutions, such as the United Nations and the International Labor Organization (ILO, which is now an affiliate of the United Nations). These efforts attest to the courageous and inspiring initiatives by policy leaders and activists who are deeply concerned about the nature and impact of work in people's lives. One of the most noteworthy contributions from the United Nations occurred after the horrific abuses of World War II: The United Nations, in the 1948 *Universal Declaration of Human Rights*, made a profoundly important contribution about human rights, which included the following statement about work:

> (1) Everyone has the right to work, to free choice of employment, to just and favourable conditions of work and to protection against unemployment. (2) Everyone, without any discrimination, has the right to equal pay for equal work. (3) Everyone who works has the right to just and favourable remuneration ensuring for himself and his family an existence worthy of human dignity, and supplemented, if necessary, by other means of social protection. (4) Everyone has the right to form and to join trade unions for the protection of his interests.[19]

Although it has been difficult to implement these admirable objectives across the full scope of the globe, the framework provided by the United Nations has established an important cornerstone for advocating for an inclusive and justice-oriented agenda with respect to work. Building on the work of the United Nations, the ILO, which actually began in 1919 following the tragedy of World War I, has sought to implement the United Nations' human rights agenda in more specific and policy-based ways. For example, the ILO has provided critically needed economic and labor policy advice to government leaders, labor unions, and the private sector in its wide-ranging approach to advocating for just policies at work.[20]

A key contribution from the ILO is a consensually agreed-on framework that identifies the minimal attributes that should be available to all those who work and who want to work. This framework, which was disseminated in 1999, is known as the Decent Work Agenda and is based on the following four principles[21]:

1. Promoting employment by creating a sustainable institutional and economic environment. . . .
2. Developing and enhancing measures of social protection—social security and labor protection—which are sustainable and adapted to national circumstances;
3. Promoting social dialogue and tripartism [i.e., close connections between governments, worker organizations, and employers]
4. Respecting, promoting and realizing the fundamental principles and rights at work.

The objective of the Decent Work Agenda has been to codify and structure the core elements of an environment that offers the essentials of stable and secure employment. According to the ILO, decent work optimally includes the following attributes: a work context that is safe physically and interpersonally from abuse or dangerous conditions; a work life that provides people with time for rest and leisure; organizational/employer values that complement the values of the employee; adequate remuneration; and the availability of healthcare.[22] The Decent Work Agenda does not include meaning, purpose, satisfaction, or other psychological attributes of a rewarding career. Understanding that the goal of the ILO's efforts are to provide a foundational base for a reasonable structure for work provides a context for viewing this agenda as a first step in developing a global framework for work that will be stable, dignified, and safe.

When considered collectively, the UN and ILO initiatives place debates about work into an explicit social and economic justice perspective. These international bodies have clearly taken a stand on what is considered to be decent and just working conditions. These standards are discussed throughout the book as we balance the psychological aspects of working with the emerging global standard of decent and dignified work for all.

Reflection and Next Steps

This brief overview of some of the dramatic changes in the occupational landscape is certainly sobering. The changes that have been evoked by the Second

Machine Age, Great Recession, and growing income and social class inequality are recasting the nature of work. The advent of the precariat class of workers augurs a trend that underscores the fraying of the tethers that connect people to work and to each other. As I argue throughout this book, our society is at a critical crossroads with respect to work. We now see the trends converging in a disconcerting way, suggesting that there may not be enough stable and decent jobs available for people who want and need to work. The policy challenges that will be required to address this problem are typically hard and, often, painful. The material presented throughout this book optimally will provide food for thought as we mull over the choices that we need to make as work becomes unsteady, unavailable for some, and unpredictable for all of us.

A Short History of Work

To more fully understand the nature of working, we need to understand the history of working. One of the major themes of contemporary working—the startling rise of technology as an instrument of change—is also an important story, going as far back as our earliest years as hunters and gatherers. The very name of this initial period of human advancement (the hunting and gathering era) embodies two work-related tasks: hunting for protein-based sources of nourishment and warmth and gathering fruits, nuts, and vegetables in the development of a diet that would ensure sustenance. Historical analyses indicated that advances in technology have traditionally played a significant role in enhancing human beings' capacity for survival and for control over their environments. The history of working in our more ancient history is closely intertwined with evolution and humanity's struggles to survive and master the environment. The earliest records of human work are found in archeological studies as well as anthropological research of contemporary communities that live without the trappings of advanced technologies; when taken together, these scholarly endeavors have portrayed a view of early humans as innovative hunters and gatherers who were constantly adapting to the challenges of surviving in often very harsh environments.[23]

The development of tools to enhance our capacity for survival is integrally related to the growth in humanity's success on this planet. Richard Donkin's book *The History of Work* conveys the complexity of survival in the distant past, when working was one of the major activities of our ancestors' lives.[24] For many of our predecessors, much of each day was likely devoted to finding food, water, and shelter and protecting oneself and one's kin from predators. Donkin described the positive trajectory of human evolution, noting that our ancestors seemed to have learned to use some rudimentary tools as far back as 2.5 million years ago. The traditional narrative of prehistoric life is one in which people seemed beset with arduous tasks, danger, and the fear of starvation. However, Donkin cited contemporary anthropological studies that suggest that some hunter–gatherers currently devote only 2 or 3 days per week locating food and water, suggesting that life thousands of years ago may not have consistently been full of work-related tasks during flush times.

At times, the hunter–gatherer lifestyle may have afforded people some time for reflection and other nonwork activities that were not directly linked to survival. As Donkin pointed out in his historical analysis of work, considerable evidence exists within the archeological findings of hunter–gatherer communities of various forms of artistic expression and the development of often-elaborate rituals that gave life meaning and a sense of purpose. Indeed, Donkin cited that evidence of artistic projects can be traced to at least 32,000 years ago, suggesting that our ancestors had the desire to make contributions to their lives that were not necessarily linked solely to survival. Another important theme of prehistoric life is the development of narratives that could be used to describe humanity's growing capacity to understand the connection between the past, present, and future. Many of these stories formed the essence of early religions and provided the necessary guideposts in the development of cultural beliefs, norms, and rituals. Thus, work was not entirely about the development of tools to enhance survival; even at our earliest phases of evolution as human beings, people sought to create meaning in their lives via the use of narratives, art, and other forms of cultural expression.

The next major transition for humanity was the movement from hunter–gatherer lifestyles to more sedentary hunter–gatherer roles, which was made possible by the growing use of food storage technologies.[25] During this transitional period, people often had more time for leisure, artistic, and ritualistic endeavors, which helped to create the infrastructure for the movement to the agricultural era. Many historians place the full onset of the agricultural period at around 4,000–9,000 years ago. Some scholars believe that notions of tedious and burdensome aspects of work began in earnest with the advent of the agricultural period. Indeed, the growth of slavery as a form of human subjugation and oppression is thought to have become systematically infused in many human societies during the beginning of the agricultural period. The nature of the work, which was routine and often very labor intensive, may have created the conditions for the growth of slavery.[26] In addition, the overall perspective of work as a burden, as reflected in the Bible and many other ancient accounts, may have evolved during the agricultural period, when work became far more regimented, predictable, and laborious.

Another outgrowth of the agricultural period was the development of more structured and hierarchical societies. Once land ownership became an integral part of many of the world's economies, social and economic differentiation of people occurred based on one's position with respect to the accumulation of land and property, which increasingly became a proxy for wealth and economic power. The rise of the agricultural period also was characterized by the development of cities, which became a focal point for global trade and for the growing rise of craftwork. The intersection of goods and services was soon accompanied by an increase in the exchange of ideas, which helped to create a growing knowledge base across the globe. The explosion in knowledge soon fostered many gains in technology, which led to the next major phase of the development of work: the Industrial Era.

As Brynjolfsson and McAfee noted, the development of the steam engine by James Watt in Scotland is often viewed as the event that kick-started the Industrial Revolution. The steam engine that was perfected by Watt allowed work to be conducted by machines in a way that radically transformed the work lives of many during the subsequent decades and centuries. No longer did people have to create the power that would drive production and labor; instead, machines could be constructed that would fuel factories, which would increasingly dot the landscape in Europe, North America, and, over time, much of the globe.

The changes wrought by the Industrial Revolution were radically transformative. First, the number of possible occupations that people could hold increased geometrically. Second, the quantity and diversity of consumer goods also grew exponentially, providing people with an abundance of options for food, clothing, leisure goods, and tools for work. Third, work became increasingly less connected to the core elements of survival and, indeed, became less central to the essence of people's lived experiences. For example, rather than growing one's own food, industrial age workers might find themselves working in a factory that manufactured machinery for other factories, thereby enhancing one's sense of disconnection from work. This experience, along with other abuses of workers, spawned the critique by Karl Marx and others about the dehumanizing and alienating aspects of work, which are perhaps most apparent in large-scale factories that are owned by investors and are tightly regimented.[27]

The advances in technology continued to reshape not only work, but also the entire fabric of human societies. By the early twentieth century, the foundation for the development of airplanes and cars was already in place. Telephones and other advanced forms of communication became increasingly common means of human interactions. Moreover, rapid improvements in healthcare led to growing life expectancies in many regions of the world. Throughout this period, work became more complex and multifaceted. For some individuals, work began to offer opportunities for self-expression, joy, and a sense of accomplishment. Typically, but not always, work that involved the development of specified skills and that tapped into human strivings for creativity, problem-solving, and connections with others provided people with the means for an enjoyable work life. At the same time, many other people were stuck in grueling, and frequently dangerous, jobs in factories, mines, transportation, the military, and security work; these jobs often were more treacherous and demanding than many of the tasks of the hunter–gatherer or agricultural periods. Perhaps the most telling feature of the Industrial Era was the sheer diversity of work experiences that people could have, often within the same lifetime.

As explored here, work grew from a core aspect of survival to a means of self-determination, expression, and an inherent part of a richly lived life. However, rather than having one set of needs override other needs that working can fulfill, the picture that emerges in this book is one wherein working can fulfill a multifaceted array of human needs that wax and wane across the life span. Work has the potential to add a great deal of meaning and richness to our lives; at the same time, it has the capacity to wither our souls in a way that few other life activities can match.

Work as a Central Role in Life: Lived Experiences

As the preceding brief history of working conveys, work has been and remains a critical aspect of the human experience. Our very survival as a species evolved based on our ever-growing level of sophistication in ensuring access to food, water, shelter, and other sources of sustenance and comfort. As I suggested previously in this chapter, work, when it is going reasonably well, offers people a profound way of feeling alive and connected to the world. Of course, when jobs are not available or are only accessible in ways that are demeaning and denigrating, working can be a major source of pain and despair.

The participants from the Boston College Working Project have given voice to the centrality of work in various ways throughout their interviews. In the material that follows, I review some of the major themes that exemplify the complex and rich ways that work is central in life. The ways in which it becomes central for people vary considerably, often reflecting the diverse levels of access that people have to the resources that promote a self-determined work life and the varied ways that people construct meaning about their lives. And, indeed, as we shall see in this section, for some of the participants, work within the marketplace was not centrally related to how they sought satisfaction and meaning in their lives. In keeping with my intention to place the voices of the participants at the forefront of this book, following the presentation of the major themes from the participants of the Boston College Working Project, I review some of the major trends in the psychological and social science literature on the centrality of working.

The Centrality of Working as a Source of Personal Fulfillment

A number of themes pertaining to the role that work plays in people's lives emerged in the interviews that the participants provided. Of these themes, the issue that emerged most frequently was that working provided people with an opportunity to engage in tasks that they loved. Mindy, a 34-year-old opera singer of Asian descent who was struggling to find her place in the music world, eloquently described the centrality of her work:

> I've always enjoyed singing. And, if you ask anyone, we sing because we are passionate and in my case, we all want to be heard and express ourselves; and, we want others to understand us and hear what we have to say. I feel singing is the best way for me to connect to others and it helps me understand the world we live in. I've always enjoyed and felt passionate about singing—it's the most effective way I feel I can communicate and express myself and it's always been there. In a way, I cannot see myself doing anything else, but if it becomes a financial struggle too long then I will get something else but find a way to keep it in my life. It's a calling and it's something I've always enjoyed.

Mindy evocatively described the sense of joy and passion that she experiences when she sings. Yet, in an artistic career that comes with financial struggles, she was acutely aware of the complexity of balancing the need for survival with the desire for a career that is passionate and meaningful to her. Her capacity to describe the significance of singing in her life is clearly reflected in her narrative about her work life. At the same time, she was aware that she may need to compromise her dreams, reflecting her capacity to balance the need for survival with her dreams for a career that will bring her meaning and joy.

The attraction of developing ideas and then implementing them in the world of work was also prevalent in the participants' descriptions of the role of work in their lives. In the next passage by Jamie, a 56-year-old White CEO of a small engineering firm, the experience of developing something new and innovative is described in a thoughtful and multifaceted way. Jamie's comments reflect his awareness of the centrality of work in relation to another central theme in contemporary life: relationships.

What does work mean to me? Well. . . . Obviously, for me it's a way of life. . . . I mean I have a wonderful family: a wife, kids. . . . Well the kids have already grown up, but that always came first, in the sense that you sacrifice. . . . I like achieving things, I mean with building companies and . . . I like being able to employ people and give them the opportunity to develop their work and satisfaction, creating things of value. So that's all part of what work is for me: it's a way of life. . . . And it's a way of satisfying myself.

For some people, working provides a direct pathway to a joyful life that is characterized by a sense of accomplishment and inspiration, especially when one is able to follow one's passions and make a living at the same time. The next participant, Rebecca, a 33-year-old Latina woman, broke out of a traditional career trajectory to pursue her dream of teaching and practicing wellness at a hotel on a tiny Caribbean island in Central America. For Rebecca, working, as reflected in the following passage, is clearly central in her life, providing her with the capacity to share her passion with others in an idyllic environment:

So really this happy, healthy concept of what my hopes are in general is to be able live a life that is in line with my values, with my morals—to really live a life, and live by example. So, for example, living a yogic lifestyle, and really living the way. . . . Living my job. So, does that make sense? . . . If you told me that I was going to be living on an island, teaching yoga and meditation, and playing drums and the ukulele. . . . I'm also a path consultant, so I inspire people to look at their path, and have positive thinking, positive psychology, and yeah, if you told me what I was going to be doing, I would've laughed.

Rebecca's experience is not typical among the participants of this project, but it does show an example of the potential of work to be a seamless connection from one's values and dreams to the realities of the marketplace. Rebecca gave up a more secure job as a makeup artist in Los Angeles to follow her dream of teaching meditation and yoga in a tropical environment. Further in the book, we explore the reasons that someone like Rebecca can make her dreams come true while others struggle considerably in finding decent and dignified work.

The Centrality of Working as a Source of Structure

Working also provides a structure for people's lives—a reason to get up in the morning. This point, which has been well explored in psychology and in the popular media, underscores that working furnishes a means of organizing one's day as well as one's relationships with others and with the world.[28] Mitchell, an unemployed 58-year-old White artist and maintenance worker, described the organizing qualities of work:

> Well I think that work kind of structures your life, and when it's not there you have to structure your own life. I mean you have to structure your own life anyway, but I think it gives you a sense of purpose and it keeps you on a schedule. . . . There's a lot of people that don't want to work and they find ways to get around it and I'm just not one of those people. I just have to have something to do, you know; I need a place to go and it may be, part of it may be, because I'm conditioned to be like everyone else that you have to go to work every day.

Yet, work can also prevent people from spending time with their loved ones. Mildred, a 52-year-old unemployed African American woman, described how work gradually became overly central in her life, encompassing time that she had devoted to her family and leisure. Her story underscores an experience that is increasingly evident for some people who find that they are compelled to work from home, in part due to the brilliant technologies emerging in modern life.

> Initially, they did me a favor by letting me go after a while because the nature of the jobs nowadays has changed significantly from when I first started working. It used to be you'd have a job, you go in, you work nine to five plus you know, hours you needed to do your project, so you'd work maybe a fifty-hour week. With the way the job was changing, you basically take your laptop home with you and you do your work at home as well as work in the office. . . . You need to be available for those questions that might come up at any time. So when they gave me the laptop that kind of interfered with my family time. . . . But when it comes time to take a laptop home with me, it's just kind of intruding on my time with my family and my son. At that point, you know, my son was eight years old, and he has special needs, he's on the autistic spectrum, and that was interfering with my relationship with my son. So, the level of stress when you have to juggle your source of income with the needs of your family and especially a child in running a household was very stressful. And I think that with my termination, I realized that stress, once it was relieved; I realized looking back that I was actually driving myself into the ground, trying to do the job.

Through their words, Mildred, Mitchell, Rebecca, and Mindy affirmed some of the ways in which working provides form and structure for people. For many people, working furnishes an anchor to a sense of time and space about life, offering a connection to the rhythm of the world. As we shall see in further chapters, the loss of work often creates a vacuum in our capacity to organize our lives, leading to a sense of anomie and disconnection that can be emotionally devastating for individuals and equally disruptive for communities and nations.

The Centrality of Working in Defining Identity

The notion that we obtain important aspects of our identities from our jobs and careers is a historic concept that dates back centuries. In fact, a review of last names often reveals occupational positions that one's ancestors held in the recent or remote past (e.g., Miller, Tailor, Farmer). The lived experiences that people have at work are often characterized by a strong identification with the roles and responsibilities of one's job. Over and over, through our interviews, we saw that participants derived meaning from their work *about their own sense of identity*; in effect, their work lives helped them understand who they were in the world. As Matteo, a 45-year-old White man, described it, his work as a musician and audio technician included periods of hardship that culminated in a prison sentence. However, his professional identity provided a sense of grounding that seeped into his core sense of self.

> Well because I'm a musician, it's part of my identity; I think it is just the nature of how men are wired . . . particularly how I am wired. I personalize it, keep it onto me—I think our identity, or my identity, is often wrapped up in my work. Both as a musician/audio-video engineer and as a daddy, and that's work for me too. I'm divorced and my ex-wife and kids are in New York still, and trying to keep in touch with them . . . and keep my fatherhood going is a challenge over the distance, especially because she has primary custody. I look at that as work too, but it's cool because both my kids take an interest in what I do.

Another participant, Loretta, a White 44-year-old former nurse who now works as a paralegal, also had a number of challenges in her life that culminated in a short stay in prison. Loretta ended up losing her nursing license because of a period of "bad choices" she made, which led to a 90-day prison term for forging bad checks. Since she left prison 9 years prior, she had been sober, with a new career where her prison record has not played such a prominent role. Even with a new career trajectory, she still was seeking to recover her nursing license so that she could rejoin the field that gave her such a sense of satisfaction and meaning.

I have always been proud to be a nurse. And every day I would come home from work, I would always have a great sense of accomplishment because I felt like I made a difference in someone's life in every shift that I worked, in some way. . . . Well I guess it's huge if I have gone through everything I have gone through just so that I can be a nurse because in all reality that's who I am on the inside and out. However, I cannot say that about the actual work that I am doing now because it's just a job and nothing else. It's not anything that I feel passionate about or anything that I see myself working in the future. I don't see myself working in the legal field forever because I am not passionate about it.

Although much of the literature in psychology, and indeed, literature in general (including fiction, plays, and memoirs), speaks to the centrality of work in people's lives, it is important to note that not everyone sees work as playing the same role. Indeed, one point I hope to make clear in this book is that the functions that working fulfills in life vary extensively based on culture, history, economic circumstances, and individual differences. Rich, a 63-year-old former computer programmer turned teacher, felt that his work life would not define him. He maintained that he derived core aspects of his identity from his roles as a parent, husband, and a dedicated fan of sports. In his interview, Rich shared his reaction to the culture in the computer industry in the 1990s and early 2000s, when supervisors would often evaluate their employees based on how much effort they devoted to their jobs:

All of the other people . . . really even the other project manager worked—they worked long hours too. Not me! I was out of there at 5 o'clock. I took my vacations. . . . I had a . . . I guess I had a little bit of job security because of my knowledge of the accounts receivable system, and the company felt I guess that I was the only one that really knew the system. So, they kind of put up with that. But my own personal feeling about that was . . . there was a song by Ernie Ford: "Sixteen Tons." . . . I really felt I never sold my soul to the company store. I paid for it a lot in all of my computer jobs, but . . . I believed in getting as much out of life as I possibly could, and to me staying there ungodly hours, working the weekends . . . for a company that was eventually going to toss you aside, was not the way to go—at least for me personally. I probably was in the wrong line of work, based on that theory, but my theory was that life was short, and I was going to get the most out of it as I could.

Rich acknowledged that his approach did not fit the corporate culture. In fact, he described a story in which his commitment to a broader identity that was not necessarily rooted in his work life led to some challenges:

And this was probably a turning point position—to give you an example of what the situation was like for me. . . . The guy in charge of the accounting department—with his assistant—went in to see me. And they had written a note, which I still have, and it said, the payroll system is kind of a mess, we need some help with it. . . . Where is Richard? Apparently he's off! (This was after hours, so 5 o'clock. . . .) And then, the bottom line, it said: "What a life!" . . . And so Bob (the supervisor) calls me into the office the next morning, and gives me the note, and he says, "Here." And he says: This is what so-and-so said about you last night. And he says: Don't worry about it, 'cause I was gone at 5 o'clock too. So I knew he had my back the entire time. I knew I was the AR . . . Accounts Receivable guy. And I knew that I valued my private life more than I valued my job. And that was I guess reflected throughout my career, in any job that I ever held: I never liked it more than I did my own private time spending with my wife, my kids, my family, my parents . . . than devoting my soul to the company store—like it says in that song. I never would do that. And now that I look back on it, I'm glad that I didn't do that.

The degree to which working becomes central to one's identity is diverse and complex. Rich's story is probably relatable to many working people who view their jobs as a means to an end—a source of survival and sustenance. However, many of the participants in the Boston College Working Project described a deep connection to their work lives, which offered them multiple pathways to a sense of meaning and satisfaction in their lives. As reflected in the next section, further insights about how people understand the role of work in their lives can be gleaned from a review of the academic literature in psychology.

Work as a Central Role in Life: The Psychological View

Within the academic world of psychology and related social sciences, the question of the role of work in people's lives has captured considerable attention, particularly within the past few decades. Psychologists working within industry and organizations (who are known as industrial/organizational psychologists) have examined this question from the perspective of how best to provide conditions that will support workers and encourage productivity. Psychologists who work individually with people in counseling and psychotherapy have examined this question from the perspective of identifying ways to help people find meaning in their work lives and, increasingly, supporting people as they seek to adapt to unemployment and precarious work. As a means of enriching the analysis of the narratives from the Boston College Working Project, I devote some space in each chapter to new and exciting research that enriches the material that has been discussed. In this section, I introduce the concept of identity, which is such an integral part of our lives and, for many people, has been rooted in our work lives.

Work and Identity

From an individual perspective, work provides people with a means of understanding themselves in relation to the social and economic world. One way of framing this understanding is via the lens of identity. Perhaps the best way to understand what the concept of identity means in psychology is to consider how people answer the question of "Who Are You?" The ease with which people present their identity by referring to their work role underscores a powerful message about how we make sense of who we are in relation to others and in relation to our own internal sense of ourselves.

Research on identity and work is generally traced back to the seminal contributions of Erik Erikson, who described the identity formation process in great depth, noting that the process of clarifying one's identity was the hallmark of adolescence.[29] Erikson's ideas about identity formation fueled decades of informative research, theory development, and practice in education and psychology. Psychologists have described how identity can be located in various spaces, including ideology, religion, relationships, politics, and work.[30] Survey research on identity has indicated that self-reports of stability and clarity have been consistently associated with positive outcomes, such as better psychological adjustment, more adaptive mental health, self-esteem, and emotional stability.[31]

As the study of identity advanced during the latter part of the twentieth century, scholars critiqued the notion of identity as a fixed state that was rooted in a developmental process that would ostensibly be resolved by early adulthood. Recent analyses of identity and work have incorporated a more intellectually expansive perspective that assumes that people construct their identities in an active and engaged way as they interact with various contexts for life.[32] For example, in Rich's case, he described how he located his identity in his personal and family life as well as in his leisure interests, with far less focus on his work life. Whereas some earlier scholars might have reported that Rich's overall identity was not clarified or integrated, a closer analysis of this case reveals that he simply chose to locate his identity in nonwork contexts. Fortunately, he was generally able to support himself and his family, which fulfilled his survival needs.

Psychology and the social sciences have increasingly been shaped by what some scholars are calling a narrative turn.[33] The focus on narrative perspectives in the world of identity assumes that people are actively participating in developing and implementing their identities. A prominent vocational psychologist, Mark Savickas, has proposed that a vocational identity is akin to a thesis that we have about ourselves in the world of work.[34] The narrative that we create about ourselves at work (and in seeking to locate work) is reflected in the patterns that we impose on our life stories. In the case of Rich, he strove to attach meaning to his life by locating his core identity in his leisure and family life, relegating marketplace work to the back seat. For other participants in the Boston College Working Project, such as Mindy, who previously described her passion for opera singing, the narrative constructed is one in which marketplace work takes the lead and provides a primary setting for the construction of one's identity.

As reflected in this chapter (and throughout the book), radical shifts in the workplace are evoking major challenges for people in creating and sustaining a coherent narrative about their identities. Two Swiss psychologists, Jerome Rossier and Jonas Masdonati, have written eloquently about the tensions that exist as people struggle to construct identities in a work world that does not readily offer stability or meaning.[35] These challenges, which can be understood as identity threats, compromise our capacity to work and to locate work with decent conditions. For those individuals who are interested in carving out their identities with a strong presence from their work lives, the failure to connect to the labor market can markedly diminish the essential connections that can be forged between one's work and one's identity. As an example, a worker who needs to change jobs and fields because of a lack of stability in his or her aspirational career would struggle to find ways of creating a narrative that includes relationships to his or her tasks, colleagues, and the overarching sense of creating and contributing. Consequently, this individual might feel less stable internally and might experience a lack of connection to the broader social world.

Although some might argue that people can locate their identities in other domains, much as Rich did, the reality of an increasingly unstable work environment is that the struggle for survival often overrides people's capacities to derive meaning from their work lives. And, while a clear and coherent sense of identity is indeed integral to well-being, the struggles created by indecent work conditions, low wages, and fears of layoffs create their own identity: one of anxiety and fear. The pull for stability, though, is a powerful need, reflecting the essential aspects of our need for survival in an environment that has often been quite hostile and barren.

Conclusion

Working is central to our lives. In mapping the changing landscape of work, the overriding conclusion is that there is a natural attraction that people have to create, contribute, and collaborate via work, both in the marketplace and in caregiving contexts. This natural tendency to work has evolved over the course of history, which has provided human beings with the challenges and resources to develop elaborate skills in managing the environment. This unique human attribute to adapt and increasingly master aspects of one's context helped to create a rich tapestry of jobs and an equally rich set of psychological mechanisms with which to understand one's work life. Even for people who do not necessarily value their tasks and responsibilities inherently, the act of working can bring people into contact with others and with the social world; in a sense, it sets the frame for many important aspects of our existence as social beings.

While work has been consistently central for humans since we were hunters and gatherers, another counterpoint has emerged in the historical and contemporary analysis of working in America. Despite relatively solid unemployment statistics, all is not well in the labor market. The rapid infusion of automation in the workplace and its coupling with growing inequality are reducing access to decent and dignified work. The tension between our natural pull to create and contribute is at risk as our society grapples with a future of work that is very hard to predict. I have argued here that a psychological perspective is essential in current and future discussions about how to proceed with creating a fair and equitable work life. In subsequent chapters of this book, I explore this theme in depth, arguing that work is essential to being fully alive in the world.

2

Being Able to Survive and Thrive

Gail, a 56-year-old White woman who had worked primarily in middle management for financial firms, entered the consulting room with a palpable sense of exhaustion and despair. (Gail is not an actual client; she represents an amalgam of clients I have seen in psychotherapy and career counseling during the past few years.) Gail was referred to me by her psychotherapist, who felt that she would benefit from intensive career counseling. We spoke on the phone prior to our first session, and I agreed that it would be useful for us set up a consultation. Like so many people in their 50s and 60s during the height of the Great Recession, Gail was laid off in 2009 and was not able to rejoin the full-time workforce. The jobs that she obtained were temporary or part-time, and each one ended at or before its prescribed end date. When she started counseling with me, she was out of work for over 3 years and was feeling quite desperate.

I began with my usual overview of the career counseling process, highlighting how I would work collaboratively with her psychotherapist and citing both the advantages and limitations of what I could offer. Gail was very clear at the beginning of the session when I asked her how I could be most useful.

> Dr. Blustein: I just need a job with benefits. I appreciate all that you would like to do for me with respect to finding a job that suits me. However, the bottom line for me is about survival: I have run out of unemployment benefits and I am a single mother of a son with special needs. I do have some savings and I have my parents still around who are helping me. But I feel so ashamed for asking them for money. What I really need is a decent job with a good salary and benefits. To be honest, I really don't care if the job is interesting or not. That is something that I used to worry about, but no longer. I need a new job in 4 weeks because I am running out of money. Can you help me?

Gail was not the only client who sought me out for help with work issues during and after the Great Recession who was more concerned with survival than with finding her dream job. Her struggles in locating work were draining her pocketbook and her sense of feeling worthwhile and independent; by the time she came to see me, she was feeling overwhelmed, frightened, and angry.

The reality of my work and of the job market is that I could not help Gail land a job in 4 weeks. After learning more about her life and work history, I worked with her on job search strategies and networking intensively for the full session; despite my best efforts, she left that session and never returned. She did not return my calls, even though I reached out multiple times. In many ways, her story is part of what has prompted this book project and this particular chapter. Although so much is written in the popular media and in the academic literature about work, the vast majority of this material, which is often very insightful, relates to people with some degree of choice in their lives. In this chapter, I focus on one of the core needs that drive the work motivation for millions of people around the globe: the need for survival.

Survival Needs: An Introductory Journey

Let us take a brief trip back in time to the campus of Brooklyn College during the height of World War II. While much of the world was embroiled in a struggle for freedom and democracy, Abraham Maslow, a middle-aged psychologist working on the faculty of the Psychology Department at Brooklyn College, was developing new ideas for a very challenging period of humankind. Maslow became well known for advocating a humanistic version of psychology, a perspective that emphasizes people's strengths and strivings for transcendence as opposed to the focus on deficits, which had defined much of applied psychology at that time.[1] The work that Maslow did during World War II became the foundation for the humanistic revolution in psychology that was just around the corner.

Maslow's Hierarchy

Using a familiar framework within the psychology of the early to middle twentieth century, Maslow conceptualized people as striving to fulfill a series of hierarchical needs. Although research did not bear out the precise order of needs that Maslow advanced, the model remains useful in the way that it frames the larger picture of humanity as striving to meet multiple sets of needs, including, but not limited to, the need for survival.[2] As reflected in the material that follows, Maslow posited a hierarchical model with five fundamental needs, with the most basic, biologically oriented needs at the core of existence, followed by relational and psychological needs, and culminating with the striving for self-actualization:[3]

1. Physiological needs: Includes air, water, and food.
2. Safety needs: Includes the resources needed for survival, such as work, health, and housing.
3. Love and belonging needs: Encompasses social and relational strivings, including friendship, family, and sexual intimacy.
4. Esteem: Defined by confidence, self-esteem, achievement, and admiration by others.
5. Self-actualization: Captures the desire to reach the full realization of one's dreams; a fulfillment of one's sense of self and potential.

As reflected in this hierarchy, the need for survival is fundamental to our existence. Maslow's model has been critiqued from a number of perspectives for its focus on individualistic and Western values as well as its assumption that we move through psychological need states in a linear fashion. However, his ideas about the importance of survival needs remain a core, although often neglected, source of wisdom within contemporary psychology. Indeed, Maslow's theory provides a useful, albeit limited, heuristic that can be used to frame how people meet their needs at work.

Survival and Work: The Psychology-of-Working Theory

Over a half a century after Maslow's seminal work at Brooklyn College, I initiated a project that aspired to a similar sort of transformative change within my own field of career development that Maslow's work inspired to over half a century ago. The perspective that I formulated is known as the *psychology of working*; indeed, this perspective is not solely my brainchild. Like Maslow, who had some wonderful mentors and influences, the psychology of working has multiple sets of "parents" who have helped to auger in a novel and revolutionary approach to understanding the role of work in people's lives.[4]

My exploration into the psychology of working began as a critique of traditional career choice and development theories, which had gradually morphed into a field that assumed that most people had a relative degree of choice and volition in their lives.[5] Interestingly, the field of career counseling did not begin with a focus on people with relative privilege in the world of work; one of the originators of career counseling, Frank Parsons, a social activist from Boston in the early twentieth century, focused on helping working class people find their way in an increasingly complicated labor market.[6] For Parsons, the Industrial

Revolution offered both challenges and opportunities. The exponential growth of the number of possible occupations that people could pursue was seemingly boundless during the turn of the twentieth century. At the same time, this growth led to an expansive immigration policy in North America, which created the "perfect storm" for the emergence of the field of career counseling. At the outset, Parsons and his colleagues were most concerned with immigrant students and families who were struggling to find their way in the world.

The early decades of career counseling (initially known as vocational guidance) were devoted to helping people find their way in the world of work. The notion of finding a job that would be maximally fulfilling in relation to one's interests, values, and abilities was an aspiration, but it was not central for many people, particularly those who were transitioning from unemployment and poverty to a stable work life. The underlying goal in the first part of the twentieth century was helping people to find a job that was stable, was secure, and would build on one's strengths.

By the middle of the twentieth century, the world of work continued to change dramatically. Thanks to the Allied victory in World War II, significant economic dividends were being experienced by many countries, especially those that did not bear the brunt of the destruction of the war, such as the United States. In many ways, the field of career counseling was a barometer of the economy; as people felt the sense of openness in their work lives, thanks to the growing availability of higher education and training, the idea of finding a career that would be not only suitable but also passionate became the dream of many people in the United States and, indeed, across the globe.[7] Underlying this shift was the notion that a rewarding career could be had by all, not just the highly affluent or privileged.

By the last few decades of the twentieth century, the field of career counseling had transitioned into an enterprise that tended to focus on the lives of people who were being groomed for white-collar, professional, and management positions in the growing economies of Western nations. It is this context that I reacted to during the early part of my career. As I discussed in the Preface, growing up in a blue-collar home in Queens, New York, left me with a deep commitment to understanding the lives of all of those who work and who want to work. Creating the psychology of working framework and theory provided me with the conceptual tools to deepen my understanding of the working class community and with the capacity to pay forward my desire to contribute to the well-being of the full spectrum of people engaged in work or seeking work.

While Maslow's work was not overtly central in my thinking as I developed the ideas for the psychology of working, his contributions were embedded in my psyche, perhaps because I trained as a counseling psychologist during a period when humanistic psychology was emerging as a viable alternative to the prevailing perspectives in the field, such as psychoanalysis and behaviorism. The psychology of working theory also explored the nature and expression of our fundamental needs within the workplace. Unlike Maslow, who viewed his needs framework as hierarchical in nature, I proposed the three needs that working can fulfill can be experienced in different degrees and contexts at the same time, as summarized next and reflected in Figure 2.1.

1. Need for survival and power: As reflected in this chapter and in Chapter 1, the need for survival and power is central in how people evolved and in our earliest relationships to work. Working, at its best, can provide people with the means for surviving and, as we discussed further in this chapter, thriving. The power aspect of this need is reflected in the striving for adaptive levels of control over the various resources needed for one's capacity for survival.

2. Need for social connection and contribution: Working is one of the major contexts for people to be with others, develop relationships, and sustain the social connections that are so integral to living a full life. In the psychology of working theory, our needs for social connection can be fulfilled by direct contact with people at work and via the sense of contribution to the social and economic welfare of one's community and society. I explore this need in greater depth in Chapters 3 and 4.

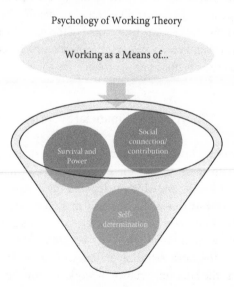

Figure 2.1 Psychology-of-working taxonomy.

3. Need for self-determination: At its best, working can provide people with a sense of feeling deeply engaged and alive in their lives. Being involved in activities that are intrinsically interesting or meaningful in facilitating our goals often yields a sense of connection to our tasks and may evoke feelings of self-determination and autonomy. The need for self-determination is explored further in Chapter 5.

These three needs provide an initial framework for understanding the psychological experiences of working. In fact, the subsequent chapters in this book expand this perspective by detailing how a wide array of work-related experiences can function to engage our sense of being in the world.

In the material that follows, I review the ways in which people make sense of their strivings for survival in the narratives from the Boston College Working Project. Following these vignettes, I highlight some important new findings from the world of psychological research and then conclude with a summary of the importance of survival needs in our work lives and in our overall sense of well-being.

Survival: Lived Experiences

One of the major themes that emerged in the participants' responses pertained to the financial aspects of work; however, a deeper analysis of the interviews revealed far more nuance and subtlety. We found that the participants' struggles to survive often generated opportunities for considerable feelings of achievement and satisfaction. At the same time, some of the participants told evocative stories of competitive and cold work environments, which became apparent as they dug deep into their histories and recollections about work.

Survival and Financial Security

The range of stories we heard about survival and the struggle for financial security was rich with insights into the complexities that have existed during and after the Great Recession, which stripped away a sense of security for so many Americans. (While recessions certainly make life more difficult for many people, the reality of our very unequal society is that a significant proportion of people struggle with survival when the economy is strong, as well as in recessions, even in the most robust economies.) One of the major themes in the interviews was the core importance of work in providing the financial resources needed for life and for caregiving. This experience was most obvious with individuals who faced poverty and a lack of other resources that are needed to get a foothold in the marketplace. From Joyce, a 31-year-old unemployed African American woman, we learn how the struggle for survival became embedded in her psyche:

> I know if you don't work, things won't ever happen, so work to me means action, you've got to put yourself out there, you've got to put it to work; whatever you need to do, make something happen for yourself. You need money; you got to go out and get a job. You need to go get your hair done; you got to work to go get your hair done. Work is action. Life is work, work is life. That's how I see work; it's life.

Jena, a 25-year-old African American woman who was unemployed at the time of our interview, conveyed a sense of desperation that was deep and profound. Jena was interviewed at a One-Stop Career Center, where she was seeking help with her job search, which had grown more and more challenging given her lack of housing and other resources.

> I see work as . . . a new form of modern slavery to me. . . . I've been out of work for almost 2 years now. And right now, I'm in desperate stuff. So I'm willing to . . . be a slave, to do whatever I need to do. . . . You do whatever the employer tells you to do, to keep the job. . . . As far as survival goals. I don't usually like materialistic things, only for things I need, so that's what I use it [money] for. And now my needs are so big because I've been homeless. I hardly have any money. When I do have money, I'm broke as a joke, because all my needs that to be dealt with. So, that's how my life is right now. . . . It's a huge challenge. I'm living with no money, and you have no money; in the USA, you need some type of money. And now, this is my second year at my local community college. I'm working; I'm striving very hard, keeping my grades up, dealing with the stress. . . . I'm having family issues; I got a lot of issues going on that are trying to distract me from focusing on my school. . . . I'm kind of stuck with asking people for anything. . . . I'm in desperate needs, so now here I am.

The fact that Jena observed parallels between slavery and her struggles to work is painfully evocative, particularly coming from an African American woman whose ancestors did in fact toil in slavery for hundreds of years. Jena also describes her hopes for upward mobility, which are complicated by ongoing family struggles, a general absence of support from others, and a lack of adequate financial resources; this upward mobility would certainly help to smooth her rocky pathway out of poverty.

Rebecca, the 33-year-old wellness director working in a resort on a small Caribbean island we met in Chapter 1, discussed how the need for survival counters the myth of seeking a career that reflects one's inner aspirations. Her comments are particularly interesting because she was able to find a way to survive while also making her dreams come true:

> So about career, so that the message that you don't necessarily follow your dreams and what makes you happy. That's not what you do for work. What you do for work is that you get an education, you build these qualifications, you work for corporations or a business, and you earn your own money that way. So these are the messages, not necessarily following dreams and passion, but rather I found that these messages stifle creativity. "Oh that's nice, but you know that's not what matters in life; what matters in life is making a good job and a good home, and good family." Sort of this message, that if you do what makes you happy; you work [and you can] "be successful." If you do what makes you happy, you end up a bum. A bum on a beach (laughing), just like me! So that's a big message from the United States.

Rebecca was actually working on a beach during this interview. In this passage and in her full interview, she described the impact of social messages about sacrificing the meaning and rewards that one can attain at work for the security of a stable job. However, her story foreshadows a theme that also emerged in the interviews about how some of the participants were able to transform their struggle for survival into a broader push toward self-determination and purpose at work.

In the next passage, David, a 55-year-old massage therapist of European and Native American heritage described having to survive with a major, chronic illness, which forced him to stay at a job that caused him considerable psychological distress.

> Well, everything is kind of a compromise. . . . The biggest one I made was to stay at [my former employer—a university] to get the health benefits. If I was truly tortured at my job at the university and thought it was awful, I might have looked, but knowing I had a security blanket there and also knowing that after a certain period of time that managers come and go so even if you have a bad one, you stick around, and hopefully they'll be gone. That turned out to be the case. I made compromises to hold that health insurance.

Amidst the stories about survival and work, the lives of rural people are often neglected or missing. The following quotation from Mike, who lives in a small town in upstate New York, attests to the challenges of finding work in communities without many options:

> I always tried to make a dollar here and there. I cut corn in the wintertime, but it was cold. I would get a Skidoo suit, all dressed up and cut corn. It was probably 15 to 20 degrees above zero on a tractor with no cab. . . . We were always trying to make dollar to keep living and we did. We paid everything ourselves. We never asked for help.

These vignettes, however brief, reveal the tip of the iceberg of the compelling, and often heart-wrenching stories of survival by the participants in the interviews. For some individuals, the need for survival was the preeminent experience that defined their existence; some would describe waking up in the morning with this worry emerging as their first thought each day. For other participants, working represents an opportunity to express their interests and values in the world, often with considerable feelings of achievement and satisfaction. (I explore these themes in subsequent chapters.) In the following sections, I describe the additional dimensions of surviving that are somewhat outside the main terrain of financial security, which individually and collectively provide an illuminating glimpse of the psychological experience of working in contemporary America.

Survival and Thriving

As we have seen, some individuals have been able to carve out meaning and satisfaction from their working lives, despite facing very real and pervasive pressures to survive. As Rebecca, the wellness director in the Caribbean, conveyed in her interview, she was aware of the demands for survival, but she had the capacity to identify her dream and ultimately thrive in a job that gave her considerable rewards. In this section, we explore the narratives that focus on how people found a way to move from the pain of the struggle to survive to a place where they could thrive at work.

Mark, a 63-year-old White educator and entrepreneur, described a fascinating journey from growing up in a middle-class family in the New York City area to reaching a high level of achievement as a business owner of various educationally related ventures. Beginning his career as a public school teacher, Mark soon realized that while he was able to cover the basic costs for his family, he did not have sufficient income to live the life that he dreamed of, which included providing the best resources for his children and nurturing his love of traveling. The next passage describes some of his inner thoughts about the transition from focusing on surviving to thriving in his work life.

> So, even though I was a teacher, I was making good money. But, it wasn't cutting it. I wasn't able to save for college. I wouldn't be able to help my kids go to camps or whatever they wanted. So, early on, I knew I had to start hustling. So, after I got my doctorate [in education], I knew I had to develop some sort of business as a second income. So what I did was become self-educated. I went to some continuing ed courses at [a local college] and other places, just to learn business, marketing and stuff like that. And I thought of business. . . . People that have niche skills will always be in demand. So, although I'm a teacher, I consider myself a teacher. I've created a niche, which is I'm an entrepreneur-teacher. How many of those are around?

Mark continued to describe his transformation from working as a teacher at a public school to running a highly successful business in speed-reading, which then grew to include other services, such as test preparation. Throughout the growth of Mark's business, he remained on the faculty of a suburban high school. Mark's narrative reveals that he was able to move from a survival mode to a work life that allowed for greater intrinsic and extrinsic satisfaction; this was attained via access to further education and training and by tapping into his own natural tendencies to engage in the world of business. In effect, he merged his two interests into a coherent career strategy.

> I've created a niche for myself. And I've been able to thrive. If I just thought of myself as just a generic teacher, I'd be competing with millions of other people; I wouldn't have thrived. Those are opportunities for others as well. So, instead of being a lawyer, don't just think of yourself as a generic lawyer, create a market for yourself. How could you apply it in a different way that can allow you to thrive? Or are you a physician? Create an opportunity for yourself, where that you're doing something that requires the physician skills, but also some other type of skill—maybe an entrepreneurial skill; maybe a legal, something else—those types of people will continue to thrive in this new economy.

From Mark's account of how he made his dreams come true, we now shift to the struggles faced by Jerome, who was caught up in the maelstrom of the Great Recession. Jerome, a 59-year-old African American former professor, described his struggle to return from a period of unemployment at the height of the recession to a new and meaningful work life.

[After losing my job at the university], I had to empty my annuity account. You know I had to empty my retirement, and start looking for a job. And it was right during the start of the recession. I mean it was right in the middle, right at the end of the Bush, and still a year left of the Bush presidency. So it was survival mode. . . . Eventually I lost my house; I put all my stuff in storage, and started looking for jobs and you know, I couldn't even tell you how many jobs I applied for. I would say well over 200 jobs. I wasn't even getting a call back. . . . I was applying literally all over the world. I got offered to go to China, and run an ESL program in Shanghai, English as a second language. So I went there and after 3 months of that, the school basically said, we don't want an ESL program. Then I was in China without an ESL program. Right around that time is when I met my now wife. And she took a job; she was a college and career counselor in China. And she decided to take a job here in South Carolina . . . but we didn't want to do long distance, so I came here with her. Now I have to do some training for a company that was working on Fortune 500 companies that was dealing with helping companies change culture. That was a yearlong training basically, and you weren't really getting paid. Then I found another company there that I thought I could help, and they asked me to write my own job description and I did. And they hired me and then things slowly started to change. . . . Then I became a consultant for this Chinese company, and then I was asked to apply for the executive director, or for the CEO [chief executive officer]/president of Big Brothers Big Sisters, and so I did and I got the job. So, I went from no job to consulting, one full-time job, and now two consulting gigs.

Delving deeper into Jerome's story revealed that he had several resources available to him—most notably his education and flexibility—that helped him to move from struggling for survival to once again working and experiencing considerable satisfaction. The comments that follow underscore the degree to which Jerome was able to draw on some elusive, but clearly evident, internal resources, which allowed him to be resilient in the face of considerable barriers:

Well, I want to be, I want to be fulfilled, but I want to create the environment where I am running to work, and not running from it. I want to build relationships with the people that I am working with. . . . I want to continue to learn, and learn something new. I want to be able to share and teach others. I want to have fun. I want to be appreciated. I want to be listened to, and I want to be mentored, to name a few.

Jerome's clear statement of wanting to be mentored emerged later in his interview, when he described the role of others in helping to inspire him and offer him support, which seemed to be critical in supporting him through a difficult period in his work life.

> I left home when I was 11 years old and grew up in a boy's school. And so, I had to grow up relatively quickly and I always had an optimistic nature and I have always surrounded myself with just amazing really good people, really solid people. So, I've had a lot of different individuals . . . a lot of really good people over my life span that have played an intricate role in my success. I call it my crystal board of directors.

Milo, a 38-year-old African American career counselor at a prestigious university in New England, described the struggles of growing up in a working-class community on Chicago's South Side. His narrative includes a subtext of how he was able to move from a world governed by the need for survival to finding a work life that would allow him to thrive.

> Growing up as a young kid in the South Side of Chicago, from a family of four who I guess would be described as working poor . . . how we thought about the world was probably very different than how someone else thought about the world. And, for me it was more imaginative. . . . My father always took me to museums, and he engaged me in the world in a way in which I thought, "Wow! So many possibilities, so many possibilities!" I never was one of those kids that say, "I'm just going to do that one thing." I wanted to do everything! And so . . . But in thinking about it, I knew that . . . God, resources were constrained. And thinking about how do you get there . . . I mean I saw it: It would be exciting to be that person, or do that thing, but how do you get there? So, I think one of the challenges and obstacles was the in-between stuff. And it's hard to quantify what that looks like. It's just like: OK, I need to get to college to get to the next step. Alright, so how do I get to college? I need to submit an application and so forth. . . . Well, my parents never went through that process. . . . Navigating it wasn't something that was intuitive. . . . So I think just navigating the challenges, and really . . . gaining understanding as you go from one challenge to the next. You know, you think, "Wow! It's really interesting not having . . . . If I only had this particular resource; it would be easy to move to the next step." So, just going to college, to give you an example, was expensive! It was easy getting accepted to college, but I mean [laughing] that doesn't help if you can't pay for it!

Milo continued to describe his journey, which involved a process of exploration and decision-making that was complicated by the barriers of racism, classism, and lack of access to social capital. Milo's powerful story attests to his capacity to develop resources by accessing the support of others and developing his own resources.

> There was always someone throughout all the challenges that I faced that said, "You know what? I'm going to push you through." And once they did, they were rewarded. I wasn't worried about the return. I knew I would deliver. But sometimes . . . you have to have someone to say, "You know? I can do this part for you." And that's essentially what happened. I finished my education. And after that [laughing], I was such a pro, I finished the education again and got my master's degree. And I guess to get back to your question, from the obstacles . . . well, you know, there were obstacles . . . and then also, figuring out the world. I was the first person in my family to finish a degree—any degree, any certificate! So I really didn't know what role I was to play in the world. I mean it's one thing to sort of look at it, and say, "Wow! I'm going to be XYZ!" But . . . wow, now that I had . . . you know, when I was getting my degree I could see it. . . . What exactly did that mean? What was I going to do? Does that mean lawyer, teacher, doctor, a pilot? I had no idea. . . . So I think the other challenge was trying to figure that out. And how I resolved that challenge was good old trial and error. . . . Doing some jobs . . . not liking them . . . talking to people in career counseling. There are a series of happenstance. . . . There was a lot of happenstance, there was, sort of learning just by being in the right place at the right time. . . . Looking at other people doing what they were doing. . . . And so I sort of said, you know what? I'm piecing things together.

As in the case of Jerome, having the support of others was critical for Milo. Indeed, the narratives that described how people were able to move from "survival mode," which is the term that was actually used by a few of our participants, to finding a work life of meaning and joy are replete with indications of factors that seemed to help people develop a more purposeful and meaningful path in their work lives. Many of the participants who were able to navigate their way out of the often-painful cycle of survival jobs reported a reasonable level of access to financial and social capital. The case of Mark, who moved from being a suburban high school teacher to being a very successful entrepreneur, affirms the importance of educational resources and the utility of having a sound job, which gave him the flexibility and security to explore new paths for himself. Similarly, Milo conveyed the essential role of social capital: He had access to people in his life and to people at the colleges he attended who believed in him and who were able to show him the subtle and often-elusive ways that people are able to navigate the unknown waters of postsecondary education and work. Yet, at the same time, Mark and Milo, as well as many others in our sample, were able to draw on their own internal resources of resilience, drive, and self-confidence, which helped them to move from the survival mode at work to the gift of a work life with meaning and satisfaction. One of the objectives of this book is to flesh out the complex array of internal and external factors that intersect, often in intricate ways, to give people enough rope to climb out of the quagmire of working relentlessly for survival.

Survival and Relationships

Another prominent theme that emerged in the narratives focused on the connection between survival and interpersonal relationships. Naturally, relationships are often at center stage in considerations of survival and work given that much of the money that is earned in working is used to support our loved ones and family members. The tension between managing the need for survival and caring for our families may cause significant distress, as reflected in the passage that follows by Jena, who previously in this chapter shared her experiences of working for survival while unemployed:

> My family, they had to help me in [the] past, but they also took money from me, did a lot of grimy stuff. . . . So just like the tip of the iceberg, it's the reason why I'm homeless now. Um, I got a crazy ass mother. . . . And so, I'm trying; it's a distraction in my life, dealing with family who does not understand how important school would be. They want me to help them, and I can't help nobody, cause I don't have . . . any money for myself. So that's what I'm dealing with right now, like, I don't know how to explain it, but . . . let's see, how can I say it. . . . They take a lot. . . . They take away from me, and now I'm . . . back where I started from.

Jena's situation is clearly more complex than conveyed in this brief passage. However, the emotional turmoil that comes as a result of poverty is evident through her narrative, underscoring the myriad and pervasive impacts of a lack of resources.

In the following passage, Robert, a 51-year-old unemployed, college-educated White man, describes the breakup of a relationship with his romantic partner, which he attributed, in part, to his inability to sustain his survival needs:

I mean part of the reason why the girlfriend left was because she didn't like that I made her sad. And you know she was unhappy to begin with so. She didn't want me to be around to, at least that's my theory is that my unemployment made her sad, even though I tried to protect her from it. . . . It made her sad. And so she wanted one less sad thing in life so—two and a half years down the drain because she didn't want to be sad. So, people you know. In many cases they just do it, they just care for themselves.

In this next passage, Patricia, a 27-year-old college-educated White woman, describes the impact of watching her father go through a period of unemployment, which profoundly affected her views of work and survival. When she was interviewed, she was working in the food services industry and going back to school for a degree in nursing, which was motivated, in large measure, by her desire for stability in work.

I don't really have a very high opinion on corporations and big companies who are outsourcing. I have a very negative view . . . partly because my Dad was laid-off last year. He worked for [a publishing company] for . . . almost like 10 years—and then before that, he worked for a company . . . that [was] bought out. And for several of the years that he was working under this company, he was sent over to India a few times to do outsourcing training. So he knew he was digging his own grave, because eventually his job would be outsourced, but at the same time his company was sending him there to do it, so what was he going to do, say no and get fired then? So, he was fired last year, a couple weeks before Christmas. And he really hasn't found a job since. Which sucks because he was getting paid I think $120–140K a year, so if a company can only offer him $80K, they're obviously not going to take him, because they think he's going to be looking for another job. So . . . I don't like corporations because you can work your ass off. . . . You know my Dad was. . . . Talk about supermodels—not "super" models, "role models"!—You know, my Dad worked really hard all throughout my childhood. Until I was about 14, he was working nights, every night. So he would leave for work around 6–7 p.m., come back at like, 4–5 (a.m.), sleep during the day as best as you can when you're a human being . . . and then go back and do the whole thing. And then he was on call all the time. . . . He was director of operations, so he was on call 24/7, and no matter how much personal time he sacrificed, how many days he could have been spending with his kids instead of sleeping during the day. . . . He sacrificed that and they still fired him before he could retire. And I just think that was . . . pretty awful. . . . So I don't have a high opinion for a government that allows companies to do things like that to individuals because of laissez-faire operations, or whatever.

Patricia then discussed her own career goals, where the need for stability and security emerged as important considerations, which allowed her to explore the healthcare world in vivo.

> I'm currently in nursing school, so I can have a career and not have to worry about getting an hourly wage and all that. . . . After my time in the Peace Corps, I was working in a rural health clinic, where I did the dispensary, dispensing medicine in local languages, and doing malaria testing, and then. . . . There was a lot of extra work too, because you had to talk to your neighbors in the local language, and explain to them . . . and you kind of help with questions that they had within the very limited knowledge that I did have at the time. And so. . . . But, you know, I saw that . . . this could be a career that I could do. And in the U.S., it's a very secure position because hospitals are run pretty well here. So, wanting . . . So wanting to become a nurse, and then maybe eventually a nurse practitioner, and not have to worry about working 12-hour days, 5 days, 6 days a week . . . would be really nice.

Finding a balance between working for survival and managing one's caregiving needs is one of the major challenges of the contemporary American world of work, particularly for people who are not privileged to have sufficient resources to afford to hire others to care for family members. Kim, a 26-year-old Asian American woman who worked as a customer service associate for a large retail store, described her experiences managing the need for survival and the need to take care of her family.

> Before I was pregnant with my first child, I was going to cosmetology [school]. I had so many different ideas, so many like, I could open up a beauty salon or I could even open up a beauty school or I could sell my own makeup or my own products. You know, so many ideas, but that was before I had a family of my own. Now after I got my certificate, I'm thinking about how hair stylists mainly they live off of their income, kind of like a commission job and if I was to get my license and work at a salon right now and not have kids, I think I would be able to do it. It's an income where, it's not a set income—the income is based on how many clients you have per day, per hour. And after I was done with school, I was like, oh my gosh, I think this is something I should have done before I started a family. This is something that I might just enjoy doing as a hobby in the future. So

that's why I can't do anything with it right now cause . . . and it's often really a competitive field to go into also. So it's all about who you know, how good of a job you do, the reputation you have. So that's something that I would do in the future but my main focus right now is just to survive with my girls actually. Have food on the table for them. Having clothes for them to wear, getting them a good education. It's kind of like their time, but I'm starting my time, too, starting my life, my career, too. But I have to give some time for them, too. . . . I'm only working [now] 8 hours a week. What am I going to do? So when I started my first semester . . . I broke down. I was going through a phase where I was . . . I didn't know what to do. I . . . yeah, it was really stressful . . . super super stressful.

Kim's struggles resonate with so many people in the United States and indeed around the globe who need to find ways to balance the demands of care work in the family context and work in the marketplace. Kim's comments touch on an important theme. The close relationship between work and relational life has in fact generated a great deal of attention in psychology and other disciplines.[8] The intensity of Kim's comments underscore the passion and anguish that goes into the balancing act that is so particularly evident when we are caring for young children, loved ones with disabling conditions, and our elderly family members.

As a means of further elaborating on the nature of survival needs, the next section of the chapter summarizes insights from the psychology literature about some of the challenges and complexities inherent in the ongoing struggle to meet the challenges of surviving.

Survival: The Psychological View

Despite Maslow placing survival needs at the core of his seminal work, psychological research on survival has not been a central issue within the study of work and careers. In this section, three specific themes from psychological research are presented and provide some insights into the nature of how people manage the struggle for survival via work: time perspective, work volition, and moving from survival to self-determination.

Time Perspective

One of the most important aspects of planning a work life of meaning and satisfaction is to be able to envision oneself in the future—in effect, to develop a long-term future orientation. Considerable research in psychology has pointed to the importance of a future orientation, which provides people with the capacity to plan ahead, delay gratification, and, perhaps most important, to feel hopeful about the future. Mark Savickas, a leading scholar and thought leader in vocational psychology, has examined the importance of time perspective for people who have some degree of volition in their work lives. Savickas and his colleagues found that a future orientation was associated with greater degrees of planfulness and adaptive beliefs about one's role in the world of work.[9] Recent studies in Italy confirmed the view that a future time perspective is associated with less career indecision and with greater levels of academic achievement in high school.[10] Brian Taber from Oakland University summarized current interventions that have been constructed to enhance the future orientation of students and clients as they consider optimal career paths. The prevailing view is that having a long-term time perspective is a positive attribute, one that can contribute to a rewarding career trajectory.[11]

Despite the conventional wisdom (and empirical research supporting these assumptions) about the utility of a future orientation, some scholars have wondered what happens to the time perspective of those who are focused on satisfying their immediate needs for survival. A recent review of scholarly contributions on time perspective and poverty by two French psychologists, Nicolas Fieulaine and Themis Apostolidis, revealed a stark truth about the intersection of survival needs and future orientation.[12] In short, when people are faced with demands to meet their immediate survival needs, their time perspectives become shorter and more focused on proximal issues as opposed to long-term plans. In a number of studies of socioeconomic status and time perspective conducted by Fieulaine and Apostolidis as well as other researchers, the findings were clear that poverty and a precarious work life are associated with a shorter time perspective. The research that Fieulaine and Apostolidis reviewed also affirmed that the shorter time perspective is a changeable aspect of one's disposition; the compressed time perspective experienced by those who are struggling for survival is likely caused by the complex and pervasive impact of economic necessity that forces people to consider their most pressing needs rather than their long-term plans. In effect, not having one's survival needs fulfilled via work or via adequate social and economic resources has a profound effect on how people view themselves in relation to time. Rather than being able to map out a dream for a meaningful work life, those mired in poverty and limited work options are often left having to live in the present, with little time and space to consider a better future.

Work Volition

When people are struggling to survive, they often have less control about their choices in life and options in their work lives. Ryan Duffy, a highly talented and prolific counseling psychologist from the University of Florida, has developed an extensive body of research identifying the antecedents, attributes, and consequences of work volition. In my thinking, I have viewed work volition as "choice in one's work life"; in fact, I have proposed that survival needs can have a profound impact on how people experience their work-related tasks and goals.[13] Duffy views work volition as a perception of choice, but is aware that this perception is rooted in a reality that is often governed by survival needs.[14]

In numerous studies conducted with college students, adults (both employed and unemployed), and veterans, Duffy and his colleagues have mapped the impact of work volition. Integrating these findings within the context of the current discussion on survival and thriving leads to a number of important observations. First, people who have greater access to resources, such as financial support, educational opportunities, and fewer external constraints, tend to experience greater levels of choice in their work lives, including the capacity to select a career that fits with their values and interests. Second, people with greater control in choosing their pathway into the world of work are more likely to experience greater meaning and satisfaction in their lives. As Duffy's highly original work shows, people who have access to the resources that promote self-determination are clearly more advantaged in their lives and are able to experience career choice privilege, one of the most coveted aspects of freedom in the contemporary world. Career choice privilege refers to the capacity to make one's work life into an integral and meaningful part of life—a gift that many of us who have career choice privilege do not even acknowledge as we consider our lives and opportunities. The narratives reviewed previously indicate clearly that those without much career choice privilege do not forget this part of their lives so readily.

Moving From Survival to Self-Determination: What the Research Shows

One of the more promising themes in the Boston College Working Project narratives is reflected in the often-poignant stories of how people managed to move from working for survival to a more meaningful and self-determined career trajectory. Several of the participants we interviewed shared stories that conveyed the importance of notable internal resources (such as resilience, confidence, and the capacity to draw on the wisdom of others) as well as external resources (such as access to good schools, financial security, supportive family members, and mentors). Individually and collectively, these resources helped some of the participants find a pathway in their work lives that provided greater satisfaction and even joy. A number of empirical studies in psychology have explored the same sets of issues and challenges, revealing important insights about the struggle to move beyond working for survival.

In research that my colleagues and I initiated during the mid-1990s, we were curious about the lives of people who did not transition from high school to college; our specific focus was on non–college-bound young adults who worked in factories, car washes, supermarkets, and other service jobs after high school.[15] We interviewed 60 young adults, ranging in age from 18 to 29, to learn more about their work experiences and their sense of opportunity in the world. Using data from the participants' family histories, we categorized the sample into a three socioeconomic statuses, ranging from low to high. Using a sample of 10 participants from higher socioeconomic status and 10 participants from lower socioeconomic status, we were able to derive some important insights about the impact of social and economic factors on the work lives of young adults during the 1990s.

The qualitative analyses were consistent and clear: For those participants from lower socioeconomic backgrounds, the choices about work were made based on survival needs; in contrast, those young adults who were from higher socioeconomic backgrounds experienced their work as a transient state, a temporary stop on a trajectory that would optimally yield a more satisfying future. This study underscored the degree to which socioeconomic status impacts on a core aspect of one's working life: the extent to which people feel hopeful about the future and their sense of being able to transcend the drudgery and anguish of working for survival. The participants from higher socioeconomic backgrounds, while not necessarily thriving in their current work lives, envisioned a more positive future, perhaps because of their access to familial, social, and economic resources that promote upward mobility.

In a recent study on the work lives of adults during the height of the Great Recession, Mike Vuolo and his colleagues conducted a sophisticated set of quantitative analyses with over 1,000 participants from the Youth Development Study to understand how the youth moved from survival jobs to "career" jobs, which is the term that was used to describe jobs that reflected greater volition and self-determination.[16] Their study revealed some fascinating trends, which complement the observations from the Boston College Working Project.

Using a longitudinal design, they found that individuals who felt that they could control the course of their lives (often known as *agency* in psychology) were better able to ride out the fluctuations of the Great Recession. This "can-do" attitude, referred to as *agentic striving*, reflects high levels of educational aspirations, adaptive job search skills, and career choice certainty, which collectively represents an active and confident approach to the tasks of creating a work life that fulfills needs for both survival and self-determination. In effect, adolescents and young adults who had this configuration of agentic-striving attributes were better able to navigate the Great Recession, as reflected by lower levels of unemployment in comparison to people who did not develop the agentic-striving skill set.

These two studies, while clearly representing just a sampling of psychological research on survival and self-determination, do provide some useful insights. First, the basic findings that we reported are in fact fairly consistent in the psychological literature, thereby reflecting some important observations about how people navigate survival and self-determination needs.[17] Second, the in-depth analyses revealed in these two bodies of work suggest that the movement between survival and self-determination is based on both social and economic forces and internal psychological resources. In the conclusion that follows, the insights from these psychological studies are weaved together with the observations from the participants from the Boston College Working Project.

Conclusion

The struggle for survival, which represents perhaps the primordial drive for people, remains a profoundly important issue for many people, as reflected in the poignant narratives of the participants whose voices comprise much of this chapter. When considering the narratives in light of the research reported in the previous section, a fuller picture emerges of the complex relationship between surviving and thriving at work. The lack of opportunities in the labor market to obtain decent work was clearly the "elephant in the room" for people trying to make their way in the world. People who did not have access to good education, training opportunities, social connections, and economic resources were often mired in the struggle to meet their short-term needs for survival. In contrast, people who had access to these important resources frequently began with survival jobs but were able to move to career paths that offered them opportunities for self-determination and for an enjoyable work life.

While these contextual issues are clearly powerful, we also saw that there was a cluster of individual attributes—as exemplified in the notion of agentic striving—that seems to help people navigate the often-rough seas of the labor market. While some of the participants in the Boston College Working Project reported that they were able to draw on their inner resources and determination, it is useful to speculate about where this inner strength comes from. The psychology literature has pointed to the importance of early childhood enrichment experiences, effective parenting, emotional support, and other "psychosocial goodies" that nurture the development of these inner resources.[18] In addition, the availability of supportive people, good healthcare, decent housing, and safe environments provides the nourishing soil for the development of resilience and agency among adults.[19] Here again, we point back to the importance of people's contexts. Parents who have access to sources of survival are generally better able to give their children the goodies that promote well-being and resilience, which is helpful in creating lives of meaning and satisfaction at work.

What is clear from this chapter is that the drive for survival is an essential aspect of being alive in the world. Creating opportunities for people to meet this integral aspect of human experience, naturally, is a challenge that will require the best of our inner spirits and a commitment to nurturing the needs of the entire spectrum of people in our communities.

3

Being With Others

Let us begin this chapter by exploring the ideas put forward by two very diverse, but thoughtful, people who have considered the experience of being with others in relation to work. One of these people created a body of work that has engendered much admiration and appreciation, yet considerable critique, across the globe: Sigmund Freud. The second individual also has made important and meaningful contributions as a musician, songwriter, and parent; however, this individual, Matteo—(also known as Participant 24 from the Boston College Working Project), no doubt lives a more circumscribed life than the world that Freud inhabited. Matteo has described the connection between work and relationships in an evocative and passionate manner that complements Freud's erudite writing. Freud and Mateo each give voice to the complex ways that work and relationships share space in our lives and create the fabric for a full and rich connection to others and to a life of purpose and meaning.

In actuality, Freud did not extensively discuss work much in his voluminous literature. However, the phrase that love and work are the hallmarks of mental health has often been attributed to Freud.[1] A close look at Freud's work, however, reveals a far more complex assessment of the relationship between love and work, as reflected in the following passage from his classic publication, *Civilization and Its Discontents*: "The communal life of human beings had, therefore, a two-fold foundation: the compulsion to work, which was created by external necessity, and the power of love" (1930, p. 88).[2] Freud's comments throughout *Civilization and Its Discontents* attest to the demands of work as a means for survival. He also proposed that work functions as a way of helping people express their inherent biological drives (referred to as the libido in psychoanalytic theory), which were often sublimated in works of art, architecture, the competitive marketplace, and other domains where people can find an outlet for their strivings for dominance, control, and achievement.[3] Since Freud's contributions, much of the psychoanalytic discourse has shifted dramatically to a focus on relational connections, which is reviewed in the next section of this chapter.[4] Indeed, these new innovations in psychoanalytic theory and in psychology in general have had a major impact on how working is now understood.

Matteo's comments about work are insightful in a more emotionally evocative way than Freud's scholarly observations, and they foreshadow many of the themes that have emerged from the narratives from the participants in the Boston College Working Project. At the time of the interview, Matteo was a 45-year-old White man who had devoted himself to his calling of a musical career in both engineering and songwriting/performance. He encountered significant challenges in his life, including a divorce, bankruptcy, and a prison term. Luckily, he was able to bounce back from some dark periods in his life; this was thanks to support from others, his faith, a deep commitment to his craft, and his own strengths: optimism and flexibility. During each of these experiences, his support system and personal qualities helped him to regain his footing. Describing his experience with bankruptcy, he explained the powerful connection between work and relationships:

> Bankruptcy—I felt like a failure in that I wasn't able to change and market myself well, or adjust to the changes in the recording industry. There was an emotional and mental impact on me that hit me, and it happened to be at the same time that my ex-wife was having an affair. So, the divorce was impending, the bankruptcy was impending . . . and my decision-making was deteriorating. And that's what led to my car accident and prison eventually. . . . That was probably the darkest time in my life, because all my identity—again, for me as a man, my identity is in my work—and you know, my marriage, and both those things were falling—my twin towers—were falling apart. The only thing I had left was my fatherhood, but I was not able to see the forest through the trees. My fatherhood was really what could have pulled me through, but I was so overwhelmed by the bankruptcy, the immense bills of the house that we just bought, and the debt that we were incurring . . . and the pressure to make sure that the bills were met, and the marriage falling apart. You know, you feel like a failure all around. As a man, I feel like I failed in the marriage, I feel like I failed in my work.

When Matteo discussed the loss of both his job and his marriage, the pain was evident, particularly as he compared these losses to the destruction of the World Trade Center twin towers during the 9/11 bombings in New York City. The analogy of the Twin Towers is very powerful and conveys a deep understanding of the complex and poignant ways that work and relationships intersect in our lives. In the case of Matteo, the simultaneous loss of work and a core relationship was overwhelming and led to a deep sense of despair and questioning about the meaning of his life. In this chapter, we explore their common foundations and highlight the vulnerability that we face in work and relationships.

In this chapter, like the previous chapters, I initially present a conceptual framework of how we are with others in relation to work; in effect, this material summarizes some core principles about how relationships and work ideally function in tandem to give our lives meaning, purpose, intimacy, joy, and a sense of accomplishment. The voices from the participants of the Boston College Working Project are presented next, culminating in insightful observations about how being with others at work functions in profoundly important and, at times, deeply painful, ways. The section that follows summarizes relevant psychological research that complements and enriches the observations culled from the narrative vignettes. The final section concludes with recommendations for future considerations for understanding and promoting the relational well-being of people at work.

Being With Others: An Introductory Journey

For much of the history of psychology and, indeed, in many other fields and policy conversations, work-related issues have been understood as fairly distinct experiences, often removed from the natural course of life, which is so rooted in families and relationships. One can easily speculate how this separation emerged. Within many cultures, economics, policy analysis, and finance have tended to dominate public discussions about work—in effect, a big picture view that is somewhat removed from the experience of people as they actually inhabit their lives. Prior to the Industrial Revolution, people generally participated in subsistence farming, made handicrafts at home, developed trades, or engaged other modes of making a living that were embedded in their families and communities. As factories expanded, people increasingly left their homes for work, which required regimented and focused activities that often resulted in less ongoing interpersonal contact with others.[5]

The natural flow of work for most people, however, cannot be truly divorced from the relational world. Even in cases when people are working alone, they may think about work in a relational way, connecting their tasks to others working on similar projects and considering how their work is contributing to others in society.[6] Moreover, losing one's job, whether due to layoffs, voluntary departures, or retirement, clearly places relational experiences of working into bold relief. People without work often struggle with isolation, a lack of meaningfulness, and loneliness.[7] (This very challenging issue is explored further in Chapter 8.)

The Relational Revolution

Freud's earliest work in psychoanalysis conceived of human beings as being hardwired to seek satisfaction for their libidos—the part of the psyche that is oriented toward sexual satisfaction and self-preservation.[8] As Freud continued to progress, his thinking evolved, and he also became increasingly aware of the importance of past and current relationships in determining psychological health. At the same time, psychologists outside the psychoanalytic tradition were developing various theories to explain what made people tick. What motivates our behavior, desires, and aspirations, including our hopes for meaningful and rewarding work lives? These are complex questions that have evoked a wide array of ideas and theories, many of which were highly circumscribed, separating work and relationships into categories that were often intellectually coherent, but not exactly in sync with the way that people actually exist. This separation of life spaces into work and nonwork contexts provided a useful heuristic, but missed a core essence of life: Work and relationships are integrated into the pores of our being, reflecting our shared evolutionary history and our shared hope for intimacy, connections, and meaning in life.

Another set of assumptions prominent during the early and mid-twentieth century affected how people thought about relationships. Models of psychological health tended to affirm the importance of autonomy in adult life. People who were more oriented toward others, who sought the input of others, and who seemed to yearn for connection could be construed as developmentally lagged or troubled in some fundamental ways.[9] These assumptions soon gave way as the discourse in psychology shifted markedly thanks to the feminist revolution and to a spirit of critical analysis about the fundamental tenets of the psychology of the twentieth century. By the end of the twentieth century, most scholars and practitioners in psychology concurred that we were in the midst of a relational revolution.[10] How did relational thinking become so central in psychology, and more recently, in studies of work and careers?

From various vantage points, including therapy offices, consulting practices, universities, and psychological laboratories, a converging view has emerged: People are hardwired to seek out, and make meaning of, connections with others.[11] This hardwiring is part of our survival apparatus and is essential in helping our very immature infants to survive. One of the mavericks in advancing the relational revolution was John Bowlby, a psychiatrist with interests in developmental psychology and anthropology, who developed a transformative perspective known as attachment theory.[12] Given the reality that human infants cannot survive on their own, Bowlby speculated that both parents and infants are born with inherent strivings for connection. For infants, the striving is manifested by needs for attachment and security; for parents, the striving centers on caregiving.[13] This matrix of relational needs helps to explain how our young survive, even in the face of harsh environmental conditions. Moreover, Bowlby and his colleagues described how attachment strivings continue throughout adulthood, creating a strong disposition in people toward being with others.[14]

Another important intellectual advance in the latter part of the twentieth century was the very creative and rich work of Carol Gilligan, a Harvard developmental psychologist, who took on some of the conventional wisdom around the evolution of moral development. Rather than affirming the view that optimal moral development would lead to outcomes rooted in individualistic and autonomous conceptions of morality, Gilligan argued that this perspective did not capture a sense of morality that is rooted in caring for others and in affirming the importance of relationships.[15] Gilligan inspired many other feminist scholars who critiqued the male hegemony in psychology, including some notable advances in career counseling, psychotherapy, and organizational consulting, which increasingly has affirmed our natural orientation toward seeking relational connections.[16]

The psychoanalytic world, which Freud and his colleagues established well over a century ago, also has experienced the transformative impact of the relational revolution. Beginning with the initial critiques of Freud's theory in the early twentieth century, psychoanalysts and therapists began to realize that sometimes a cigar is just a cigar: A client who is feeling lonely, isolated, or anxious about relationships may indeed be experiencing the natural disappointments of relational life, with its unpredictable twists and turns. Thanks to the insights of very creative relationally oriented psychoanalysts (such as Winnicott, Fairburn, Mitchell, Wachtel, and many others), the relational revolution has transformed Freud's initial ideas about the impact of early development and the nature of our psychological constitutions.[17] Like Bowlby and Gilligan, the relational theorists now affirmed the critical importance of people throughout the life course, including, but not limited to, childhood. One of the most important of the relationally oriented psychoanalysts, Heinz Kohut, described our need for people as analogous to our need for oxygen: an essential ingredient in sustaining life.[18]

The Relationships and Work Landscape

So, how does this relational revolution affect our understanding of people's lives at work? As I present throughout this chapter, relationships and work have a complex and intersecting impact on each other. For the most part throughout the twentieth century, psychologists, career practitioners, human resource professionals, and organizational consultants have viewed the adaptive worker as an independent person who is able to function well without leaning too much on others. In fact, some of the decision-making models used in career counseling in the mid- to later twentieth century highlighted the importance of independent decision-making, eschewing the input of others, and often interpreting such behavior as a sign of dependency.[19] However, the relational revolution soon seeped into the psychological study of working, culminating in a sea change in the intellectual landscape of work and careers.

As in traditional psychology, input from feminism and multicultural studies fostered a needed critique of the predominance of models of work and career that reified independent and autonomous functioning.[20] By the late twentieth century, the foundations for a more integrative perspective of work emerged, with a strong impetus from the relational revolution. A number of innovative scholars in psychology and related fields offered ideas, informative research findings, and practice recommendations based on the position that work and relationships share considerable space in our lives.[21] In addition, similar ideas emerged from organizational studies and from other discussions about work in sociology and other disciplines.[22] In fact, a close examination of the natural conversations that people have about work, as illustrated in Studs Terkel's classic book, *Working,* and in so many other bodies of literature, reveals that people often consider work and relationships as intertwined experiences in their musings about life.[23]

As suggested by this new wave of scholars in the psychological study of work and careers, the emerging relational theories and perspectives have significant potential to reshape how we think about work and careers in the twenty-first century.[24] When considering the various theories and perspectives collectively, a number of assumptions about the interface of work and relationships emerge:

- *To work is to relate:* This simple, yet brilliant, phrase by Hanoch Flum, a gifted Israeli psychologist, underscores a point that has been neglected in how we think about work and relationships.[25] The very essence of work is relational in nature: Working offers people a structured place in the world, often with prescribed roles and expectations, which are embedded in relationships. Moreover, many work tasks involve being with others, infusing life with opportunities for connections that are often integral to the well-being of individuals and communities.
- *Career choices and decisions occur in relational contexts*: The inherent process of mulling over one's career options and implementing decisions involves a clear movement from an individual's internal experience to a more social context that is populated by people and internalized figures

from one's past and present. Moving into the world of work forces people to attach themselves to people and organizations in a way that is often one of the main venues for relational engagements throughout life.[26]

- *Relationships vary in their impact:* Not all relationships at work are necessarily positive and affirming. Flum described the unfortunate experience of being both recognized and rejected at work, which may be manifested in bullying, a process that regrettably is inherent in many workplaces as well as other social spaces.[27]

- *Relationships vary in their dimensions:* The research on social support in general and on the role of relationships at work has identified several dimensions in which people are in connection with each other at work.[28]

  - Emotional connections: Some of the relationships that take place at work provide people with emotional support; in effect, the connections that are forged at work and outside work have the potential to furnish a critically needed buffer for people, helping to assuage the stress of work and to provide a sense of connection, meaning, and purpose.[29]

  - Instrumental connections: In addition to the importance of emotional support, some relationships are instrumentally helpful to people at work. Instrumental support can include the role of networking in the job search process, mentoring, providing people with skills and knowledge needed for given tasks, and other hands-on forms of assistance.[30]

- *Relationships occur in real time and are also internalized into our psyches.* A major contribution of the relational perspectives within psychoanalytic theory is the observation that people internalize salient aspects of their relational patterns over the life course. In the relational theory of working, I proposed that the internalization process also plays a critical role in our work lives, an idea that is directly linked to some of the most important advances in psychoanalytic and developmental psychology.[31] Past relationships at work, supervisory experiences, and the cumulative impact of one's relational patterns outside work (with the most vital relational influences stemming from our family of origin) create internal psychological frames in our minds that play an important role throughout our lives.

As discussed in the first chapter of this book, the shifting nature of work has generated a great deal of anxiety for people; for many people who work and who are seeking work, the fragility of the workplace has perhaps made relationships even more important. The material that follows explores the complex, and often unexpected, ways in which being with others at work is integral to feeling alive and engaged at work and in life.

Being With Others: Lived Experiences

The interviews with the participants from the Boston College Working Project revealed that people generally understand their work lives and relationships as co-occurring in shared spaces. Even when the questions did not pertain to relationships, many of the participants discussed how people help them to make meaning of their work lives and how the support of others (or lack of support) was so significant in their lives. The first dimension that is explored in this section describes the various emotional valences that relationships evoked at work.

Relationships at Work: The Good, the Bad, and the In-Between

The participants covered a wide swath of emotional experiences with respect to being with others at work. The most common theme described the positive aspects of relationships at work, which often provided a critical resource for people and helped them to get through some challenging times. Gloria, a 48-year-old African American parent education supervisor, described her feelings about the possibility of working from home, a common location for many who are telecommuting rather than going to an office or conjoint workspace:

> People always ask me why I wouldn't work from home: because I think I'm too sociable. I just can't be at home, I would get too distracted . . . and I want to be around people. I don't want to be stuck at the house, I think that would isolate me and I don't think that would work for me.

Similarly, Robert, a 51-year-old unemployed, college-educated White man, described the sheer pleasure of working with people you enjoy.

> In my first job out of college, I worked for a small comic book company; that was fun. I did that for 18 months and the company downsized. . . . And it was a very small company so there was a lot of bantering back and forth. And a lot of fun and we used to meet in the conference room every day for lunch. You know, it's not so much about the work. . . . When I think about my jobs . . . what I liked about them are the people.

Interestingly, Robert's career trajectory was not as satisfying as his life progressed; his recollections of working at the comic book company remained an oasis in his memory of a time when his work life brought him a sense of comfort that was elusive later in his life. While many of the participants described the positive aspects of relationships at work, some reported that their relational experiences were tinged with conflict, sadness, regret, or even abuse. Robert's experiences in his career after his stint with the comic book company convey an emerging brutality in the workplace that dramatically shaped the essence of his interpersonal relationships on the job.

> Obviously I did something wrong in my professional life. I guess I'm old enough to remember when you used to work for companies. And you know you'd stay there for decades. And you'd grow old and retire from them. . . . And I guess my thoughts are too outdated, because when I was doing that, other people were kind of covering their own ass and they're are the ones with the jobs. I don't blame them; I just feel like I'm two decades behind. Because I just thought working hard was enough, and it really isn't. You really just got to look out for your own self. I mean, its cut-throat. . . . No employer really cares about you so you have to care about yourself. . . . You're not a person. You're an asset. So, you're no different than a computer that they'll upgrade when they have to.

Robert's narrative is painful in its portrayal of the work world treating people like commodities and not like fellow human beings. This theme emerged in quite a few of the narratives, underscoring the sense of the labor market becoming a more dangerous relational space for people who do not have much power to control their work lives.

Jerome, the 59-year-old higher education professional we heard from in Chapter 2, attested to the interpersonal climate during a layoff:

> I remember the day they were letting me go from the museum, and my mom had passed away 2 days earlier, and the time they were letting me go literally like at 1 o'clock in the afternoon. And that was the exact time my mom was being cremated, and so I sat there pretty numb. You're talking about conflict, but it was more inner conflict, because I didn't have anything to say to them. I absolutely had nothing to say, except when they did it, I asked them if they were done, and if I could go home now. And then I went home, and then that evening I came back and cleaned out my stuff and that was it. But on a level they knew my mom had died. But their level of insensitivity just really told me that this was not a place I needed to be. Probably the worst, you know one of those things that will always stick with you. You know, there's things that happen at work; that will be one of those that I probably will never forget because it was coupled with such a traumatic event.

Jerome's vignette strikes a powerful note in conveying the harshness of relationships at many work environments. The narratives from the participants in this project tell a story that is often lost in statistical analyses about the contemporary workforce. Market forces, which prevail throughout many economic sectors around the globe, and particularly the United States, are often inconsistent with a kind and gentle work climate, which is what many of the participants seemed to long for as they told their stories about their lives.[32]

Power Differentials in Relationships at Work

Some of the conflict at work takes place within the structure of sanctioned supervisory or hierarchical relationships. The problems that people experience with their bosses and supervisors at work have naturally attracted considerable attention in thoughtful examinations of work.[33] Susan, a 60 year-old White woman, shared her experiences as a top-level administrator at a small, private higher education institution. She recounted a horrific relationship with her supervisor, which culminated in considerable psychological distress. At first, Susan was delighted to have a job that she coveted—working in an institution that she valued, where she felt that she could make a positive difference in the lives of students from poor and working class backgrounds:

> And then, little by little, strange things would happen. . . . By the second month, the first month was great, but the second month I had strange feelings and I just couldn't figure out what was happening. . . . I sat down with the president and she said, "Well I think you have a problem." She looked me up one side and down the other and she was like, "Well you seem to be" and then she could never finish her sentences. She said, "We're so happy to have you here. But you seem like you just don't know how to be with the faculty." And she never could really get at the problem. I would leave every night not knowing what I had done right or otherwise. I can't really explain what happened. That's why I said it was abusive, but I didn't know it was abusive. I kept thinking, "Oh, well, I'm just doing a really bad job." I would get there at 8 every morning and I started to work about 16 hours a day, so, instead of getting better at what I was doing or figuring out what I was doing wrong, I got literally sick. I got sick. I worked as hard as I could work, so I wrote new programs, I wrote curriculums. . . . I think it was a big setup. They wanted to hire somebody with the credentials I had. . . . They knew I could do all of the things that they needed, but they were really just abusive people.

Susan's evocative description of feeling so unwelcome at her job and feeling abused by receiving ambiguous yet negatively tinged feedback suggests a sense of being tossed into a dangerous relational climate that was highly anxiety pro-voking and frightening. Thankfully, she received feedback from others who left her job prior to her that the problem was not related to her, but to a toxic super-visor who created a harsh and unforgiving work context.

Another complex relational issue for some of the participants occurred when they were in supervisory roles. Rachel, the young woman working on a trop-ical island, described the struggle she faced when she needed to terminate an employee's contract:

> I had to fire someone recently. I've never had to do that; I've always recruited and hired but never fired. This was an ex-pat from Canada. We hired him to do massage services, and anyway, overall we were not happy about his services, but then he got caught stealing a camera. So, that was a deal-breaker for sure, and I had to let him go. A part of me wanted to give him a second chance, because the circumstances surrounding it, where it could've maybe warranted a second chance. But the truth is, all those locals [indigenous people from the island] and all the employees knew about it, and I could imagine what they were saying, where if that was us, we would be fired immediately. . . . I am generally speaking a very emo-tional person. I have to let you go, how are you feeling about that, tell me what's going on, how are you doing, and taking care of that person emo-tionally. And in this instance, I did not do any of that, and I was like gosh you know, am I turning into a sociopath? This doesn't feel normal to me, to not be emotionally involved with this person, about their needs, their worries. I'm starting to question, about why I was okay with it, and then I moved on.

Rachel's touching description of having to fire a colleague underscores how challenging relationships can be at work, particularly when they are nested in structured hierarchical roles. Rachel's vignette resonated with many other participants who described the various ways that their supervisory relationships affected the quality of their work experiences.

The constant in the narratives for most of the participants was a sense that relationships and work were dynamic and complex; different jobs and diverse relationships influenced people in ways that were not always predictable and that shifted across their life spans.

Balancing Work and Family/Caregiving

A perennial issue in conversations of people about work and relationships has to do with the struggle to balance work and family/caregiving responsibilities.

The two passages provided next attest to some of the pathways and reactions that people had about the ongoing challenge of finding a balance between work and family. In the first vignette, Jack, a 55-year-old White corporate executive, describes the historic dimensions of balancing work and family:

> In many aspects of my life, I go at 100 mph. . . . Not to say I'm not grateful for my family, but that was a real struggle trying to balance work and family life and, maybe that was in my early to late 20s where you worked 60–70 hours a week. At [my employer during my 20s], I worked a lot, traveling and when I was at home; it was hard to detach. It had its minuses and pluses. But to answer the question [about balancing work and family], that's something I struggle with a lot, life balance and for the last couple of years I haven't been working full time and I seem all out of sorts.

Jack's honesty is telling. He described the pull to immerse himself in work, noting the advantages, but also acknowledging that the experience had become integral to his sense of aliveness in the world. As he adjusted to working less at his current stage of life, Jack commented how he felt that something was missing in his life. In this next passage, Aaron, a 48-year-old Asian American general in the US Army who was deployed overseas during the interview, shares his personal and professional insights about balancing work and family:

> Family is always the top priority; work obviously helps to take care of family, you have to do well at both. I have had people come up and tell me in my neighborhood at one of my previous jobs, a guy came up to me, saw me playing with my girls and he said he always sees me out with my girls around the base and he says it is a good example for all the other troops, a lot of commanders become workaholics, I always made an effort to be home for dinner and to be able to see my kids off to school.

Later in the interview, Aaron focused on his own struggles to balance work and family, which became a challenge during his long deployments overseas.

> I try to talk to Susan [his wife] probably four or five times a week. Obviously with FaceTime, it is really convenient, even if we can only talk for a few minutes. . . . I don't know that it is as good to keep interrupting their life. . . . This is my eighth deployment and I have never had FaceTime or Skype available in the past. This is a huge difference. I mean as you can imagine it used to be 5- to 10-minute phone calls, and I think really people kind of built up walls with their families and they just kind of separated to kind of endure it. And then they just had a big homecoming, but here you

can really stay connected and I think that makes a big difference. As you can imagine with a population with 5,000 plus people, we have our issues, any normal population does and most of ours, to be honest, [occur] when people are depressed, angry, you name it, it is generally about a relationship.

Aaron's narrative is rich with insights culled from long periods away from his family as well as the very daunting task of managing large numbers of troops who also face separation from their families and friends. His perspective about the care with which he approaches this balancing act conveys considerable wisdom about how to manage work and family in a natural and thoughtful way. In addition, Jack and Aaron, as well as many other participants who we interviewed, reported that their families provided authentic support for them as they faced challenges in their work lives. Indeed, a key subtheme in the narratives about balancing caregiving and marketplace work was focused on the importance of maintaining a deep connection to one's family, both to receive care from others and to provide care for family members. (This issue is explored in greater depth in Chapter 6.)

Internalizing Others: Creating Soothing Support

The notion of internalization is one of the more complex ways that being with others functions for people in their work lives. As indicated previously in the chapter, the overall pattern of relationships in life, particularly in early development, creates the psychological framework for a lifetime of internalized psychological structures that function metaphorically as a bookshelf that organizes one's relational experiences. These relational structures help to create internal frameworks (or *schemas*, as they are often known in psychology) that play a major role in how people manage work, subsequent relationships, and their overall capacity to soothe and regulate themselves.[34] One of the ways in which people develop internalizations is via the process of admiring others in their lives, including at work. By locating others at work who exhibit some combination of being highly regarded, interpersonally warm, charismatic, and competent, people may experience a sense of idealization, which can support existing internalized structures and, at times, can create new internalizations.[35] As an illustration, Jeffrey, a 47-year-old White unemployed former computer professional, describes a deep appreciation of a supervisor who helped him develop a positive motivating and inspiring internalization.

There's people who seemed to carry . . . I don't know, the strengths of their jobs and some charisma that you want to follow them . . . as opposed to somebody who's just good and demands something of you. I'm not sure how to explain that, but most people that I enjoyed working for did really well and they expected you to do well, and you did 'cause you didn't want to let them down. As opposed to somebody who wanted you to do well or they're going to fire you because you are not a good employee.

Jeffrey's description captures the sense of admiring others at work in a way that affirms the importance of respect and admiration in creating a welcoming frame with which to understand the role of others at work. Having someone to look up to at work can help people in feeling alive and connected to their jobs; in a sense, people can derive significant psychological resources and support from others, even if their connection is based on a form of idealization as opposed to a direct relationship.

In the next passage, Jamal, a 41-year-old African American higher education professional, described how a counselor early in his college education helped to shape his goals, but more importantly, provided a powerful and soothing form of internalization.

I was in the program called EOPS, Equal Opportunity Programs and Services, for students who are either first-generation college students, or low income, or all of the above, and he (my counselor) I guess when I looked back at it, he cared. He showed an interest in my academic future, and he took time out with me during our appointment to give me advice about what classes I should take, and what would be classes that would work for me and probably not work for me. And so he encouraged me and he also recommended that I maybe should be a counselor myself. So, he obviously saw something in me and he encouraged that and empathy he showed me was something that was inspiring.

Jamal conveyed a poignant memory of a mentor and counselor who was able to see some attributes in himself that he was not able to identify himself. The pathway from a comforting relationship to a soothing internalized figure who can be evoked readily during stressful times is difficult to map precisely. However, the exemplars set by Jeffrey and Jamal provide some glimpses into this subtle, but important, aspect of being with others at work.

Networking and Instrumental Support

In addition to the emotional support and the provision of ideals and role models, being with others at work can help in instrumental ways. Many of the participants described the diverse contributions that others made in their work lives and in preparing them for work. Milo, the career counselor we met in Chapter 2, describes the importance of a professional at one of his undergraduate colleges who provided specific instrumental emotional support to him when he was in a vulnerable place in his education.

> I met with a woman at a community college in Chicago that had a director of financial aid that someone recommended that I meet with. And when I met with her, I talked to her, I told her about my story. I told her about my background and some of the courses and things I was engaged in. . . . And she looked at me and she heard my story. And she said, "Someone like you should be in college. You should be in college." And she was so sorry to hear all of the things I had to go through. And this woman was not affiliated with any college that I was applying to. It was a community college in Chicago, just someone had recommended to me to talk to her. And she . . . I don't know exactly what she did, but she created a waiver on the system in my name, so that when I applied to any college in the system they would see me as an independent student. And that's how I was able to continue my education. If it wasn't for her, I would be delayed in finishing my degree, because I would not have been able to get the financial aid that rewarded someone with my type of grades and my type of experience.

Milo's story conveys the importance of emotional support as one of the strongest threads that serves to help instrumental support become maximally effective and meaningful. The fact that the financial aid advisor was able to understand Milo's experience, both the content and emotional tone in his presentation, seemed critical in providing the right type of support at the right time. Milo's story also describes how one person with access to important information and resources can make a transformative change in one's life trajectory.

In the next passage, Cynthia, a 43-year-old African American unemployed dental hygienist, describes her initial reluctance to engage in networking, but eventually attended a networking group at a Boston-based One-Stop Career Center, which had a transformative impact in her thinking about finding work. Cynthia's story of unemployment began when the large group medical practice where had worked for over a decade decided to eliminate its dental services, leading her to a period of long-term unemployment. Her comments about networking follow in response to a query from the interviewer about her job search path.

> Don't be discouraged by what you see; use that to push further, and don't be afraid to share who you are, let people see who you are. And the

contacts . . . stay connected . . . stay connected. Because I think that the one thing that I didn't do which I learned from this place is networking. Not just getting cards, but connecting with people. I generally would keep things in a professional way and I wouldn't share my personal information. So I always feel like you keep your work and your private life separate but somehow they intertwine.

Cynthia's comments affirm the mixed messages that people receive about integrating their relationships and work lives. While it is not clear if Cynthia's initial reluctance to network hurt her job search in the first few months of her unemployment, she did realize that being with others and tapping into these relationships for job leads was an important part of her struggle back to full-time employment.

One of the most viable types of instrumental support is provided under the rubric of career counseling and job coaching.[36] In the next passage by Bob, the 51-year-old career counselor-in-training we met in Chapter 2, explains the way in which a career counselor at a One-Stop Career Center helped him to make adaptive decisions about his current circumstances and future plans.

He's the veteran's service rep here and he deals strictly with veterans. And when I met with him, he just said you're not going to be doing accounting anymore. I kind of knew that. I was relieved to hear that. I said well you need to tell the people at Voc Rehab because they think I'm going to find a job there and they want to push me to start looking. I don't have a lot of time. I'm 51 years old. I don't want to spend 6 months looking for a job that's never going to materialize. I need to do something else. And he asked me, well what are you interested in? What would you like to do? And it didn't take me long. I said frankly what you're doing. And he said really? I need an intern. Where do I sign? So that's what started things.

In addition to providing instrumental and tangible support, being with others at work is part of a foundation for networking, which has become so essential to the job search and career transition process throughout many nations across the globe.[37] The examples of networking provided here reflect one particularly important way for others to provide instrumental support; indeed, like the initial example by Milo, networking often encompasses both emotional and instrumental support. For the next contribution on networking, we have an opportunity to hear again from Matteo, who so eloquently opened this chapter with his moving rendition of losing his twin towers of love and work early in his adult life.

The networking group was all about establishing relationships with people, and it was because of that—here, at this One-Stop Career Center—that, somebody said, "You know I know a guy that works for a company that staffs audio engineers." . . . And that one connection . . . I called the guy up, set up an interview . . . filling out the application process and everything and . . . now I got the job. Wow! So, relationships are really key, beyond filling out applications, beyond all the other crap. And I even told them, I said, "You know I have a background. If you do a background check, I did prison time." "We don't care. We don't do background checks on guys, we give them a second chance." Wow. That was pretty cool. But there's not too many companies that really do that. So, relationships. . . . That's how I balance my life.

Matteo's story underscores one of the most compelling aspects of networking, which can be critical in helping people to overcome obstacles in their work lives. Yet as we explore in the next section and throughout this book (particularly in Chapters 7 and 8), not having access to social networks is one of the primary ways that classism and marginalization are transferred from one generation to the next.

Being With Others: The Psychological View

The narratives presented in this chapter tell a richly evocative story about the various ways that being with others shapes and influences contemporary work experiences. Recent research enhanced this view and helped to point the way to important implications for public policy as we mull over the future of work.

The Role of Attachment and Social Support at Work

A prevailing finding in psychological research is that people who feel attached to others and who experience social support fare better at work and in life in general.[38] As we shared previously in this chapter, John Bowlby's attachment theory provided the conceptual undergirding for understanding how relationships function to sustain mental health and to foster adaptive exploration and transitions. In brief, the experience of being able to rely on others for emotional support helps to create what Bowlby called an internal working model that shapes our relational experiences and expectations. (An internal working model is akin to the internalizations mentioned previously; these are beliefs, expectations, and schema that are formed from our earliest attachment relationships and are subsequently modified in attachment bonds throughout the life span. I consider an internal working model to be analogous to bookshelves in our minds that have a prearranged shape and structure, which helps us to organize our relational and psychological experiences.) The attachment bonds that are formed early in life are in fact mutable and can be reshaped by relationship experiences in many domains of life, including work. So, how does the attachment story impact work? Considerable research has been conducted indicating that secure attachment orientations help people explore themselves and their external worlds and to make decisions that are necessary in the transitions required by contemporary work.[39]

A number of years ago, my colleagues and I at the University at Albany were intrigued by the existing conventional wisdom that young people needed to feel a sense of independence and autonomy in order to progress in their career exploration, in decision-making, and ultimately in committing to a career choice. Based on one of the team member's doctoral dissertations, we found that college students who reported independence from their parents were no more likely to be decided about their careers than their peers who seemed to be struggling in differentiating from their families. In a follow-up study, we included a measure of parental attachment along with a measure of psychological independence, which yielded very different and very revealing results. College students who reported simultaneous experiences of both conflictual independence and attachment to their parents were most likely to be making progress in this critical movement into adulthood: choosing and implementing a career plan. The inclusion of a measure of attachment completely changed our thinking and helped to transform my views about the role of relationships in the study of work and careers.[40]

Subsequent studies over the past two and a half decades since the publication of this study have generally supported the basic premise that we identified in 1991. People who experience support from their family members, peers, teachers, and others in their lives are better able to negotiate complex work-related tasks.[41] Buttressing this view within the realm of social support (which assesses one's overall access to people who can provide emotional and instrumental support) is research by my talented colleague Maureen Kenny and her colleagues from Boston College. In an intriguing study with urban high school students, Kenny found that connection to one's family members, access to nurturance from others, as well as a sense of rootedness in one's social network were associated with school engagement and with optimistic attitudes about one's work lives.[42]

In a longitudinal study by Matt Diemer from the University of Michigan, which followed poor youth of color from the National Educational Longitudinal Study from high school into adulthood, participants who experienced direct career support from their parents were more likely to report work role salience 2 years after high school.[43] This finding is particularly significant given the plethora of barriers that exist in the educational and career development experiences of poor and working class students of color. An international qualitative study of middle-aged and older working women by Jenny Bimrose and her colleagues reported a similar impact with respect to social support. Specifically, one of the members of the Bimrose et al. team from Germany, Simone Haasler, reported that the women in her sample indicated that social networks were the key ingredient in supporting women making career transitions.[44] Haasler also described how being with others helped the women in her sample make meaning of their work lives via thoughtful discussions and reflection.

From various vantage points in the research literature, the conclusions are clear and compelling: People who have secure attachments and who are well connected to supportive family members, peers, and others in their lives are well positioned to weather the storms that are such a common occurrence in the contemporary world of work.

Mentoring at Work: Another Way Forward

In the actual workplace, support from others is also considered essential, as reflected in the narratives from the previous section. Falling under the rubric of mentoring, relational connections at work have long served a critical role in lives of people around the globe.[45] Mentors can provide both emotional support and instrumental support, as described by the participants from the Boston College Working Project. In a comprehensive review of the mentoring literature at the workplace by Chloe Tong and Kathy Kram, the research evidence was parsed, and the following picture emerged[46]: People who have access to mentors tend to do better in their careers, as demonstrated by faster promotions, better job performance, and greater levels of job satisfaction. In addition, Tong and Kram differentiated between formal mentoring and informal mentoring; formal mentoring is structured by an organization, whereas informal mentoring typically takes place outside the structure of a workplace and occurs organically based on relationships among people in a given workplace. Interestingly, informal mentoring seems to provide more robust benefits for people, perhaps reflecting the strength of a relationship that is formed based on natural connections that people develop at work.

One of the most important new concepts in the mentoring literature is the discussion of development networks.[47] Developmental networks refer to clusters of people who serve as mentors; this phenomenon is akin to the notion that it takes a village to raise a child. Applying the developmental network notion to the world of work, it would seem that an optimal relational matrix among working people would involve some of the attributes that Shoshana Dobrow and her colleagues reported in a summary of existing research. Dobrow identified the following four attributes of an adaptive developmental network:

1. The mentors, known as developers, are directed toward facilitating the protégé's career.
2. There are generally about four or five developers, in contrast to the dyadic relationship in most mentoring situations.
3. Developmental networks entail a broad array of people, including people from within and outside the protégé's organization.
4. The content of the relationships in a developmental network is expansive, encompassing diverse amounts and types of support.

The picture that emerges, then, from the research literature on mentoring is that relationships and connections are not secondary or peripheral factors in our working lives. We exist in relational matrices in our families and at work: People need others to understand their experience, to learn "the ropes" of a given work climate, and often to actually get a job. Mentoring is an essential attribute for our well-being in a working context that is increasingly ruled by market forces and profit margins.

Social Network Research

The role of developmental networks just described has broader implications in the relationship–work interface. Let us consider the role of social networks in general as people are struggling to get a foothold into the world of work. The view that is emerging in the job search literature is that social networks are critical in providing emotional and instrumental assistance for people who are out of work.[48] As we shall see in greater depth in the discussion of unemployment in Chapter 8, the relational connections that people have are strongly facilitative of an effective job search.

As Steven Vallas, a sociologist from Northeastern University, has described in his very thoughtful book on work, social networks may be a major factor in accounting for gender and racial differences in career mobility and attainment.[49] Studies cited by Vallas pointed clearly to the pervasive role of social networks in the job search and attainment processes. For example, studies by various scholars in sociology and psychology have documented that an increasing number of job openings are filled via social networks and not traditional job postings.[50] In addition, women and people of color in the United States tend to have less powerful social networks, which functions to sustain inequity. The impact of social networks therefore has important implications across the spectrum of the working experience. People without access to support early in their education and training often lose out on the possibility of learning about viable careers; people seeking to transition to the world of work after school will tend to replicate their social status, based to a large extent on the nature of their social networks. Furthermore, people at work will tend to seek developmental networks that are most likely to enhance their careers, which may preclude selecting people who are generally on the margins of the workforce (people of color, people without adequate financial resources, people with disabling conditions).

Work–Family Balance

Another issue that emerged in the narratives that is also very present in the research literature is how to best manage the work–family balance. Indeed, this is perhaps the most researched area within the domain of relationships and work; as such, it is impossible to summarize this broad body of work in this space. The focus of this discussion is on the issues that have driven this project: What are the most compelling findings from the research on work–family balance that can inform our thinking about how society can adapt to radical transformations in the world of work?

A review of the literature on the work–family interface by Sue Whiston and Rachel (Gali) Cinamon provided informative insights into the nature of how people negotiate the overlapping demands of work and family.[51] As noted in the first chapter of this book, the changes in the world of work are forcing major reappraisals of work and family. Following the trends identified in the past decade or so, many people inhabit both roles simultaneously throughout their lives, with shifts often occurring continuously throughout each day. At the same time, people who have been left out of the American dream and who are struggling to obtain decent work are often left to lean on their families, which was a common refrain among many of the participants in the Boston College Working Project.

An initial recommendation by Whiston and Cinamon is to consider the full array of impacts that work and family can evoke in the natural course of people's lives. As a result of this perspective, scholars in the work–family interface community increasingly are considering the notion that there are important benefits that occur for people who are engaged in both work and family roles. The recent impetus of research has indicated that positive outcomes can accrue for people who are engaged in healthy work and family responsibilities; indeed, scholars now think of how work and family can facilitate gains in each domain as opposed to focusing on work–family conflict. According to the research in this field, positive engagement in relationships and work are central to promoting mental health, points that were outlined at the outset of this chapter. In relation to the changes taking place in the occupational landscape, the notion of work and family facilitating growth in each sector would seem like an important source of protection from the rocky seas of a labor market that treats people as commodities. As I have detailed in my earlier contributions, having a sense of satisfaction from work and family can serve as a powerful inoculator against the unexpected winds of change that can so dramatically change people's contexts in both their relationships and their work lives.[52]

Conclusion

In this chapter, the intent was to create a clear and compelling picture of the space shared by work and relationships. Indeed, the twin towers' metaphor that Matteo described at the outset of this chapter provides a useful visual icon of the connection between work and relationship. The Twin Towers in New York City were separate but were connected at the base; indeed, I recall visiting the Twin Towers in the early 1970s when I worked as a messenger during one of my summer jobs as a college student, which gave me an opportunity to observe their construction, which was a very powerful experience for me. What I noticed was that the entire project was interconnected at the base, with a shared foundation that gave rise to both buildings. As I reflect on the material presented here, I am struck by both the strength of our commitment to work and relationships and the vulnerability of our lives at work and in relationships. Like the Twin Towers, our dedication to work and relationships stands strong and proud as integral aspects of our identities and communities. However, there is an inherent vulnerability as well; much as these Twin Towers stood up to great heights, they were open to the unexpected twists and turns of life.

As we know clearly from the psychological literature, being with people is central to our health and to our sense of meaning in the world.[53] Moreover, work is one of the places where we are embedded in the social world; indeed, for some people, the connections that they make at work may be the only sources of relationships in their adult lives. Therefore, mulling over a world without sufficient access to work has grave implications for the core of our humanity. As the personal stories compiled as part of the Boston College Working Project coupled with the research and theoretical material shows, people find their relationships at work to be very meaningful. As automation and the rise of precarious work reduce stability in the labor market, corollary changes are likely to ensue in our relational lives. Indeed, people from the Boston College Working Project spoke about the sense of disconnection and aloneness during periods of unemployment and underemployment, observations that are increasingly common in public and academic conversations about work and relationships.[54]

Another important theme in the material covered in this chapter is the importance of relationships in fostering decent and optimally meaningful work lives. Whether the source is via structured mentoring or the informal support of one's family, people rely on each other to manage the ever-complex tasks of gaining access to decent work and of managing the workplace. Yet, at the same time, empirical research and the narratives from the Boston College Working Project express the very real experience of harassment and other negative relationships at work, which undercut our capacity to derive meaning and benefit from others.

A premise that runs throughout this book is that the experience of working that has been associated with stable access to survival, meaning, connection, and self-determination is eroding. Without a thoughtful and intentional focus on ensuring that our human rights as workers are safeguarded, we are likely to see growing abuses in the relational context of the workplace. (Broader implications about the future of work are outlined in Chapter 9.) Solutions to these problems will require a critical and comprehensive analysis of the relational dynamics at work within the context of a broader public debate about working in general. Ensuring that our human rights are protected will further require that we establish policies that allow informal and formal relational connections to flourish in the workplace. However, much as the Twin Towers required a firm structural foundation, our relational lives necessitate the firm framework that a stable, decent, and dignified working life provides. Without stable work, people will feel increasingly untethered to the social bonds that are so essential for our feelings of well-being. In the subsequent chapters, the nature of people's experiences at work is further explicated, with the intention of painting a fuller picture of the intertwined nature of work, which powerfully shapes so many core aspects of being alive.

4

Being Part of Something Bigger
Than Ourselves

Becoming a passionate scholar, practitioner, and advocate for understanding the role of work in people's lives has been a richly rewarding journey, beginning in a compact apartment as a boy growing up in eastern Queens, New York. In this small apartment, I began to develop some interest in knowing more about the nature of work. As an example of this growing fascination, I recall disliking playing board games, which I thought were not a good use of my time (which actually was not all that committed during this period); I felt that we should be playing sports, watching sports, or listening to the exciting new rock and roll that captured my imagination. However, I somehow developed a keen interest in the board game called Careers, which I loved. For some unexplained reason, this was the only board game that I would ever play. In this warm, loving garden apartment on the edge of Queens, I also learned an important lesson about how work can help us feel that we are part of something that is bigger than we are. The teachers of this lesson were my parents, who were not trained in the academic world; they were schooled in the college of hard knocks, which encouraged them to go all out in ensuring that their two sons received the best education possible.

My father, Harry, was a sheet metal mechanic, working with Pan American Airlines, which was a secure and stable job for him, yet also very strenuous and physically draining. He had struggled to get a position with an airline for many years and finally landed a job with Pan Am when he was 46. His job was not easy; he often came home from work with his hands cut up. He felt exhausted after spending the day in a large, drafty hangar working on the fuselages and other metal components of aircraft. My mother worked as a sales clerk in the cosmetics counter at a department store in our neighborhood called Mays. (Those readers who grew up post World War II New York City and Long Island will recall that Mays was a long way from Macy's, another New York retail institution.)

One day in my early teens, my mother began to talk about her work and described how much hardship she faced growing up during the Great

Depression. She shared an observation with me that has always stuck with me to my core: "David: Your father and I do not have glamorous jobs, but what we do makes a difference. We did not necessarily select these jobs, but these were our only options. When I work with the women on their cosmetics, I feel a sense of accomplishment about helping them to feel good about themselves, often with very inexpensive products that they can easily afford. And, your Dad likes working on the planes. It has been his dream to be involved in aviation. So, you should always feel proud of what your parents do." I am not sure if I said something vaguely disrespectful about their jobs, which may have evoked this discussion, but I feel so pleased now that I can recall this interchange and describe how their message inspired this chapter and, indeed, many other endeavors throughout my career.

That working can yield a sense of contributing to something bigger than ourselves is a wonderful gift that, when it is going well, work can generate. In this chapter, I explore the basic contours of how work can function to enhance our connection to the world outside our families and ourselves by bringing meaning and purpose to our lives. Beginning with a discussion of how work can promote the feeling of being part of something bigger than we are, I draw on stories from the participants of the Boston College Working Project to show how this experience can manifest in all kinds of careers. A selected review of recent research from psychology concludes the chapter, along with recommendations for creating workplaces and opportunities that foster the valuable, yet elusive, sense of feeling that one is part of a culture and community.

Being Part of Something Bigger: An Introductory Journey

What is the feeling that my mother spoke about so eloquently many decades ago? The sense that work can yield a connection to people and places has long been understood as integral to our understanding of work. However, working also provides people with a more subtle sense of connection to the broader social world, even if meaningful relationships are not necessarily present in our jobs. As my mother suggested, her work and the work of my father provided them a sense of connection and attachment to the world. In retrospect, I imagine that they were able to see themselves as part of a larger whole: a system of cogs and wheels that helped to keep society afloat. In a sense, they experienced a buy-in into the world of work and, more generally, into the larger world that framed their lives. By identifying the importance and meaning of their work, the subtle connections that link people, communities, and institutions became less of an abstraction and more of an experience that they participated in and contributed to.

This experience of feeling part of something bigger than ourselves is a wonderful reward for work, one that is often less obvious. Seeing the fruits of their labor in the new makeup patterns of the shoppers at Mays or in the jets taking off safely from Kennedy airport allowed my parents to experience their work as contributing to something greater than themselves. In effect, their work provided them with a sense of meaning and purpose in life, despite the fact that they did not find the work to be consistently engaging and stimulating.

In this section, I highlight the importance of being able to contribute to the greater good, which I propose is a critical, although often neglected, aspect of work. I initially review the underpinnings of how we understand human strivings to contribute to the social good, which is followed by a review of the seminal work by Howard Gardner, Mihaly Csikszentmihalyi, and William Damon on good work.[1]

The Natural Desire to Do Good

Throughout human history, many theories and ideas have been advanced that seek to explain the variability in people's behaviors and feelings about trying to do good in the world. Certainly, the capacity of people to be inhumane and cruel to others mars our history and our current landscape. Consider, for example, the behavior of US soldiers during the My Lai massacre in Vietnam in 1969, which is a painful exemplar of the worst in our natures. Citizen-soldiers, many of them young men drafted out of impoverished homes, were given orders to kill women and children in a village that had been abandoned by the Vietnamese men of fighting age. As we know from history, many of the soldiers complied with the orders for this terrible atrocity. Yet, interestingly, at least three of the soldiers refused to obey their orders and sought to protect the innocent civilians of My Lai.[2] This incident captures the most obvious and painful aspects of the human capacity for cruelty. However, in the efforts of a few soldiers to care for others, the seeds of the striving to do good are evident, albeit overshadowed by the horrific outcome of this painful event in American history.

While it is beyond the scope of this book to examine the underlying nature of humankind, I propose that while people are clearly complex, under optimal conditions, most people have the capacity to do good and to exhibit selfless behaviors, often at great risk to themselves and others. In this context, psychologists have been fascinated with prosocial behavior for a number of decades; this interest, in part, grew out of another gruesome event that also took place in Queens, New York, in the mid-1960s. A young woman, Kitty Genovese, was stabbed to death while other people in her building ostensibly heard the attack. Although there has been some debate about the actual number of people who may have understood the nature of the attack, this tragic event raised an interest in understanding how people manifest prosocial behavior.[3] The Kitty Genovese murder has taken on an almost mythic quality in psychology and the social sciences, arousing a grand debate about how people negotiate the challenge of trying to exercise altruism throughout their lives. One of the implications of the response to the Kitty Genovese murder has been the development of knowledge about how people decide to become bystanders in the face of violence and how people decide to engage in prosocial behavior.

Prosocial behavior refers to the tendency for people to help others, to feel for others, and to contribute to the broader social good.[4] Although the research literature in psychology has examined the more obvious manifestations of prosocial behavior, a growing interest by scholars interested in work and careers has yielded important insights about our striving to do good in our lives via work.[5]

Good Work: Contributing to the Social Good

One of the most prominent psychological studies of prosocial behavior in the workplace is the seminal collaborative work by Howard Gardner, Mihaly Csikszentmihalyi, and William Damon, aptly titled *Good Work*.[6] These very prominent psychologists, who were all serving as fellows at the Center for Advanced Study in Behavioral Sciences in Palo Alto at the same time in the mid-1990s, became interested in applying moral development to the workplace. They decided to conduct in-depth interviews with over 100 geneticists and journalists, including new practitioners and more senior professionals, with the hope of understanding how people contribute to the social good via their work.

By studying geneticists and journalists, Gardner and his colleagues were certainly examining working people who had a fair degree of choice about their career directions. Moreover, the "Good Work" project was focused on the work lives of professionals who chose their career direction in large measure to enact their desire to contribute to the overall social good. The findings reported by Gardner and his coauthors in the late 1990s foreshadowed some of the changes that we have witnessed to date in the world of work. Gardner and his associates found that the geneticists were able to maintain fairly close adherence to manifesting their ethical values in their work. However, the journalists reported more diverse experiences, wherein they were often pressured to act against their inherent desire to "do the right thing" in their jobs. The distinctions that they observed between these two very noble professions were understood to be related to the demands of their occupational lives and the broader changes in the social and economic order.

For the most part, the geneticists were able to implement their values in their work lives; the pressures that they experienced did not generally result in major ruptures in their prosocial behavior. In contrast, the journalists were beginning to experience the massive changes spurred by the introduction and growth of the Internet in the world of media and communication. Journalists reported that the profit-driven nature of their industry, coupled with the growing threats from Internet-based information sources (which, in fact, have transformed this profession radically since the time of the Good Work project), created a shaky ground for them, significantly constraining their capacity to do good work. Gardner and his colleagues provided a very thoughtful analysis of their interviews, culminating in a sharp critique of the demands placed on professionals by the market-driven economy, which increasingly has placed profits over people.

The focus on contributing to the broader good is also reflected in John Budd's compelling book, *The Thought of Work*, which summarized the various ways that work is understood within contemporary labor studies.[7] Budd devoted one of his chapters to the function that work provides as a form of service. Like Gardner and his colleagues, Budd considered the role of work in furnishing people with a sense that their efforts are contributing to the broader social fabric. Budd also highlighted the role of caregiving work and the efforts that we devote to maintaining our households as a means of enacting our desire to serve via work (which I explore further in Chapter 6). He noted as well the tension that exists between the more collectivist spirit of working for the greater good and the individualistic strivings that are clearly an integral part of the world of work in the United States and other Western nations.

The broad sketches provided by Gardner et al. and Budd create a clearer sense of what my mother referred to by noting the contributions that she and my father made in their not-very-glamorous jobs. However, the contrast of my parents' experiences with the careers of journalists and geneticists generates several questions. First, to what extent can people who have access primarily to survival jobs attain a sense of doing good in the world? Second, what does this experience feel like? And, third, how can people attain this sense of doing good in a world of work that is increasingly challenging our sense of autonomy, self-determination, and dignity? The rest of this chapter provides some responses to these questions, while also highlighting the challenge of being able to find meaning and feel a sense of purpose when work challenges one's dignity and decency.

The Elusive Experience of Being Part of Something Bigger Than We Are

Being able to experience meaning at work is actually elusive for many people, particularly when they have little choice about their work lives. However, the need to experience a clear sense of being affirmed for a given job is not necessary to feel that people are contributing to something bigger than themselves. A recent book by David Zweig has sought to explore the nature of jobs that are "invisible," highlighting how people who are out of the public limelight create lives of richness and satisfaction despite the lack of social recognition for their work.[8] In Zweig's insightful book, *Invisibles*, he describes the unsung heroes of the workplace, such as a guitar tech, an engineer for a building under construction in China, a cinematographer, and an interpreter, who develop great skill and passion for their work without seeing the fruits of their labor recognized. Zweig concluded that not everyone needs to be affirmed publicly for their work. The "invisibles" who were interviewed for this book recounted three specific attributes that helped to give their work lives meaning:

1. Ambivalence about recognition
2. A commitment to meticulousness
3. A savoring of responsibility

These attributes convey some of the essential ingredients that work can provide, even when people do not receive external affirmation for their efforts. Similarly, Mike Rose described the work lives of hairdressers, plumbers, carpenters, and waitresses in his wonderful book, *The Mind at Work*, where he made a compelling argument that the workers who seemed to sense a level of meaning and contribution in their work were able to use their "minds at work."[9] They were able to problem-solve, express their ideas, be creative, and engage in activities that they could master. In a sense, they were able to take something from themselves and bring it to their tasks and their jobs. In addition, many of the workers understood how their work contributed more broadly to the social good, much as my parents did in their work. Taken together, Zweig and Rose suggested that contributing to the greater good is not an experience that is exclusively granted to those with privilege and highly skilled careers. The complex mosaic of individual attributes and workplace characteristics that help to create the conditions for a life of meaning and purpose at work is harder to discern. The sections that follow provide some depth that may help to flesh out the details of a good working life.

Being Part of Something Bigger: Lived Experiences

Much as the chapter was inspired by the observations of my mother, who shared an insightful observation about the world of work, we now turn to the stories from the Boston College Working Project participants, who conveyed poignant descriptions of the role that social contribution plays in their work lives.

Meaning and Mattering

Many of the participants commented thoughtfully about the various ways that work evoked a sense of meaning and mattering. The notion of work having meaning refers to the sense that one's efforts and labors are personally meaningful to an individual's goals and values.[10] Mattering, a concept that was popularized in the recent career development literature, refers to the experience of having one's work matter in relation to the broader social community.[11]

Mildred, an unemployed woman who was introduced in Chapter 1, who was completing her college degree during a period of unemployment, described how working optimally could furnish a connection to a meaningful life.

> [Working is] a big part of my family's outlook. It's like either you're working for your family; you're working for your community; you're working for your job that pays you, but work was supposed to be part of a function of what we did. We've always enjoyed work. . . . I want what I do to mean something to someone, that it makes their life better or is something that people should be aware of or it helps people who need something. So it's not just a paycheck that I'm looking for when I'm working. I'm looking for a sense that I'm helping people; there's a product that needs to be out there, there's something that needs to be said to someone, there's something that can help someone else along the way. Whenever I approach work, it has to benefit someone, and that's where I get my enjoyment from—these feelings of what I'm doing matters.

Mildred's views capture the positive essence of work that provides meaning and mattering. Throughout her interview, Mildred embedded the experience of meaning in relation to work in herself and her family's values and not necessarily in the attributes of the job. Mildred had been laid off from a job with a startup and was unemployed for a number of years before returning to college to complete a degree that she had started decades earlier. Her commitment to a work life of meaning seemed to function as a way for her to manage the stress of being unemployed; in a sense, her determination to derive meaning from her work provided her with a source of resilience as she faced jobs that often did not provide easy access to satisfying and purposeful activities.

The experience of deriving positive meaning at work seems to function as a firm foundation in creating a pathway to a work life that provides a sense of doing good in the world. Milo, the 38-year-old career counselor who shared his impressions in previous chapters, provides a richly textured analysis of how he finds meaning at work.

> So work . . . to me is a vehicle for how people connect their talents to the world. . . . I guess that's how I see work: it's how we get things done. It's how we translate . . . as a society, as a world, our skills, our abilities, our values . . . into action, into making things happen, into improving, moving, and shaping. . . . Without work, we don't have a society, we don't have anything. Work is defined in a macro sense in my view as well as in a micro sense. It's getting up in the morning. It's sweeping the floor. It's making your bed and getting your kids ready to go to school. . . . I see myself in the larger component of work as being part of the continuity of society, of values, of ideas—a reflection of shared beliefs and shared goals.

While Milo and Mildred (along with many participants) shared positive impressions about how work functions to provide a sense of meaning and purpose, some of the participants described how work detracted from their experiences of meaning. Susan, the 60-year-old woman introduced in Chapter 3 who struggled so much in her job at a private community college, described how the challenges of work caused her to question the capacity of work to provide meaning and mattering.

> I think now that things have changed so much. . . . The thing that I think work should fill and I'm not sure how we're ever going get to this point because I think work should be a place of family. I think it should be a place of family because most of us—not all of us—but most of us are at work more than anywhere else, so I think it shouldn't be a contentious place. It shouldn't be this stressful place. It shouldn't be this, "Are they gonna like me today?" "Am I gonna do good today?" "Am I gonna be fired today?" "Am I gonna be hired today?" "Am I gonna make more money today?" It should be a place of family.

Susan's frustration about her work situation is palpable in this passage. She once worked for a major public school system in a leadership position and was, at this point in her life, coming back to work after a period of unemployment that resulted in her taking a job at a department store as seasonal help during the holidays. As indicated in the passage that she contributed in Chapter 3, she was working at a community college in an emotionally abusive situation that led her to worry constantly about whether she would have a job the next day. This destructive experience detracted from her capacity to experience the sense of being able to be part of something bigger than she herself, which had been the case in her previous positions.

Meanwhile Joshua, a 45-year-old unemployed White man who was a stay-at-home dad taking care of his children, conveyed a complex and ambivalent discussion of meaning at work.

> I've gone through a process [of career coaching] where you do values-based work, and sort of explore what your own core values are. Sometimes you can emerge with like: What is your purpose? I don't have a problem saying that my purpose is to disrupt the way that people work—and to make the workplace more humane. My dad worked for the federal government for 40 years, and he used to say these things like . . . this is the saddest thing I've ever heard—"I'm in the twilight of a mediocre career." And he used to say that sort of shit all the time. "In the twilight of a mediocre career. . . . " That is the saddest thing to hear when you're like 12. And that same idea, that: Am I projecting that kind of self-pity on my kids?

Joshua presented deep ambivalence about his current situation as a stay-at-home dad; his full interview revealed that he was not able to gain access to marketplace work and focused instead on taking care of his children while his wife served as the primary breadwinner during the time of our interview. The legacy of his father's unsatisfying work life seemed to eat away at him, amplifying his sadness and a sense of resignation.

Contributing to the Social Good

Optimally, work contributes to the social good, either directly via careers that involved helping others, or indirectly, as my parents described, by helping to keep the machinery of society moving in a constructive direction. Many of our participants described the direct experience of contributing positively to others via one's work. Gloria, a 48-year-old social worker from the Midwest, told us the following:

> Work means a lot to me. I think it's important because I'm able to help people and I'm able to help families and I'm able to give families information and that sense of community. . . . All these different resources that you can pick up to help support you if you are out here trying to make ends meet and trying to have a healthy family and trying to get ahead. So there is a lot of resources and information out here that everybody doesn't

know about. That helps me to be able to help somebody else. And that's why I really like home visiting.

Gloria attested to the rewards of engaging in helping activities as part of one's work life. The appeal of a job that allows for direct caring for others was further described by David, a 55-year-old White man, who worked for decades in public service and in higher education and who was transitioning to full-time practice as a massage therapist. David described the profoundly important impact that helping others had in his life.

> What does work mean to me? A lot of it is a sense of pride, satisfaction, and a sense of accomplishing things. It has always been important to me to be doing work that I consider very helpful to mankind and very helpful to the goodness of mankind. For example, I do believe that we have to have a military and a military presence. I am glad we have that, but I want nothing to do with it. So, being in education was really important to me. Being there for the better social good is important to me. This wellness thing is all about that too. So, being helpful to society in my efforts as I work is an important factor to me.

David described his transition from a career as an administrator at a large private university to his own business venture in massage therapy as reflecting his hope to do good in the world with a gift that he discovered later in his life. Both Gloria and David elaborated on the capacity of the helping professions to provide a life of meaning and contribution. While both of these individuals (as well as other participants from the Boston College Working Project) described the gift of working with others in a helping capacity, their paths generally reflected intentional planning that allowed them to implement career goals that were consistent with their values and capacities. Of course, as we know well from the literature in vocational psychology, not everyone shares the same interests and personal preferences. A life of helping others can provide some with an incredible sense of joy and accomplishment, whereas for others it can be tedious or emotionally exhausting.

Indirectly Contributing to the Social Good

While less present in the interviews than other categories in this chapter, some of the participants gave voice to their sense that their work was implicitly helping to enhance the quality of life more generally within society. In the next passage, Jerry, a 60-year-old White flooring salesman, described the informal ways that working provides a sense of contributing to the social good.

> A big part of the satisfaction I get from working is being part of something bigger than myself; that's got to be part of it. I've left positions before because they didn't feel like there was a mix between me and the rest of the environment. I want to be an active part and a valued part of a bigger picture and that's huge. That's probably the bigger, more important thing to me really than anything else about the job in that I would be willing to work for less money if I felt like there was value, that I was valued by that company which is kind of the situation I'm in right now.

Jerry suggested that part of the sense of meaning comes from working in an organization where people valued the contributions of the employees; in effect, his description and the rest of his interview suggest that the feeling of contributing to the social good may be reflected in the specific community of workers focused on shared tasks and responsibilities.

A similar sentiment was conveyed by Vicente, a 51-year-old Latino man who was a former banker and was working as a career coach during the interview. Vicente's comments that follow convey a deep sense of contribution from his work as a branch manager of a bank.

> In my case, when you're impacting people's lives in a positive way—that's when it doesn't feel like work. So becoming part of something bigger where you do good, you do good to others. The means at which you do it, it doesn't really matter. What matters is how you impact in other people's lives. So whether I'm a teller or a branch manager or a regional manager, it doesn't really matter; what matters is how you treat the person or the people in front of you. In my case, I love being at the regional level because of my ability to impact more people. There's only so much you can do where you're a teller compared to when you're a regional manager. You have a greater voice.

In contrast to the vignettes by Jerry and Vicente is the observation by Sierra, a 29-year-old White woman working as a supervisor in a call center. Sierra commented that her work does not provide her with a sense of contributing to the social good, either directly or indirectly.

> I just don't feel like I'm a productive member of society. You know, like I'm not a doctor saving lives, or I'm not a firefighter putting out fires. . . . You

know, I just feel like my job is just. . . . It doesn't make a difference in this world—my job.

Sierra's comments are a critically important counterpoint to the positive experiences that were described in Jerry and Vicente's passages and an equally important message in relation to the material reviewed at the outset of this chapter. Clearly, not all working people are able to experience the sense of meaning, social contribution, and purpose that is so much part of the grand career narrative in the United States.[12] In the next section, I explore the sense of meaning that may be available in the capacity of work to have a positive effect on people.

Creating Meaning by Impacting Others

Several of the participants described the application of their specific talents and skills as a means of making an impact on the lives of others emotionally, artistically, and experientially. Mindy, an opera singer, described her experience in working via her artistic expression.

Something that happened 10 years later was a performance at a concert with the Singaporean youth travel group. We went to Spain to sing a beautiful Russian composition and I remember an old lady coming up to us and she didn't speak the language but she was trying to say something to us and we had trouble understanding and finally she gave up and just said with both her hands up to her eyes demonstrating tears. And I think for me that was significant because it just made me realize how powerful music can be in connecting people. It really transcends cultural and language boundaries and music has the power to connect people in that way because the world we live in is very complicated, lots of strife, tragedy and terrorism and we constantly try to make sense of what happens. . . . And I think that's my way of contributing to making the world a better place. . . . I think in the United States, you find diverse people and I find talking to people we have different cultures, beliefs, practices and rituals and at the end of the day we respond to music the same way. Emotionally, we all react the same way to things, happy things that happen in our life and tragedies and the common humanity connects us even though we have different religions. I feel that music and opera tap into these common elements of humanity which is why I think music has such a strong tool to connect people from all over the world with our feelings and our emotions.

Mindy highlighted the special feeling that she has when she is able to move people in emotional, almost transcendent ways. In a different field, Rachel, the 33-year-old wellness director, discussed how her work provided a means for her to have an impact on her clients' well-being.

> There is a certain responsibility here that has a positive meaning in a sense. The responsibility to people who come to yoga and to meditation, which was an interesting thing to me. . . . I really like serving, and teaching yoga and teaching meditation, and really helping people getting in touch with their true voice, and their authenticity. Inspiring transformation in people, and so the responsibilities and duties of being a wellness director, because I am overseeing the entire wellness program, creating and developing, and streamlining, facilitating, and managing.

Of course, the opportunity to move people spiritually, artistically, and psychologically is not available to many people who were interviewed. However, for those who are fortunate to find a job that allows for deep self-expression, work can be a powerful process of sharing part of oneself. In a sense, this kind of experience represents a peak experience at work, one that is often found in the arts, sciences, teaching, helping professions, and related fields. However, one can also inspire gratitude in others by helping to repair their homes, fix their cars, and make the lives of others easier and more satisfying.

We can see that people are creative in finding ways of deriving meaning in their work and connecting their efforts to the broader social good. In the section that follows, recent research from psychology offers further insights into the complexity of connecting work to life outside our immediate economic and psychological worlds.

Being Part of Something Bigger Than Ourselves: The Psychological View

Recent research from psychology has examined the nature of how people experience work, with findings that enrich our understanding of how, for example, my parents, standing on their feet in often uncomfortable spaces, found work that was, for the most part, meaningful. In this section, I explore a few areas of inquiry that individually and collectively point our way toward insights into how we can enhance the quality of the working experience for people.

Work as a Calling

The notion that work can be understood as a calling has become an increasingly popular way of thinking about many of the issues that we are exploring in this chapter. Two very creative vocational psychologists, Ryan Duffy and Bryan Dik, have devoted extensive thought to the nature of calling.[13] According to Duffy and Dik, *calling* encompasses three components: a sense of being externally summoned to one's work, via spiritual beliefs, family influences, and social or national needs; seeking meaning and purpose at work; and most relevant to our current discussion, engaging in work that allows for a broader contribution to society. Duffy, Dik, and their research associates have been clear that calling is not simply the province of the privileged; people who are working at not very glamorous jobs may also experience a calling, much as my father experienced when he finally was able to fulfill his dream of working in aviation for the flagship airline of the United States.[14]

So, how does the notion of calling help us to understand work as a form of prosocial behavior and as a way of establishing meaning and purpose at work? First, the fact that seeking prosocial work is associated with a sense of being drawn to a given line of work suggests that the capacity to contribute more broadly is part of a larger quest for people: to find meaning and to engage in purposeful work. Second, the research evidence on calling indicates that only about one third to one half of all working people in the United States report that their current job provides them with a sense of calling. Third, working at a job that satisfies one's sense of calling has been associated with life meaning and overall satisfaction. Thus, it appears that being able to contribute, among other attributes, is an important aspect of work, one that is often overlooked in contemporary conversations about work.[15]

Having the capacity to fulfill one's sense of calling certainly seems to be an aspirational aspect of work; however, Duffy and Dik noted that there is a dark side to calling.[16] People who experience a profoundly deep calling for a particular line of work (such as artists, musicians, and the like) and who are not able to fulfill their dreams are often left in a state that is frustrating and, at times, depressing. In addition, Dik and Duffy reported significant distinctions in the lives of those who are living a calling versus those who are clearly aware of their calling but not able to implement it in their work lives. As in other research on career choice privilege, people with higher incomes and greater levels of educational attainment were more likely to experience a calling and live out their calling. Research on calling has also revealed that people who are deeply moved by their calling are more likely to foreclose on their career choices, engage in work that may not be a good fit for themselves, and be exploited by their employers because of their intense commitment to their work.[17]

As Duffy and Dik have noted, the experience of a calling is not universal, and opportunities to fulfill the dream of a meaningful and purposeful work life are not distributed equally. One of the recommendations that Dik and Duffy provided is that the capacity to experience calling may be enhanced by crafting jobs that are aligned with the natural striving that many people have to engage in a work life that offers deeper rewards than simply a pay check and survival.[18] In the next section, the research on job crafting is highlighted, with a focus on how changing work environments can promote a sense of meaning and connection to a broader social mission.

Crafting Work to Enhance Meaning and Contribution

The idea of designing work so that it maximizes productivity goes back to the beginnings of industrial psychology over a century ago. More recently, this psychological technology has been adapted to meet the more human needs of working people: to create lives of dignity, decency, and meaning at work.

In an intriguing book by Barry Schwartz, *Why We Work*, based on his highly popular TED (Technology, Entertainment, Design) Talk, the question of why we work is explored and related to the notion that jobs can be crafted to enhance motivation and meaning.[19] Schwartz made a compelling argument that work is central to our psychological well-being, above and beyond the acquisition of money and resources for survival. Schwartz proposed that work, while not inherently central for many people, has the potential to be rewarding both intrinsically in relation to our well-being and extrinsically in relation to our need for survival and financial welfare. Using recent findings from psychology, management studies, and other disciplines, Schwartz argued that work can be intentionally structured to foster greater meaning and connection to the broader social good. Schwartz observed that the individuals who seemed to thrive in less-than-attractive jobs did have some unique personal attributes that helped them to engage and expand their responsibilities to make them more pleasant, challenging, and personally meaningful. These attributes can be best understood as proactivity, which reflects an individual's tendency to take action to maximize one's life and circumstance, as opposed to being passive.

Of course, our experiences at work comprise far more than our individual attributes: The context of the work environment is critical, as reflected in the new research on job crafting.[20] Schwartz proposed that we can redesign workplaces so that people can engage in job crafting, which is defined by the intentional design of work environments that help people to feel more engaged at work. As a means of integrating the voluminous literature on job design, I turn to the advice of Bryan Dik, Zinta Byrne, and Michael Steger, who edited a fascinating book that included input from scholars in organizational psychology, vocational psychology, and management on how to enhance meaning and contribution at work.[21] The major themes that emerged in this book revealed that many people do find their work to be a central part of their lives; indeed, some people experience a deep sense of calling at work that is described by some workers as evoking spiritual feelings.

However, a number of the chapters in the book by Dik and his colleagues revealed that significant barriers exist for many people in being able to internalize work as an affirming aspect of their lives. First, the lack of choice in selecting one's line of work was a common thread in shaping how people attributed meaning to their work lives. Second, Dik and his colleagues integrated observations from the chapters in their book in developing clear steps that people can use to experience meaning and a sense of purpose in their work lives. Included in these recommendations were the following suggestions:

1. Enhance the level of respect and dignity that people experience at work.
2. Provide employees with a real sense of autonomy in their work tasks and in their work lives in general.
3. Ensure that employees understand the nature of their organization's functions and goals; similarly, provide people with clear instructions about their work tasks.
4. Furnish employees with a deep reservoir of knowledge about how their interests, values, abilities, and talents fulfill the responsibilities of their position.
5. Leaders and work organizations should be designed to foster a good fit between workers' attributes and their work responsibilities.
6. Organizations should be focused on promoting the greater good, which optimally will enhance the meaning that workers can experience in their jobs.

These recommendations reflect a set of values about work that may or may not be available for many workers in our society. Like much of the existing literature on psychology and work, the implicit assumptions underlying this advice is that people have some degree of flexibility in their work lives. One way of drilling deeper into this material was provided by Dik and Duffy in their chapter on calling and career interventions, which explored how work settings and people can enhance not only their meaningfulness at work, but also their capacity to do good in the world.[22] From a personal perspective, Dik and Duffy advised that people may first need to focus on discerning their calling. Using the traditional career counseling framework as well as an easily accessible self-help book, they developed the following recommendations;[23]

1. Encourage active discernment: People should look deep into themselves as well as actively explore the world to experience an engaged and active discernment.
2. Connect gifts with existing options: In a sense, this part of the process is akin to the search for a good fit in the world of work—the standard recommendation of career counseling.
3. Explore social fit: In addition to seeking a field that is good fit for one's internal attributes, Dik and Duffy recommended considering what society would benefit from and how one's talents can meet these needs.
4. Align career goals with life goals: In a thoughtful spin on the traditional career development narrative, Dik and Duffy suggested that people consider their career goals in conjunction with their life goals, realizing that not all of one's strivings for meaning, purpose, and prosocial activities will be met via marketplace work.

When considered collectively, the recommendations from these scholars offer innovative ideas about how to enhance work for people. However, the gap observed by Duffy, Dik, and others regarding those who experience a calling and live a calling is troublesome and underscores an important theme in this book.

Conclusion

The search for meaning and for a connection to the greater social good has been a vital part of humanity for many centuries; these themes are evident in nearly all of our religions and in many philosophical traditions from the West and East. Indeed, even during the Holocaust, people struggled to find meaning in their lives, as so eloquently conveyed in Viktor Frankl's classic book, *Man's Search for Meaning*.[24] Finding a job that furnishes opportunities to feel alive and healthily embedded in the social fabric of one's world is indeed a great gift in life; in many ways, it defines one of the core attributes of feeling alive in the world. Within the world of psychology and management and in the popular press, seeking a life of meaning at work is viewed as an integral aspect of having a good work life.[25] Indeed, the now-classic book by Gardner and his colleagues, coupled with Schwartz's popular book, convey a world wherein it is possible to craft one's job, even a job without much intrinsic reward, to create a meaningful work life. Moreover, my parents, who often struggled to find stable and dignified work, had a reasonably optimistic view of their jobs, as did many (but clearly not all) of the participants in the Boston College Working Project. However, a deeper analysis of the challenges of developing a work life that provides a connection to the social world in a positive and healthy way reveals a broader set of implications for contemporary and future workers.

One of the themes of this book is that people vary considerably in the extent to which they can express their hopes and dreams in the world of work. While career choice privilege is certainly an important factor in the extent to which one can attain a life of meaning and purpose at work, the picture is far more complex. Some of the individuals who were interviewed in the Boston College Working Project struggled to feel connected to the broader social world, even if they were in the driver's seat in their career plans. A major insight that can be gleaned from the interviews and the psychological research in this area is that the nature of the working climate is essential in providing people with the means for creating meaning and purpose at work. Clearly, the levels of dignity, autonomy, and self-determination that people may have in choosing and managing their lives at work vary greatly. Consideration of the interview vignettes reported in this chapter coupled with the insights from the research literature suggest that people need to experience human rights at work; they need to be able to manifest the rights that were detailed in Chapter 1, including the capacity to have work that offers "just and favorable conditions of employment . . . an absence of discrimination . . . and other means of social protections."[26] In my view, ensuring human rights at work and the availability of decent work for all are the foundations of a work life that can promote the social good and a sense of being part of something bigger than we are.

Once the essential elements of work are in place, the advice from the scholars on calling and job design may be useful in creating more meaningful work. However, with some notable exceptions, the prevailing ethos in the literature on work creates a set of expectations that may inadvertently blame the victims for not being able to attain a life of meaning and purpose.[27] From Rose's wonderful analysis of the importance of the mind at work to Schwartz's compelling synthesis of why we work, a prevailing story about work and career seems to be one that empowers individuals to create their own lives of vitality and purpose. The participants from the Boston College Working Project, while often optimistic about the capacity of work to give their lives a sense of meaning, also described the sense of abject terror in the face of often-brutal working conditions and the ongoing struggle to find and sustain decent work. The contrasts between the participants' voices and the optimism shared in the psychology and management fields attests to the distinctions between working for survival and working for self-determination (which is explored further in this book). Some people have access to lives where they can feel a deep connection to their work and the broader social impact of their efforts, while others struggle to find work and, when they do, are often stuck in jobs that seem meaningless and empty.[28]

Moving forward into a world of work that is increasingly unstable, particularly for people without access to twenty-first century skills, offers both opportunities and potential pitfalls. An overriding theme in the narratives and the research in this area is that intentionality and purpose are essential in creating work environments that offer opportunities for social contribution. My position is that intentionality needs to take on a broader scope, above and beyond a specific work organization or setting. Continuing to embed the conversation about meaningful work in an individual perspective or an organizational framework reduces our collective sense of responsibility for shaping a fair and dignified work world for people. Yes, of course, there are some notable individual differences, such as a proactive personality, that can make a difference for some people in their capacity to have a life of meaning and purpose at work. However, the challenges that exist in the workplace now require far more complex solutions than simply trying to craft better work environments. In the realm of creating work that promotes meaning, purpose, and a connection to the larger social world, macro-level solutions will be needed, such as creating policies and regulations that will ensure decent work for all. (Please see Chapter 9 for a review of these macro-level solutions.) Devoting most of one's adult waking life to marketplace work is part of the contract of contemporary life in America—ensuring that the experience of work is connected to the broader social world provides people with a buy-in—a sense of being part of something bigger than themselves. As reflected in the chapters that follow, I believe that creating the social and economic structures that ensure that people have ready access to work that is meaningful and interconnected to the social world is essential for people to engage fully in the gift of life.

5

Being Motivated and Being the Best
We Can Be

Developing and sustaining motivation is one of the most significant aspects of work; it consumes a great deal of time and effort for people who are seeking a work life that offers a sense of meaning, purpose, and engagement. The entire process of discerning how people become motivated to work has consumed scholars, practitioners, and workers themselves since people started to organize their survival efforts into work projects, positions, and responsibilities. Rather than duplicating this rich literature (much of which originates from industrial/ organizational psychology and related fields), my focus in this chapter is the striving for motivation in a world of work that offers increasingly fewer options for people to find meaning and stability in their work lives.[1]

To begin the story, I take us back to a period over a decade ago when I was working on two major projects, each of which characterized the starkly contrasting experiences of working on a task I loved while also needing to work on a project that I dreaded. (As shown in this chapter, these two experiences captured intrinsic and extrinsic motivation, respectively.) One project entailed writing my first book, *The Psychology of Working*, which was a complete passion of mine.[2] I felt a deep calling to do this work, which reflected a desire to transform the conversation in my field of career development to embrace those with less-than-optimal options. This book, which took 5 years from start to actual publication, was a labor of love. Rarely did I ever feel that I had to force myself to work on the writing or research that was needed to write this book. Instead, I often used my writing time as a reward for other, less interesting, projects. Although it did seem daunting to write an entire book on my own, the phase of life in which this project unfolded was perfectly matched for the task. I was in a major personal transition, and my first book project gave me an anchor—a sense of meaning and purpose for which I felt deeply grateful.

In contrast to the joy of the *Psychology of Working* project was the onerous self-study for the PhD program in counseling psychology at Boston College, which I was directing during the same time frame that I wrote my first book. During the period when I was completing my book, replete with the excitement of picking out artwork for the cover and locating colleagues to write reviews for the back cover, I was leading our doctoral program's writing efforts for our self-study, which is essential in obtaining reaccreditation from the American Psychological Association. The self-study, which is a mammoth project involving a detailed narrative and extensive supporting data, was simply not a good fit for my skill set or interests. The narrative of the self-study was reasonable and manageable; in fact, I received a lot of help from my colleagues who were contributing specific sections to the project. However, I also had to work on organizing scores of tables that involved very detailed information, which gradually started to drive me to the edge of my chair, not with excitement, but with frustration, tedium, and a disconcerting lack of attention to details. The project soon became painful for me to work on; indeed, I told friends that I "felt my skin crawl" having to go through reams of data and organize the presentation into coherent tables. I did not feel particularly skilled with these tasks, which left me feeling considerable self-doubt about my capacity to do a good job on this project; moreover, this task took place in a context of public evaluation by my colleagues at Boston College and the accreditation community, which included many valued friends and colleagues. In short, I felt that this project would always reflect back on me (especially if something did not go well). I recall taking long breaks by walking around Walden Pond in Concord, Massachusetts, which was a modest drive from my house, to restore my sense of balance and peace.

So, what do these two stories show about being motivated at work? First, it is clear that I have had considerable privilege in my work life, what I refer to as career choice privilege in this book and in other recent contributions.[3] Having a chance to write articles and books on topics that I love is clearly one of the most cherished gifts in my life, one that reflects the privileges that I have attained and that have been granted to me, based on my gender, social class, educational resources, and race. Second, I do experience intrinsic motivation when I have a sense of purpose in a project and when the tasks fit my skills and values. Third, the process of trying to motivate myself when the tasks are not interesting to me is clearly more complex. I took on the leadership of our doctoral program, knowing full well that I would need to write the self-study and lead the program through the site visit and accreditation process. While most of the tasks of providing program leadership fit my skills and interests, some aspects, such as dealing with highly specific details, often made me anxious and frustrated. I would avoid the tasks, and when I finally immersed myself in the work, I developed simple rewards for myself, like listening to songs that I loved after 2 hours of work or taking a walk.

I share my story here to illustrate how even a professional with a self-determined career will at times struggle with motivation. Moving beyond my own story leads me to the hundreds of therapy clients and research participants I have listened to who have given me in-depth exposure to the nature of work in contemporary America. I have been amazed by the resilience that people display, often against great odds. Some of the people I have spoken with have struggled with abusive and brutal supervisors at work; they have described experiences of bullying that have taken my breath away. I also have been amazed at the doggedness of people who have worked hard to motivate themselves to look for jobs, often with little external support or feedback. Others have dealt with jobs that have been tedious or physically exhausting, leaving them without hope of finding meaning and purpose in their lives.

Yet, most people manage to get up each day and get to work on time, despite significant obstacles. At the same time, clients and research participants have described feelings of accomplishment and pride about their work efforts. Some have written books, created masterpieces in music and art, and contributed to the enhancement of personal and community well-being. In the sections that follow, I explore the world of motivation and work, beginning with an introduction that places this issue into a historical and psychological context that frames the subsequent review of narratives from the Boston College Working Project participants.

Being Motivated: An Introductory Journey

The experience of being highly motivated for work is a cherished state in life. Some people devote their entire lives to seeking the perfect job that will give them a sense of meaning, connection, inspiration, and achievement. In the material that follows, I first place the journey of being motivated in a historical context, tracing the story back nearly 100 years to a fascinating project on work and psychology. I then explore one of the most exciting descriptions of the sense of being engrossed in one's tasks—flow—a prized state of being that many yearn for throughout their lives.

The Hawthorne Effect

The history of work motivation in many ways captures some important themes within the history of psychology.[4] In fact, reviewing the trends about work motivation is sort of a greatest "hits" of applied psychology, featuring some of the most important intellectual stars and themes of the past century.[5] While many key events can be identified, perhaps the one that I heard about the most in my various undergraduate and graduate classes was the famous Hawthorne study.

In the mid-1920s, the Committee on Work in Industry of the National Research Council asked Elton Mayo, a well-known Harvard Business School professor, to explore questions about motivation and productivity at the Hawthorne plant of Western Electric outside Chicago.

Mayo conducted fairly elaborate experiments, albeit with a very small sample of eight workers, to provide research evidence that would support the use of greater illumination in factories. The underlying hope was that a relationship between greater illumination and productivity would help to compensate for the higher electricity costs of the lighting fixtures that Western Electric was hoping to market.[6] What the research team found in the Hawthorne studies was intriguing and has engendered many important movements within the psychological study of working. While the Mayo team initially set out to study the impact of changes in lighting on factory workers, they soon decided to use their experimental method on a wider array of personnel practices, such as changing break times, introducing flextime, and providing free tea and snacks.

The findings from the Hawthorne studies were very promising; each of the interventions yielded notable improvements in productivity. The results were initially interpreted as supporting the view that paying attention to workers, particularly providing them with a place to feel heard and affirmed, would result in greater motivation and productivity. Indeed, the message from the Hawthorne study helped to inspire the growing human relations movement, which became a major aspect of the organizational psychology world in the mid- to latter part of the twentieth century.

On closer examination, the Hawthorne studies were quite flawed; in fact, these flaws actually illuminate some issues about motivation and work that dominate this chapter. For example, the small number of participants were highly motivated to cooperate with management because their participation in the project shielded them from mass layoffs, which were taking place during the time period of the study (i.e., Great Depression).[7] In addition, two of the sample members were removed from the project, which certainly complicated the findings further given that the remaining participants were very motivated to stay in their reasonably safe working context. These points notwithstanding, the Hawthorne study did lead to an interest in attending to the voices of workers. In retrospect, the research evidence supporting this conclusion was not that compelling; however, the oral history of this project took on a life of its own in psychology and management. The contours of this project, as reflected in the fact that the workers were seemingly desperate to ensure their survival, is a subtle lesson from this study that regrettably remains a critical issue in the experience of being motivated at work.

Following the Hawthorne study, work motivation soon grew to have a much larger role in psychological studies of work and careers. For individuals who were in less skilled positions, the focus of inquiry was on providing the conditions that would support active participation at work, less turnover and absenteeism, and productivity gains. For those who were in more privileged positions, motivation tended to focus on enhancing self-determination and meaningfulness. By the 1970s, the full impact of the human relations movement had become far more impactful, leading many people as well as scholars in search of the conditions that might facilitate feelings of engagement, purpose, and achievement at work.

Flow: The Golden Experience of Motivation

Throughout this book and, indeed, throughout much of my career, I have focused on work as an activity that is often motivated by our need to survive. This perspective emerged as a counterpoint to the notions of work as a source of fulfillment and self-determination, which were pervasive in my professional life and, more broadly, in the culture of post–World War II America.[8] As I entered the workplace in the 1970s, a new concept emerged that started to attract a fair amount of attention in public conversations about work: flow. The concept of flow, developed by Mihalyi Csikszentmihalyi, a brilliant psychologist who emerged out of the ashes of postwar Europe into the halls of the most prestigious universities in the United States, captured a time and place that still resonates in our thinking about work and motivation.[9] Indeed, the notion of flow is still a notable part of the hopes and dreams that people talk about when they consider their working lives. On occasion, a client who I worked with in the midst of long-term unemployment would harken back to the dream that work could lead to that kind of state of joy and engagement.

Csikszentmihalyi developed the concept of flow initially in observing artists and musicians, whose complete sense of connection and corresponding feeling of near-ecstatic abandon while engaged in their tasks, intrigued him. The concept of flow reflects an engrossing sense of absorption in a given set of activities that is often experienced as "being in the zone." For people who are in a flow state, time either stands still or moves incredibly quickly; the sense of being engrossed in a task or project is experienced as an enjoyable state, one that often results in a complete sense of focus that allows people to avoid unpleasant or anxious thoughts and feelings. As reflected in the extensive research that Csikszentmihalyi has conducted with a wide range of people, the sense of flow can be attained by people in diverse activities, including, but not limited, to marketplace work. Flow also was not limited to people who were engaged in highly skilled tasks; Csikszentmihalyi found that a diverse array of people,

including cattle ranchers, factory workers, and homemakers, among others, reported attaining flow states at some points in their lives.

According to Csikszentmihalyi, flow states are characterized by the following
experiences:

1. A pervasive feeling of concentration on a specific task.
2. A deep sense of engagement and a feeling that action and awareness are
   impossible to disentangle.
3. A feeling of control in relation to one's tasks.
4. Significant interest and contentment about the content and process of the
   tasks at hand.
5. A distorted experience of time.

A curious aspect of flow is that it cannot be reliably predicted.
Csikszentmihalyi found that flow states are most likely to occur when an individual has greater skill than average and is engaged in tasks that are more challenging than average. However, extensive research by Csikszentmihalyi and his
colleagues has identified the critical role of subjectivity that is inherent in flow
experiences. Flow is more likely to occur if people believe that it is occurring
and if they are open to the experience. Interestingly, research also reveals
that the experiences that evoke flow states are often autonomously chosen,
underscoring the critical role that career choice privilege has in the realm of
work and well-being.[10]

The notion of flow certainly seems compelling to people and scholars.
Research on this experience has been extensive and is a common thread
in many self-help and positive psychology treatises on work.[11] And, while
Csikszentmihalyi noted that homemakers and factory workers may experience flow, the reality is likely that privilege is critical in understanding who
has access to flow states. In the material that follows, the Boston College
Working Project participants provide a contemporary counterpoint to this
brief introductory journey of motivation, underscoring the exuberance of
being in a job that is totally engaging as well as the despair of a painful work
life and periods of unemployment that undercut one's sense of being alive in
the world.

Being Motivated: Lived Experiences

The issue of what motivates people to work, to look for work, to manage stress
at work, and to seek the joy of accomplishment and creation in the workplace
occupied a central role in the interviews. The sections that follow review the

major themes that arose in our interviews and include many of the important concepts in work motivation more broadly.

Creating and Accomplishing

The opportunity to be involved in activities and tasks that allowed people to create and accomplish was the most common theme in the extensive comments about motivation. While not quite a flow state, the sense of having an opportunity to use one's skills and abilities in making something happen, helping people, or creating something was a clearly articulated objective and experience of many of the participants.

Suba, a 29-year-old South Asian man who worked as a process engineer, spoke about his sources of motivation. His situation was complicated by the fact that he lived apart from his wife due to dual-career issues; he also indicated that he struggled to find his path earlier in his life and felt very fortunate to have discovered material science and engineering, which felt like an optimal fit for him. With these points in mind, his thoughts on how he experienced his work life affirmed the essential role of creating and accomplishing.

> I have been through times when I am not working and when I am really struggling. And those times when I was not working and I was not creating value were the times when I was really depressed. And I just don't want to feel that again. I want to feel that I have created value in life, that I'm not just existing, but I'm living my life.

Suba described how the experience of creating value, both for himself and his employer, gave him a sense of purpose and meaning. He described elsewhere in the interview that his contribution to the creation of glass (which was the focus of his material science work) helped in the construction of houses and buildings, for which he took great pride.

The next interview introduces Mildred, a 52-year-old woman who had returned to undergraduate school in midlife during a period of unemployment. Mildred discussed her hopes for her work life, which seem particularly compelling given that she had suffered an extended period of unemployment leading up the interview.

> I want to do something for someone that makes their life better or is something that people should be aware of, or helps people who need something. So it's not just a paycheck that I'm looking for when I'm at work. I'm looking for a sense that I'm helping people; that there's a product that

needs to be out there; there's something that needs to be said to someone; there's something that can help someone else along the way. When I was working at my old company, when we first started out, we were one of the first companies that came up with a way of helping people learn how to cook, because our company is focusing on cooking, and we were focused on teaching people how to make cooking something that's part of their daily life. I enjoyed that concept, and I really was thrilled about doing that work. Whenever I approach work now, it has to benefit someone, and that's where I get my enjoyment from—these feelings of what I'm doing matters.

As Mildred recounted, the sense of accomplishment that work provided was key in ensuring that she felt motivated in her work. Even as she was ramping up for a new job search, the fact that she was able to feel such a clear sense of creativity at work in the past became a driving force in her considerations of how to develop a new career plan. Similarly, for Joshua, the unemployed man we met in Chapter 4, the complications of seeking a job that provided a sense of accomplishment and creativity (which Joshua described as "purpose") are detailed in this passage.

I've lost a couple of jobs because I went out and got experimental over the last couple of years because I became purpose-based, and I wanted to find something new and exciting . . . and the truth is it didn't work out; that was somewhat risky. That's hard because on one level, I know full well for me to be fulfilled as a human being, I'm going to have to take a couple of risks that take me to a place that is more purpose-based, or that follows my curiosity, than sitting in a place in big corporations—which I think is just as risky. So, I took some risks to go into other environments that have affected us financially.

As Joshua described, the search for an opportunity to feel deeply motivated at work was deep and pervasive; in his case, he ended up in a period of unemployment, which he was struggling to make sense of during his interview. His vignette speaks powerfully about the human desire to engage in a work life that helps people to feel alive and engaged.

Intrinsic Motivation

To engage in activities and tasks that one actually enjoys and finds meaningful represents perhaps the optimal state of work; in this context, work, at times, can become akin to play and can lead to the cherished flow states we described previously. Indeed, the experience of creating and accomplishing, as described in the previous section, is often a manifestation of intrinsic motivation. As an example of intrinsic motivation, Sandrine, a 41-year-old, French-born White biologist who was looking for work at the time of the interview, described what motivated her to get out of bed each day.

> Two things: One thing is I cannot bear being inactive. I used to be super active in the past. So I cannot stand at home. What motivates me first is when the sun rises, I like that. Second, I want to do something in my life. I want to be useful. And if I don't do something, I'm useless. So definitely I feel useless (now that I am unemployed). And definitely I don't like this feeling. So, what motivates me is the people waiting for a cure or at least for alternatives. So maybe I'm not going to save the life of this patient. But at least I'll try. The most important things for me are the patients are waiting for us.

Sandrine described her desire to be productive and connected that desire to her sense of calling to do research in the life sciences, which she viewed as helping to improve the quality of life for others. Hence, her love of the activities of research was enriched by the meaning that she attached to her career aspirations. In the next passage, Charles, a 25-year-old White magician educated at an Ivy League university, described his experience of feeling powerfully connected to his work. Charles represents a minority of the participants who elected to follow a somewhat risky passion, despite the reality that making a living as a magician was more challenging than many other fields.

> I love magic; it is very easy for me to sit in a room for 24 hours and think of magic ideas and work on magic ideas; that is not a challenge, that's awesome. . . . For me, work should be intellectually engaging and one step more than that it should be intellectually challenging. . . . It is about finding those comfort zones and those upper limits. I feel like work happens in those areas, work happens where you are comfortable and towards your upper limits. . . . When I am creating a show . . . work is the research, work is the scripting and the editing and it is hours and weeks and months of all the background that you need to get towards the upper limits, which is where it kind of stops being work. It is where you hit that runner's high. . . . You have put in these 20 miles of real work, whether it be physical, emotional or mental and suddenly you reach a point where it ceases to be work and it becomes this self-fulfillment, and I think many people are perfectly happy in the comfort zone. They are perfectly happy doing the work.

Charles described an experience in conceptualizing and presenting magic that is akin to the flow state that was summarized previously. His choice of being a magician reflects the culmination of a dream that began when Charles was a boy and began to explore the world of entertainment and performance. As spokespersons for the many participants who recounted their experiences of intrinsic motivation, Sandrine and Charles gave voice to the desired aspiration of finding a means of survival that also feels interesting, challenging, and, at times, fun. The counterpoint to intrinsic motivation is extrinsic in nature, which is explored next.

Extrinsic Motivation

As many readers were admonished in their youth about chores and school-work, life is not a bowl full of cherries (a common refrain from my father; interestingly, I did not like cherries at the time). The participants conveyed powerful vignettes about their struggles to stay motivated in the face of often-considerable obstacles. In the first passage, Mark, a 63-year-old educator who shared his insights in previous chapters, elaborated on his journey from working as a teacher to becoming an entrepreneur of educationally related businesses. He initially took a job at an elite high school in a suburban region that sustained his life financially but left him feeling lifeless. He then began to pursue various educational businesses, which soon took off and gave him a new lease on life. Here, he described how he dug deep to develop the motivation that was needed to manage his "day job" and take the risks needed for his passion: the world of entrepreneurship.

> I hope I haven't sounded Pollyannaish, but I do genuinely believe in what I'm telling you. Life has been good to me. I've been fortunate. Sometimes, when I feel weak, I try to summon the energy I imagine deriving from my dead natural father, who I never knew. He has kind of given me some strength if I feel weak, that he has inputted it. Sometimes, when I was younger and I had doubts as a beginning entrepreneur, and I had fear; I would see the faces of my young children and that I had to feed them. And I would use that as a source of strength; I would try to get sources of strength wherever I could to drive me forth and that did work.

Mark's description of his career trajectory underscores how extrinsic motivation, at times, can lead to experiences that are closer to intrinsic motivation. As Mark realized that his public school position would not satisfy his thirst for greater autonomy and creativity as well as his need for an income that would support his family and his own desire to see the world, he engaged in serious self-reflection, which ultimately led him to a business that was more intrinsically motivating. In the passage that follows, we move from the world of market work to care work, where we meet Meryl, a 45-year-old White former training and development specialist who worked full time caring for her three children.

> What motivates me? Well . . . there is no choice. I have three little people who are counting on me to help them get dressed, out the door, with their lunches, with their homework, with their sneakers. So, it's not like I have the luxury of lying in bed wondering, "should I get out of bed today or not?" There is, there is no choice, so I don't really think about it that way. I guess what motivates me is just their well-being.

Like Mark, Meryl described her motivation as having extrinsic roots, but also shifting to intrinsic when she reflected on the long-term objective of ensuring the well-being of her children. In each of these cases, the participants described bumping up against some aspect of life that evoked a response; however, they were able to generate meaning and purpose from their activities, thereby making the work more palatable. However, for a significant portion of the participants in this project, work was primarily motivated by the need to survive. Sierra the 29-year-old woman working as a supervisor in a call center who contributed to Chapter 4, shared a powerful lesson in how work can be deadening in the following passage:

> I want to go to work, and I just want to be happy. As soon as I walk through the door at my current job, my whole mood has shifted from the moment that I woke up and got ready for work. I'm singing in the car, I'm happy, I'm enjoying my drive to work, I'm smelling the fresh air, I'm enjoying life. And then as soon as I step into this hell-hole, it literally just kills my mood and I find that I'm not friendly to my co-workers. . . . I'm very brief, and I choose to avoid certain people. . . . And I just feel like you should just really love your job. And I know that I've said that so many times. . . . You really should just love your job. It should truly make you happy. You should be proud of your job. You should want to go to work. When I was home sick yesterday, deathly ill—I had to go to the doctor because I had a viral infection—I was joking around at work today that a day at home deathly ill with a viral infection is a better day than being at work.

Sierra's story is often overlooked in narratives and media descriptions of motivation and work. Throughout Sierra's interview, she spoke passionately about her efforts to create more meaning and dignity at her workplace, which was characterized by a harsh management culture that detracted from the workers' sense of autonomy. In the following section, some of the psychological tools that people use to enhance their motivation at work are described.

Personal Attributes as Sources of Motivation

Both in the interviews that we conducted and in the psychology literature, the role of personal attributes as a source of motivation emerged as a powerful mechanism in understanding the way in which people manage to keep themselves going in spite of often-harsh barriers. Consistent with many of the most important theories of work motivation, the articulation of personal goals represents one of the best internal tools that people can rely on to feel motivated.[12] In the first passage, Jena, a 25-year-old unemployed woman who was attending college, described the function of goals in helping her to stay focused and positive.

> So I got goals . . . dreams. So I want to own . . . I wanna have my own empire, so that motivates me . . . to keep going, and to try to save as much money as I can, put some money in a bank account, and invest. . . . It sort of helps me to keep going every day, which is the reason why I wanted to go to school.

In addition to goals, a number of participants described their dreams for a better future as providing a powerful motivational force in their lives. Jamal, the 41-year-old higher educational professional who contributed to previous chapters, described his capacity to draw on some intangible aspects of his character as resources throughout his life.

> I would really have to say that there was something about my spirit, and early on, I just was an old soul. I have always been a very independent person. I have always been a leader. I have never been someone that followed other people. I have never been someone who prescribed to group think or how other people think about things. . . . I take pride in being who I am. But I would have to say there was something in me that saw the surrounds that I was in and I knew that the only way that I was going to get out of this was through an education. No one told me that. No one cultivated any of that in me. I just knew, and I can't pinpoint what that was, but I knew that this was not for me and in order for me to get out of this I needed to get an education.

Jamal grew up in a very impoverished urban community and faced significant obstacles in putting this plan into place, including racism and problems within his family or origin. While he clearly had intelligence, great interpersonal skills, and passion for his work, this passage (and indeed, his entire interview) conveyed a sense that he was able to dig deep down into a reservoir of personal attributes that helped him to achieve his goals.

Another important attribute that emerged in the interviews was competence; when people feel competent in a given set of tasks, they are more likely to feel motivated.[13] Scott, a 29-year-old White public high school teacher, attested to the motivating properties of competence in the following passage:

> I think that's why I love my job, because there is that challenge. And I know that it's gotten easier every year. And I think that's why it excites me the most that I'm getting better at it. And I know there's a lot more to do, more to learn in a lot of areas, but the difference that I see in part of our recertification to get our license is that there's a reflection involved and I am a significantly better teacher than I was years ago, so that's exciting.

A number of other personal attributes emerged in the interviews, including spiritual beliefs, optimism, and a strong work ethic. Taken together, these themes, coupled with the vignettes reviewed in this section, suggest that the nature of work motivation is certainly complex, involving both aspects of individuals and their context. In the following two sections, two of the most important features of the work environment are reviewed, including the relationships that frame people's lives at work and the sense of competition, which is often a function of both relationships and work-based policies.

Relationships and Motivation

Relationships are essential in nearly all aspects of work, including the process of feeling engaged and motivated. In a very tangible way, Kerri, a 23-year-old unemployed African American woman, recounted how a previous job as a day-care worker provided her with a relationship-based source of motivation:

> I enjoyed my previous job! The kids just. . . . They put a smile on your face. It's different from retail. It's different from working at a restaurant. It's like you're telling yourself, "Ughh, so miserable." . . . You don't want to wake up on the wrong side of the bed every day. But with the day care, oh my Jesus! The kids, they put a smile on my face, working from 9 to 5.

This theme is further explored in the next passage from Fran, a 62-year-old White business manager from Alaska, who described her main motivation for work in vividly relational terms.

> My primary reason for working on that job is because of the socialization. To be able to socialize with 3- to 5-year-olds and the people who work there, the staff is wonderful. . . . My socialization opportunities in my daily life is challenging because I live on an island. I can isolate very easily out here, and so that's my number one goal. . . . It's usually the people, the people I work for.

Interpersonal problems also can contribute to a lack of motivation. In the next passage by Kim, a 26-year-old woman who worked as a customer service representative for a large department store, the role of relationships as a barrier to motivation is described with eloquence and anguish.

> Before I got hired at this store, I planned on just staying with the company for 2 years, leave just until I was done with my degree, but that didn't happen. So, oh God . . . I have pros and cons. How I feel about [name of store] right now? How I feel about my job? I think I just go. I just go because I feel like I have to. I don't like the environment. I love the people, but in terms of the associates, the coworkers, I feel like there's a battle between associates and managers, and that's one of the things I saw while I was a supervisor, where I was in the middle between the upper manager, the store managers, and the assistant manager. People . . . I don't think their voices were being heard from . . . whenever they had problems/issues. Now I think it's all about retaliation. And I think that's really wrong, very judgmental. If you say something, you would have to be careful who you say it to, how you say it or else there will be retaliation.

In her comments, Kim suggested that a deeper examination is needed of how competition and other forms of relationship tensions may affect people's experiences at work. Indeed, the intersection of relationships and motivation is complex and nuanced. At times, relationships at work or in other parts of one's life can provide the nutrients needed to foster motivation; at the same time, when these relationships are in a state of flux or crisis, the impact at work can have a negative or distracting effect, undercutting our natural desire to create and contribute.

Competition and Motivation

While competition is one of the hallmarks of the neoliberal economic system, its impact on individuals is complex and clearly relevant to this discussion of motivation. In the first passage, Talih, a 32-year-old medical resident and researcher from Turkey, describes the role of competition in her work life.

> Yes, [this job is] too competitive and it was built to be competitive. People are worried that they are going to lose their grants; they are going to lose the positions they have. If you're not the best, they won't keep you, they won't pay you and everyone has families or they are trying to get a visa or they are trying to get a green card so everybody is worried they won't be able to take care of themselves or their loved ones. So, I think that the work culture just promotes it to be competitive and sometimes people, do unethical things to be more competitive.

Talih's description conveys the sense of competitiveness that pervaded many aspects of her residency, particularly the research part of her work. Her comments were echoed by many other participants, who reflected on the price that they paid at work that often enacted a powerful negative influence in their lives.

At the broader level, competition brought on by globalization generated some thoughtful comments in these interviews, reflecting a common theme in the political discourse about work across many nations that are reeling from the impact of market forces. The following passage by John, a 56-year-old chief executive officer of a mobile marketing firm, describes the broader economic scene that has sent shock waves across many regions of the United States and other nations that have struggled to maintain competiveness in a global environment.

> [Work] started to be unfun, yeah that's probably the right word—an unfun experience, because of the level of intense, and almost unreasonable, competition that was coming from the Asian companies. Back in the day when . . . when cellular was young, making mobile phones was complicated and difficult, and the design, you must understand, was very elaborate. Most of the Asian companies were not there yet. They were. . . . They had great manufacturing prowess, but not design prowess. But . . . unfortunately in a lot of these countries they don't have a very high respect for intellectual property rights, so as time went by, we found that a lot of the companies that we were outsourcing our manufacturing to, little by little, learned what we did, how we did it, and basically started to steal our designs. And then, we're competing with them, or they were competing with us. And, of course, they would do anything to win market share, which means to sell it below their cost. So they were in all of the markets eventually, just beating us up like crazy, with crazy prices . . . and it was . . . not fun anymore. . . . You know, we were a public company

with . . . we have our responsibilities to our shareholders to [have] results quarter by quarter, which was becoming virtually impossible to do given the pricing pressure we were under.

As John noted, competition within the economic and financial marketplace helped to drive his experience of work as well as the work lives of millions of people around the globe. The impact of the global market and the more proximal influence of interpersonal competitiveness are reviewed further in subsequent chapters. However, Talih and John's experiences certainly suggest that the well waters run deep and wide when people are reflecting about competition at the workplace.

Most of the participants in the Boston College Working Project spoke extensively about the role of motivation in their work and overall lives. Taken together, what seems clear is that feeling motivated at work is not a given; people struggle to feel alive and engaged at work, often at great psychological expense. While we did observe some of the participants drawing on powerful inner resources, the reality of work for many of the people we interviewed is that their sense of feeling motivated was often a function of how much privilege and access to opportunity they experienced during their lives.

Being Motivated: The Psychological View

The field of psychology is no stranger to the world of work motivation. In doing a deeper dive into the psychological aspects of motivation, I have selected two specific bodies of knowledge that will inform how we put the puzzle together about the impact of work in an age of uncertainty. Both of the perspectives presented represent alternatives to the traditional views of motivation, which have often assumed that individuals have a relative degree of volition in their work lives and that their internal attributes (e.g., personal goals, self-efficacy) can help them to develop and sustain motivation, even in the face of considerable obstacles. While these factors are no doubt critical in understanding what motivates people, the picture is more complex than a linear relationship between internal resources and action.

Self-Determination and Work

In the early 1970s, academic psychology was in the midst of the behavioral revolution, which assumed that behavior was generally contingent on external factors, such as rewards or social approval. For example, motivating workers was thought to be a direct function of the incentives and punishments that were linked to the work situation. In the clinical world, psychoanalytic theory held sway, using a set of ideas that essentially viewed human beings as hardwired by biological drives that motivated behavior.[14] Into this deterministic mix emerged humanistic psychology and a more optimistic view of people as the authors of their life story.[15] This intellectual brew created the climate for new innovations about how we motivate ourselves for tasks that we enjoy and for tasks that we find tedious and onerous.

In a number of experiments with college students in the early 1970s, Edward Deci, a psychologist from the University of Rochester, found that people who enjoyed tasks were more engaged when they did not have external rewards linked to activities that were intrinsically interesting and motivating.[16] In fact, when the participants of these studies were given rewards for intrinsically motivating tasks, they felt less in control and ended up being less motivated. The extensive research that these early studies generated soon blossomed into a fully fleshed out framework of human behavior and motivation known as self-determination theory.[17] While it is impossible to summarize the entire breadth of this work in a few pages, I highlight a few central points that are critical to our thinking about work motivation during this current period of such flux in the labor market.

1. *Intrinsic motivation:* The longed-for experience of feeling authentically connected and engaged in a set of activities is clearly the gold standard of motivation. Within self-determination theory, intrinsic motivation is understood as being shaped by conditions within the environment. People who are inherently motivated to engage in a given task are more likely to continue their work if they are feeling autonomous and competent. Receiving negative feedback or harsh criticism can undercut an intrinsically motivating experience.

2. *Extrinsic motivation:* The reality of many work experiences, and, for that matter, the job search while unemployed, is that we do not necessarily enjoy the tasks that are needed to develop and sustain our work lives. Extrinsic motivation refers to activities wherein the outcome is separate from the actual enjoyment of the task. For example, many jobs require that people perform tasks that are tedious and even painful; however, the rewards of financial resources and survival provide a powerful motivating link. In self-determination theory, Deci and Ryan have thoughtfully demonstrated that people can experience various levels of autonomy and authenticity in their tasks including both intrinsically and extrinsically motivating experiences.[18]

The decades of research that have been conducted on self-determination theory have identified three attributes of the context that can support both intrinsically and extrinsically motivating work tasks, as reflected in Figure 5.1 and summarized below.[19]

a. *Autonomy,* which is often viewed as the key that unlocks motivational engagement, is the essence of what Deci discovered in his early experiments. People whose behavior was not linked to external consequences felt autonomous and were less likely to lose their intrinsic motivation. Similarly, autonomy is critical in helping people to find meaning and value in extrinsically motivating activities. In short, people need to feel free and experience volition in their lives; it is a gift that keeps on giving.

b. *Competence* was also mentioned in the early descriptions of intrinsic motivation and has become central in understanding extrinsic motivation. If we feel skilled in a given task, we are more likely to gravitate toward it, even if it is not necessarily interesting or compelling.

c. *Relatedness,* as initially discussed in Chapter 3, is a critical aspect of life and is integral to our work lives as well. In self-determination theory, relatedness is the third leg of the stool that supports our motivational efforts. Indeed, research has indicated that feeling connected to others at the workplace helps to enrich a job or set of tasks that may be inherently dreary.

So, how these do these pieces fit together to create a sense of self-determination, which is the essence of this very innovative set of ideas? For Deci and Ryan, the reality that not all work and related efforts to survive are interesting is obvious.

The self-determination model of working:

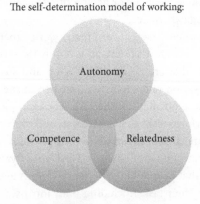

Figure 5.1 Self-determination theory.

In their research, they have identified the usefulness of autonomy, competence, and relatedness as critical aspects of the context that can foster a feeling of engagement and autonomy. In the case of extrinsic motivation, these three factors can help people internalize their motivation by providing meaning and authenticity, above and beyond the tasks at hand. In other words, we may find activities meaningful if they help us to achieve our goals and are consistent with our values. However, these experiences can be further enhanced by ensuring that people feel autonomous, competent, and related to the others at the job. The experience of self-determination, therefore, is possible for those who are involved in very compelling and flow-like activities and is also possible for those who have not had a chance to enact their dreams in the workplace.

In considering self-determination theory in light of the changes in the world of work detailed in the first chapter of this book, a number of questions emerge that were implied in the narratives from the Boston College Working Project. First, to what extent are work environments currently able to provide autonomy, competence, and relatedness? In an era of increasing disparities between highly skilled and less skilled workers, I fear that the core elements of providing decent work, which arguably ought to include autonomy, competence, and relatedness, may be eroding.[20] Second, how can people mobilize to ensure that work is not only available but also nurturing of self-determination? Finally, how can self-determination theory help to inform public policies about work? I have more to say about this in the conclusion of this chapter and in the final chapter of the book.

Organizational Justice and Motivation

As reflected in the discussion of self-determination theory, motivation is a process that entails an understanding of both individuals and their contexts. Another late twentieth-century movement that has sought to unpack how the environment affects motivation is organizational justice. In brief, people often shift their motivation based on their perceptions of fairness within the workplace. Researchers in management and organizational psychology have determined that employees are strongly influenced by their views of how resources and tasks are allocated at their jobs.[21] For people who believe that their efforts are not valued similarly to their colleagues, motivation may diminish, leading to less-than-optimal work experiences and engagement. The underlying notion of the organizational justice movement is that people are highly attuned to the question of whether they are being treated fairly and equitably. The impetus for this research began in the early 1990s and has blossomed, leading to a number of important observations that illuminate our understanding of work motivation during the current era.[22]

The first question that we need to explore is why employees care about organizational justice. In a thoughtful synthesis of the literature on organizational justice, Russell Cropanzano and his colleagues identified three significant factors that contribute to the importance of organizational justice.[23]

1. *The long haul*: People joining work organizations are interested in how they will fare over the long term. An organization that establishes fairness and equity in a clearly evident way will provide workers with the capacity to predict how their effort will be rewarded over time.
2. *Social implications:* As reflected throughout this book, work is a social arrangement that provides people with ongoing contact with others and with opportunities to compare one's treatment with others. An organization that values justice conveys that it cares about its employees, thereby providing a greater sense of connection among the workers and between the workers and their tasks.
3. *Ethical implications:* People care about equity as an inherent value with clear implications for the workplace. Workers who are able to identify an evident level of justice at their jobs will feel more engaged and motivated based on their buy-in to the organization's principles.

How does organizational justice build the framework for motivation? Cropanzano and his colleagues have elaborated on the motivational processes that have been linked to perceptions of justice. First, the perception of justice is not always based on fact; the research literature is clear that people will construct their own narratives about the formal and informal justice policies at their jobs. Second, justice has been found to build trust, which then enhances a worker's connection to the organization and its mission. Third, considerable research has indicated that perceptions of justice improve performance: People work harder and are more motivated when they understand that their efforts will be judged fairly. Finally, justice facilitates the development of organizational citizenship behaviors, which include treating others well and demonstrating high levels of conscientiousness.

The flip side of the organizational justice perspective is the identification of the consequences of organizational injustice. Workers who perceive injustice may retaliate at work, are likely to become disengaged, and report lower morale. However, the overarching story of organizational justice is that it is an essential aspect of the complex puzzle of work and motivation. People need to know that they have a voice in their working lives, an observation that emerges throughout this book. Moreover, organizational justice provides a benchmark that allows people to establish their effort and goals in broad daylight. Optimally, people should know what aspects of their work are likely to lead to positive feedback, affirmation, promotions, and a secure sense of stability in a given job. The organizational justice literature is a bright light in work motivation in that it clearly implicates the context as a resource that can nurture or undercut our natural striving to engage in meaningful and valued work activities.

Conclusion

The material presented on work and motivation is rich with implications for individuals and for the broader collective that forms our social world. The participants from the Boston College Working Project shared powerful stories that suggest the ways people can derive so much inspiration from their work that it literally propels them through considerable obstacles to attain work and perform, often at great expense to themselves and their families. Some of the participants did in fact attain a level of flow that has become the aspirational standard for people who feel the spark of their dreams in their work lives. The narratives were flush with stories of creativity and accomplishment, even for people who were not necessarily in jobs that fit their personalities or values. Throughout this chapter, the reality of motivation is evident, as articulated in self-determination theory: People are often able to feel deeply engaged, even when the job is not necessarily that interesting.

Yet, a notable proportion of people we interviewed described dreams that were often deferred or never even conceived of because they had lost hope that work could be meaningful or enjoyable. Many of the narratives stood in stark contrast to the psychological literature, which has focused, for the most part, on people with a relative degree of choice in their work lives.[24] The addition of the self-determination and organizational justice theories provides a broader perspective about work motivation that complements the perspectives that were observed in the interviews. So, as the world of work becomes increasingly fragmented and unstable, where does that leave our inherent desire to engage in work that is motivating and self-determined?

Multiple answers to this question can be inferred from the material presented in this chapter. First, the strong focus on individual attributes as driving forces in work motivation is certainly understandable given the circumscribed view of work from the lens of middle- to upper middle–class scholars who were studying their peers. However, a broader view is required at this point in time in order to fully understand all people who work and who strive to work. Yes, attributes such as clearly articulated goals, self-confidence, proactive personality, and resilience, among other personal assets, are all critical; indeed, reams of academic papers have been devoted to understanding these factors.[25] They will continue to be important as we understand work in the coming years and decades. However, the narratives and the newer psychological models of motivation tell a more complex story. People need to be in environments that offer justice and fairness; the experience of justice is a major motivator for many people.

I argue here that the focus on organizational justice needs to be broadened to include the structure of work and the treatment of workers. The excerpts included in this chapter (and in other chapters in this book) convey the intense striving that people have to gain just a foothold in the labor market—a chance for stability and a place to create projects and, it is hoped, experience the joy of accomplishments. Perhaps it is time to consider justice, writ large, as a human right within the workplace that is needed to nurture our striving for creativity, contribution, and purpose. Without a safe and secure place to try our hand at whatever we can perform, create, or serve, people are often left feeling disengaged and desperate in a world of work that is increasingly eroding. The observations that are evident in this chapter create a clarion call for social policies that will provide a comfortable frame around our work experiences. The neoliberal economy seems to be stacked against those who do not have ready access to the tools for the twenty-first-century labor market.[26] However, the psychological consequences of continuing to emphasize profits and reduced labor costs are clearly a problem. Underneath the frustration and bitterness of some of the participants lies a deeper resentment, the sort of feeling that has led to the radical shifts in the political system in the United States and other countries. What seems clear from this chapter is that people have a natural striving to be involved in work that fires their spirit and engages them in some authentic way. In the subsequent chapters, particularly in the closing chapter, I focus on how work needs to be restructured so that it provides people with real opportunities to feel motivated and alive.

6

Being Able to Care

Roberto entered my therapy office about 6 years ago, looking exhausted, depressed, and somewhat embarrassed. (Roberto is a fictional case based on an amalgam of clients I have seen since the start of the Great Recession in 2008.) As a well-educated 58-year-old Latino man with a master's degree in business administration, Roberto had worked in human resources in the private sector consistently for the first 25 years of his career. At 53, Roberto was laid off by a global company that manufactured pharmaceuticals at the outset of the financial downturn in 2008. He was out of work for 2 years and then got another job in human resources for a small software startup. This job lasted 18 months and ended when the company was bought out by a larger organization that took over all of the human resources functions.

When Roberto sought me out, he was unemployed for 3 years and was becoming increasingly depressed, despite a very strong marriage to Rosa for over 25 years. Roberto was interested in reinvigorating his job search; he also was struggling with depression and was hoping to work on his diminished mood and energy level. Interestingly, Roberto was quite engaged during his unemployment periods in caring for his daughter, Isabella, with Down syndrome. Throughout the therapy process, which lasted for 3 years, Roberto struggled considerably with his self-esteem and with often-intense feelings of shame because he was not able to obtain a decent job. The profound sense of loss and pain that he felt was palpable.

An interesting theme emerged in my work with Roberto that provides an illuminating overture to this chapter about the tension between marketplace work and caregiving work. (As I noted in Chapter 1, I view work as encompassing the activities that we do both in the paid marketplace and in our personal and community contexts, where the efforts are often directed to caring for others, ourselves, and our communities and do not result in remuneration.) Roberto devoted a great deal of time, effort, creativity, and passion in caring for his daughter, Isabella, who was between the ages of 17 and 20 during the time span of the therapy process. Roberto also was caring for another daughter, Maria, who was 2 years younger than Isabella and did not have any developmental delays or other significant concerns. Throughout Roberto's therapy sessions, he recounted how important it was for him to be a good father and caregiver. Yet, at the same time, he described how he preferred to obtain a job in human resources in the marketplace (where he would be paid for his efforts), which he felt was his true love and passion.

One of the core conflicts in the therapy process was Roberto's deep ambivalence about the meaning that he attached to his caregiving during the period when he was unemployed. While I worked on helping Roberto to create an affirming narrative that would support a more realistic and compassionate view of his caregiving efforts, he struggled in accepting this reframing. In a sense, Roberto became stuck in the more widely accepted narrative that work for money is all that matters, and that the caregiving that he was doing was something that just had to be done. While Roberto stated that he did not derive much overt satisfaction from his care work, he clearly felt attached to both of his daughters and felt comforted in knowing that he was so engaged with them. The prevailing internalized view that caregiving was not that essential for his sense of identity overshadowed the actual experience, as if the true nature of the meaningfulness of his work could not rise above the forces of the powerful social messages that valued marketplace work above nearly everything else.

As I mulled over this case and others throughout the years, I certainly understood that people struggle to balance work and family, a well-known issue that is part of our public conversation about contemporary life. However, I discerned a deeper sense of conflict about how to understand the ways in which people relate to their caregiving efforts. In many ways, the question of how people engage in caring for others and its relationship to work has taken shape as a major dilemma in considerations of work. I also began to read deeply about the role of caregiving as a gendered activity that is very often done by women throughout many cultures around the globe.[1] In my reading and reflection, I began to understand a deeper meaning about caregiving and learned about the highly contentious debate about the social and economic impact of caregiving. In short, a fundamental question that has been debated for many decades regards the extent that caring is part of our working lives.[2] Despite the challenges that are present when caring for others and despite the marginalization of care work, I sensed from Roberto and other clients that it is a core aspect of being alive in the world, albeit one that is often not affirmed by others or by our social and economic systems.

In this chapter, I explore caregiving in depth and in relation to marketplace work, identifying some of the complexities that are integral to these two essential aspects of human experience. To gain a broad and deep perspective on this issue, I explore this terrain initially from a historical lens and then move to some of the core assumptions about caregiving within psychology. The participants from the Boston College Working Project give further insights that are followed by new advances in the psychology of care and working. At the conclusion of the chapter, I develop a position based on a vision of caregiving that is economically rewarded, socially affirmed, and dignified, which befits this core aspect of being alive in the world.

Being Able to Care: An Introductory Journey

Considerations about caregiving and work have been part of the dialogue about labor, psychology, well-being, and gender for nearly two centuries.[3] While caregiving and care work have been central responsibilities and functions in human history for eons, the relationship among caring, gender, and work are beset with challenges that are becoming even more pronounced as work in the marketplace becomes more precarious. In addition, the role of gender is the "elephant in the room" of caregiving and work, in that women are most often expected to manage care work in their households and are also encouraged to pursue care work in the marketplace; both of these sets of expectations markedly limit the autonomy of women as they navigate their lives.[4] These processes result in a loss of earning power, lack of access to positions of control and empowerment in their lives, and very real constraints in being able to implement their dreams.[5] In this section, I review the terrain of caring and work, beginning with an examination of the nature of care as a fundamental human attribute, followed by an exploration of the relationship between caregiving and work.

The concept of care has been considered both a form of work and a form of love and connection.[6] Scholars from psychology, economics, sociology, and feminist studies have all explored the nature of caring and care work.[7] From an economics perspective, care is generally thought to encompass a subset of work that entails caring for people, either within one's relational orbit (such as parents taking care of children) or within the marketplace (such as nursing aides working with the elderly).[8] From a psychological perspective, caring is viewed as a bond that encompasses giving emotional support or instrumental assistance (such as bathing a child), typically to someone who is close to the caregiver.[9] Other scholars view caring as taking place with people who are less intimately connected to the caregiver, such as volunteer work and community work; moreover, self-care is increasingly understood as a critical aspect of caregiving.[10] Furthermore, caring is viewed as part of an intimate relationship that involves giving as opposed to receiving kindness and care. (That said, many scholars do believe that caregivers experience deep satisfaction and connection in caring for others.) When considered collectively, the psychological view of caring is complex, multifaceted, and deeply rooted in our natural tendency to connect and contribute to the welfare of others.[11]

The Nature of Caring

Caring has been integral to human evolution and development. Indeed, scholars who examine the nature of humanity often describe caring as a core function that has been instrumental to the survival of our species. Perhaps the most notable contributor to this perspective is John Bowlby, a well-known British psychologist, psychoanalyst, and scholar who has revolutionized our thinking about attachment and caring.[12] Bowlby, who was introduced in Chapter 3, developed the comprehensive perspective known as attachment theory, which has explored how people develop emotional bonds to each other, particularly within the child–parent dyad. As discussed in Chapter 3, attachment theory helped to fuel the relational revolution, with significant implications for our understanding of people within their work lives.

A key feature of Bowlby's thinking is his expansive theoretical perspective that encompassed psychology, psychoanalytic theory, ethology, cognitive sciences, and evolutionary theory. While the attachment bond of children to their caregivers has received most of the attention in psychology, a corollary ingredient of the attachment process is an internalized desire for people to care for others. Bowlby argued persuasively that adults have a strong caring motivation that is manifested in a wide array of ways.

Consistent with Bowlby's broad-ranging thinking about attachment, caring is thought to occur based on genetic predispositions, learning, and cultural expectations. Naturally, one of the most obvious ways in which the caring tendency is expressed is in the behavior of parents with their own children. However, caring is also revealed in the intense emotions that are evoked during periods of separation when adults miss their children or others who they are taking care of, such as elderly parents or an infirmed family member. I am continually reminded of the caring motivation when I see adults gravitate to infants who are not in their family or relational orbit, even strangers, just to comment on their cuteness or to interact. This process has always underscored for me how integral the caring motivation is in our lived experience.

According to Bowlby's research and the input of subsequent scholars, caregiving is an essential aspect of the attachment process.[13] Without a natural tendency to care for others, it is hard to imagine how humanity would survive, especially when faced with the daunting task of taking care of infants who are dependent on adults for many years. Consider how difficult it must have been for humans to survive in the wild while caring for their young, who could not even walk on their own or feed themselves.

The core of Bowlby's contributions have centered on the parenting dyad; however, more recent innovations have identified the attachment–caregiving bond within romantic relationships, friendships, and less intense relationships, such as with members of our communities.[14] As discussed further in this chapter, considerations of the fundamental nature of the caring motivation represent a new and exciting development in psychology that has implications for our thinking about caregiving and work and indeed for the future of work.

Caregiving and Work

Caring and caregiving, as core aspects of human experience, naturally have broad implications in our work lives. From a definitional perspective, Mary Sue Richardson, a highly innovative counseling psychologist who has helped to put caregiving on the "work and career map" within psychology, has provided a very thoughtful taxonomy of caregiving and work. She initially proposed that work can occur within two contexts: market work and personal care work.[15] Market work is defined by the signature feature that people are paid for their efforts. In contrast, personal care work refers to caring for others without financial remuneration. Personal care work can include caring for children, family members, and others within our communities. Richardson expands this view to encompass caring for oneself, nurturing one's relationships, and contributing to one's community; in effect, personal care work contributes to the broader social good.

Richardson also developed a similar definition of relationships, which she viewed as integral to understanding how people engage in contemporary life.[16] (Indeed, her perspective in counseling psychology is known as counseling for work and relationships, which underscores her compelling position of establishing relationships and dignified work as equal partners in our overall understanding of how people engage, and create meaning, in their lives.) For Richardson, relationships also have two specific contexts: the personal care domain and the marketplace.[17] Richardson's agenda in advocating for these equal, but distinct, definitional boundaries is rooted in her concern about the marginalization of caregiving and personal care work within psychology and, indeed, throughout nearly every aspect of life. I resonate deeply with this position, which has formed one of the core pillars of my contributions within the Psychology of Working Theory and that informs my thinking in this book.

Concerns about the treatment of caregiving within the marketplace have been central in early feminist critiques of the labor market.[18] In short, caregiving within both the personal care and the market spaces has been highly gendered in the United States and in many other nations and communities.[19] Women assume the majority of caregiving in their households, even when they are working in the marketplace at levels of intensity that are as high or higher than their partners. The impact of women carrying the burden of care work has been profound and pervasive, particularly among poor and working-class women. In the points that follow, I summarize some of the trends about caregiving and gender that continue to plague families and communities that struggle to create equitable relationship and working conditions[20]:

1. From a broad anthropological vantage point, caregiving work has been and continues to be primarily conducted by women across many cultures around the globe.[21]
2. Women who pursue careers in the marketplace are often encouraged (either covertly or overtly) to consider work that involves considerable caregiving, such as teaching, nursing, counseling).[22] These career decisions are one of the reasons (although not the only reason; see Chapter 7) that contributes to women earning less than men who are able to consider a wider array of careers.[23]
3. A consistently challenging issue is that women who take time out of the marketplace to engage in personal care work experience broad and substantial negative impacts on their subsequent marketplace work. As reflected in an incisive analysis by Suzanne Bianchi and her colleagues, women who engage in personal care work in lieu of marketplace work face the following consequences:[24]
   a. A loss of income, often due to being out of the marketplace and facing what is known as a "motherhood penalty";
   b. Discrimination in the marketplace in terms of hiring and advancement opportunities;
   c. Loss of leisure activities due to the intense demands of caregiving; and
   d. Reduction of retirement savings.
4. These various forces collude to marginalize caregiving in social, economic, and psychological spaces. In short, caregiving is not often considered to be work by many in that it does not produce wages, retirement benefits, or other economic resources for people.

In addition to the gendered nature of caregiving, race, social class, and sexual orientation create an intersecting set of influences that can have devastating impacts on people navigating both work and family. Low-income families tend to have fewer financial resources to support caregiving tasks, such as funds for cleaning their homes, caring for the elderly, and childcare.[25] In addition, poverty creates a crescendo of negative factors that reduce opportunities for more training and education, thereby limiting work opportunities, often circumscribing their option to marketplace care work, which is generally not well paid. Individuals who care for others for pay and then need to care for their families face significant challenges, including burnout, which is a common outcome for intensive and long-term care work.[26]

While the picture that is being painted here certainly seems dismal, it is important to note that care work for some is a calling and an intentional and planned lifestyle or career choice. People who enter caregiving professions and occupations often feel deeply committed to their work and spend considerable time and effort in training for their marketplace roles. (In fact, I consider myself to have experienced a calling for care work, having served as a provider of counseling and psychological services for over three decades.) Indeed, this same experience ensues for parents who choose to stay at home with their children and serve as their primary caregivers; indeed, for many people (both men and women), it represents the culmination of a meaningful and purposeful dream. Financial and social costs, however, are associated with this decision and reach far into a caregiver's life span, as reflected in the points mentioned previously. The reality is that care work in the personal care context and marketplace is often, but not always, done by people who likely did not select this trajectory and often feel that it was all that life offered them.[27]

Although research has revealed that men within the United States are doing more personal care work than at any time in the past two centuries, John Budd, a labor relations scholar, argued that a "cult of domesticity" exists for women that continues to weave a controlling thread throughout their lives.[28] Budd's argument is that the inaccurate belief that women are somehow biologically and psychologically oriented to caring for others has created a set of false dichotomies that function to support the status quo. These dichotomies include the tension between production and consumption, competition and caring, and the public marketplace forum versus the private household. According to Budd, these dichotomies represent belief systems that are ultimately false and that serve to sustain the cult of domesticity.

One of the fundamental dichotomies in this discussion is the question whether people engage in care work for love or money.[29] One of the major threads of this debate is essentially an extension of the cult of domesticity. If women are inherently more satisfied and more capable of providing care, why should society or our economic systems figure out ways to provide economic benefits, social rewards, and enhanced sources of purpose and meaning for care work? As explored in the next section, the participants from the Boston College Working Project reflected deeply on this question and related concerns, providing some insightful perspectives that enrich the contributions of scholars and policy analysts who are exploring these complex questions.

Being Able to Care: Lived Experiences

To examine the relationship between caring and work, we intentionally asked the participants to reflect on their experiences and impressions about these essential aspects of life. The responses to this question and to other queries in the interview process were illuminating and provided some useful ideas that inform our understanding of the role of care work in this age of uncertainty.

Nature of Caregiving

The participants shared feelings and insights about their caring, both in their households and in the marketplace. Betsy, a 43-year-old African American woman who had worked as a dental hygienist before being laid off, described her intense feelings in caring for her mother and her aunt. Betsy's mother passed away in a hospital, but her aunt had a more extended illness that allowed for direct caregiving, as described in the following passage:

> It [caregiving] was a gift. My mother was in the hospital and I wasn't able to take care of her hands on. My aunt was able to go home [prior to passing away]; she wanted to live in her home. She was so powerful at the end; she wanted to be in her home. I was with her and singing to her when she left. We were holding hands. It was a gift to take care of her in a way that I couldn't take care of my mom, hands on. My girlfriend who was a nurse, she showed me how to wash her and how to take care of her. That was the best gift ever.

Betsy's moving discussion of caregiving provided a counterpoint in her interview that focused on so many sad events in her life, which had recently been characterized by long-term unemployment.

Rich, the teacher, described a touching narrative where he experienced a horrific layoff (described further in Chapter 8) and then contracted a deadly form of blood cancer a few years later as soon as he became established as a tenured high school teacher. During his illness, Rich took on the leadership of a support group of fellow survivors of this particular type of cancer. When asked about the relationship between caregiving and work, he replied with the following comments:

> I think [that caregiving is] very important. I can't really say [that running the support group has] saved any lives, but certainly I've saved people a lot of money by researching. . . . When I was first diagnosed and realized that this could be an expensive proposition, I was brought right into the local

oncologist's financial advisor and she told me a number of ways that patients could get financial assistance. And I took those ways, and I told every member of our support group about them, and. . . . And I know for a fact that I've saved people a lot of money. But in other ways too, I think. In our group we're about to put people in contact with doctors, nurses, and the like, that deal with this disease, and I think we've been able to accomplish a lot. . . . It is engaging, and I think it's the most important work I've ever done in my life.

Rich's full interview was infused with his disappointments in work. However, his contributions to this support group were a bright spot for him, one that gave him considerable meaning and fulfillment.

Meanwhile, Kerri, a 23 year-old unemployed African American woman, who had become the primary caregiver to her grandmother, described the complications of intensive caregiving work:

[My grandmother] is still sick; she's in a nursing home now. So it was like, I wasted . . . not to be mean . . . but like I wasted the whole time I got out of high school taking care of my grandmother when I could have went to college, and got what I needed to do.

The challenge for Kerri, and for so many who devote extensive time to care for people in their families, is the opportunity cost. When Kerri was interviewed, she was homeless and using the services of an urban One-Stop Career Center to figure out how to enter the labor market. Her skill set was not readily viable in an increasingly high-tech marketplace; in effect, her interview conveyed a sense of her being catapulted out of her home when her grandmother could no longer manage herself and had to enter a nursing home. At that point, Kerri became homeless and was faced with a world that was unforgiving to her about her lack of marketable skills.

For many, caregiving feels like an obligation, a form of service to children, parents, relatives, and community. Yet, the stories described by the participants were, for the most part, complex, revealing a capacity to tolerate ambivalence and nuance about the often-unexpected challenges that emerge in taking care of one's loved ones. Caregiving was rarely all good or all bad; it was presented as a part of life, a textured exemplar of life with all of its joys and hardships.

The Relationship Between Caregiving and Work

The participants seemed to struggle to understand the relationship between caregiving and work. Indeed, the challenges that exist in the academic community about how to make sense of how caregiving and work intersect were mirrored within the lived experiences of many of the participants in our interviews. In the first passage, Bob, a 70-year-old White small business owner, recounted the struggle he faced in taking care of his wife, who was very ill for 10 years. This story about his care for his wife was generated as he reflected on the question of whether caregiving should be considered work:

> Well, with my wife being sick for 10 years . . . at times, it was work, yes, because I think it was over 10 years, the grueling gets to you after a while . . . not only monetarily, because it cost a lot of money to care for someone at home or in a home. In my particular case, my wife was at home all the time, either at home or in the hospital. I don't know if I considered it work, but at times it was quite grueling and upsetting. There were times when I would be working out of town. . . . There was a time I worked for a company on the road for many years and I would have to stay over at hotels. I would take off if my wife was at Yale hospital, I would take off and spend a few minutes with her, go to the job in Danbury, work there and then come back and stay at Yale 'til late. . . .That was quite challenging. The ride home at night was quite a long ride, trying to keep your eyes open coming home and then starting all over again the next day. Like I said it's a thin line between work and just a lot of pressure, I never considered it work I guess, I just considered it something that you do. That is an extraordinary situation, 10 years is a long time for someone to be sick.

Bob's mixed views on this issue reflect his deep emotional pain of managing the primary caregiving of his wife while taking care of his business. This narrative speaks volumes about the intensity of caregiving, which, at times, morphs into personal care work, often with substantial emotional and physical consequences. In the next story, we hear from Clark, a 34-year-old White stagehand, who reflected thoughtfully on the question of whether caregiving is a form of work:

> I can see it [caregiving being a form of work]. But it also depends on what it is. If you have an elderly relative and you have to bathe them because maybe you're not ready to get an aid, or you can't afford an aid, so you have to be the aid, then I can see that as work. But if it's your child, like changing diapers and making food or part of normal, everyday life, you have to do it for yourself, so what's a little bit more. But I can see it from both aspects. I guess you could say from yes and no.

A similarly nuanced perspective was offered by Talih, the physician, who shared the following observation:

I actually think [caregiving is] the way I refresh myself and how I charge my batteries. I mean doing housework is work, like laundry and I really think that I don't like it, but you know cooking with my son or playing with him or going to the park with him, it's not work. And it's like I try to call my mother every day when I'm going to work; it's just a way to relax and to hear her voice and talk to her about things, and it's just something enjoyable, I don't see it as a work.

Other participants had more unequivocal views on the question of whether caregiving should be considered a form of work. Dick, a 55-year-old White in-structional aid and artist, recounted an increasingly common story that reflects a challenge for many people as older people live longer, often with considerable health and cognitive challenges:

Oh, yeah, absolutely [work is a form of caregiving\. What I'm going through with my mother, and being her health proxy, coming to see her and making sure she gets the right care—that is definitely a job. Especially with aging, as people get older, they are less and less able to take care of themselves. . . . Well, especially now because my mother has dementia and I am her guardian; it's important for her to have family, and I seem to be the only family member who's making the effort to go and interact with her. People in wheelchairs and stuff need a lot of attention. Yeah, it's an-other job. . . . I'm actually feeling I have a very rich life and even though it's challenging.

Dick's situation certainly was hard and seemed to inform his position that caregiving is a form of work. The four examples presented here reflect the tip of the iceberg of an extensive set of narratives about caregiving and work; it seemed clear that people had a lot to say about this issue. Interestingly, while the question was worded in a way that would have created dichotomous responses, a number of the participants, including Clark and Bob, provided more nuanced answers, reflecting the inherent complexity of managing the tasks of caregiving in a society that so clearly values marketplace work.

Work–Family Relationships

Deeply embedded in considerations about caregiving and work is the very hotly contested issue of work–family balance and conflict. Many pages of journal and magazine articles as well as self-help books have been devoted to helping people find a balance between work and family. The participants in our interviews also had a lot to say about this, as reflected in this first passage from Loretta, a 44-year-old paralegal who provided the following description of her struggle to balance work and family:

> So it's difficult for me to work an 8–5 job because I am used to being home with my kids all of the time, so that is kind of frustrating I guess. I think that when I'm at work and I'm not really engaged because I'm thinking more about what I'd rather be doing or who needs me at home because my kids are used to having me there all the time, or whenever they need me. I'm used to being there all the time, and now I can't do that. So I struggle with that when I'm at work, and I think my work product probably suffers a little bit because of that and also in my personal life, it's the same. I am used to making my own hours and working whenever I want to work so it has changed my own personal life because I was able to do whatever I wanted during the day and take care of things.

From Mary, a 64-year-old White social worker, we see a retrospective view of work–family struggles as she mulls over her past in light of having grown children and a father with dementia who lives some distance away.

> In the past, some of the obstacles have been a lack of time in my personal life. I spent a lot of time on my career and in some ways I am a little regretful of that. I could have spent more time with family, especially when my kids were younger; however, they seemed to come out okay. But, it would have been nice to be at home a little bit more with them when they were younger. You do have to sacrifice some for a career. And that was part of my sacrifice.

Mary's description attests to the psychological consequences of making decisions about work and family, choices that often have deep resonance and reach well beyond the years when the conflicts are most overt. Framing these decisions are factors such as the potential for satisfaction that one has at work, as well as an equally important appraisal of one's relational life, which Mary alluded to in other parts of her interview.

The complexity of managing work and family was further elaborated by Vicente, the 51-year-old former banker who was currently a career coach:

> In the beginning, it was work–life balance, and it wasn't that I didn't like working 'cause I loved what I did and so my work became 24–7. I would get out of work and I would be going to an event where I would be teaching people how to apply for a mortgage or I would be doing a

seminar on how to build or rebuild credit because I happened to speak the language. Work–life balance was a challenge and I sacrificed my life, my family per se—my relationships because of work. My message now is around a holistic approach to personal well-being where work is part of it, but it's not everything. And the second thing is redefining success 'cause in the environment which we live, success has been defined as how much more money you can make, and the reality is that I came to a point to where money is not what defines me. So how can I manage myself in such a way that will allow me to work, do what I love still and still have the lifestyle that I enjoy and still spend quality time with my family. . . . So, in Colombia, people work hard, but at the same time, they make family a priority and it doesn't matter—family comes first.

Vicente's passage attests to the complexity of balancing work and family, particularly during the years when one's children are young. Like Mary, Vicente reflected on his life history, charting the different ways in which he managed work and family. His final comment about his Colombian heritage speaks to the role of culture, which often helps people connect to broader sources of support and guidelines about how to manage work and family.[30]

Taken together, the participants spoke eloquently about caregiving and work, underscoring that this is indeed a major concern for people as they manage their lives. The vignettes that were selected convey some of the richness and ambivalence that exists around the questions of how we make meaning of caregiving and work. What does seem clear from these interviews is that this issue was emotionally evocative and that people were struggling to balance their lives, particularly during the times of the most intense demands, such as taking care of ill loved ones, managing early childhood responsibilities, and caregiving elderly family members. While there were not many detailed comments on care work in the marketplace, some of the participants, especially women from impoverished backgrounds, often described how their options centered on providing care for others, typically at very low wages.

Being Able to Care: The Psychological View

A number of new contributions on caregiving and work have been developed that have the potential to respond to some of the concerns raised by the Boston College Working Project participants and optimally inform public policies that are clearly needed to support people in both caring and marketplace work contexts. In this section, we highlight two of these new perspectives; the first is the caring motivation, a new perspective offered by Ofra Mayseless, and the second contribution is Mary Sue Richardson's analysis of caregiving and work. These perspectives, coupled with the insightful vignettes presented in the previous section, inform recommendations about caregiving that conclude the chapter.

The Caring Motivation

In a bold and innovative book, *The Caring Motivation*, Ofra Mayseless, a very creative Israeli psychologist, makes a compelling case that human beings have an inherent motivation to care for others.[31] This motivation is thought to be a fundamental and central organizing component of our motivational states that informs our attitudes and drives our behaviors. Mayseless presented compelling evidence that we do not simply care for others because "it has to be done." Rather, she proposed that the desire to care is part of our "true spirit." Mayseless took an aspect of human behavior that has been marginalized in many aspects of life (including our lived experience, work, and relationships) and elevated it to the same level of importance as other inherent human motivations, such as our desire for affiliations and achievements.

In effect, Mayseless has deeply mined the relational revolution (presented in Chapter 3) and elaborated on the full dyadic relationship processes that occur in our connections with others. In considering the caring motivation, we can now understand relationships not only as a desire for love and connection (i.e., being on the receiving end of a caring relationship), but also the complementary need to care for others. In contrast to the prevailing notions of human motivation as governed by self-interest or selfishness, Mayseless presented very compelling evidence that people are hardwired and socialized to want to care for others. Although many scholars and clinicians have described caregiving, including, of course, John Bowlby in his classic work on attachment, the exhaustive treatment by Mayseless, in my view, has yielded a new paradigm about caring.

A full description of Mayseless's contribution is beyond the scope of this book. However, I focus on its applications to our understanding of people as they manage caring in general as well as caring in both the personal care and marketplace spaces. An ongoing debate in psychology and the social sciences is how caring roles and responsibilities are distributed to men and women and how we reward caregiving. Mayseless affirmed the gendered nature of caring in that women are more often expected to engage in nurturing types of caregiving in dyadic contexts, and that men are more likely to express their caring motivation in larger social groups. For example, research in psychology indicated that women are likely to prefer caring for children or aging parents, while men may manifest their caring via community contributions, such as volunteering as a board member at a church.[32] The controversy that is drawing out much discussion is the extent to which these differences are biological or genetic in nature. Like many developmental psychologists, Mayseless suggested that both socialization and biological factors are at play, and that these influences are mutually impactful. Other scholars (including myself) would view the impact of family experiences (particularly in one's family of origin), culture, and social expectations as serving as the prevailing factor in defining how one's caring motivation is experienced and expressed.[33]

Another question that emerges in thinking about the caring motivation is the issue of how realistic this rather positive appraisal of humanity is in the face of many acts of selfishness and cruelty, both in interpersonal relationships and in broader social contexts. This is an important issue, one that Mayseless addressed directly and thoughtfully.[34] Although she argued that the caring motivation is a fundamental aspect of our makeup, it is also characterized by individual differences (i.e., people vary across all sorts of dimensions) and diverse social and cultural expectations (i.e., societies vary in what they expect from people and how they teach people to manage their lives). It is notoriously difficult in psychology to develop theories that will be truly universal. And, as many people know from their lived experiences, people vary greatly in so many ways, including, of course, their relationship behaviors and responses. In this context, Mayseless has raised a good point about individual and social differences. She also indicated, for example, that not all caring behavior is kind and gentle. Taking care of children or an elderly parent with dementia may involve setting limits in a way that may hurt the feelings of the person who is being cared for. In addition, caring for one's own community or social group may involve being unkind or aggressive to other groups, for example, by creating forceful consequences for people who threaten one's community. Despite the obvious limitations of considering that all people are kind and caring at all times, the caring motivation notion, in many ways, may be foreshadowing a caring revolution in psychology, and a caring revolution in the workplace, which I believe can help to inform needed policy changes with respect to the work in the marketplace.

So, how does the caring motivation affect our thinking about working during this very dramatic period of transformations in the workplace? The caring motivation, in my view, has powerful implications for our discussion, much as the relational motivation has transformed our views of human behavior and working. As indicated previously in the chapter, many jobs involve caregiving, such as nursing, teaching, and providing direct care to children, the elderly, and individuals with disabling conditions. In addition, caregiving provides work opportunities for many poor and working-class adults, particularly women of color and immigrants in the United States, who often toil in very difficult circumstances with inadequate wages.[35] Regrettably, the infusion of caregiving into an occupation seems to be associated with the feminization of that field and an associated reduction of wages, benefits, and advancement opportunities.

A question that emerges in considering the Mayseless contribution and other bodies of work on caring is to what extent social expectations can be shifted so that policy changes will result in improved working conditions for those whose primary role in the marketplace is in caregiving. Optimistically, I have witnessed the relational revolution result in major changes not only in psychology, but also in the world of the helping professions and other sectors of society.[36] One dramatic way to change the conditions of personal care workers is to reduce the inherent sexism that exists in relation to the distribution and affirmation of caring roles. (This point is elaborated in the conclusion of this chapter.)

Another powerful implication of the caring revolution is the potential loss of the relationships that exist at work when work is not available; as reflected in previous chapters, working often (although not always) provides people with opportunities not only for social connections, but also caring and nurturing others. If we follow the logic of Mayseless's position, having opportunities to care for others is central to our meaning and purpose in life. A close look at many workplaces reveals that the occupational world provides multiple opportunities to mentor others, care for people in times of distress, and provide instrumental assistance to both customers and fellow employees. Of course, one viable possibility of a society in which automation and artificial intelligence result in diminished requirements for marketplace work is the very real option of people having more time to do caregiving. As I highlight further in this chapter, this provides both an opportunity for society and a risk.

The caring motivation contribution also has important implications for a psychologically enriched discussion of the relationship between work and family. As some of the participants noted previously in the chapter, the issue of work–life balance is a major dilemma for people and often eludes easy answers. Considering the caring motivation in relation to the struggle for people to navigate meaningful connections between family and work provides some important insights that may be useful for people struggling with work–family conflict. One application of the caring motivation is that it affirms our need to care for others and places this motivation at the same level as many other motivational states, such as the needs for achievement and self-determination, that define many marketplace roles. Given the centrality of caring, work–family dilemmas may be responsive to broad policy levers that would provide financial and social support for care work in one's family. While this will not solve all of the work–family problems that exist, reducing the marginalization of caregiving would go a long way to creating an equally affirming playing field for life in both family and marketplace work contexts.[37]

Caregiving and Work–Family Relationships

One of the greatest challenges in truly being able to care is to find the time and space to engage productively and fully in caregiving. Balancing work–family responsibilities clearly transcends the caregiving part of life given that people also strive to develop and sustain relationships, engage in leisure, exercise, hobbies, and household tasks. However, the struggle to engage in caring is a central theme that pervades both the academic literature and lived experiences of people when considering balancing work and family. A fascinating and highly influential chapter written by Mary Sue Richardson and Charles Schaeffer provides important grist for the mill in thinking about how to understand the work–family nexus in light of shifting work demands and changing gender norms.[38] Richardson and Schaeffer began their discussion by reviewing the evolving nature of the work–family balance, highlighting the following noteworthy trends:

1. Two ever-widening groups characterize the United States now, with vastly different experiences in their work and family lives. Affluent and well-educated adults are faced with too much work to do, but often have resources to outsource some of their care work, generally to underpaid women of color or immigrants. In contrast, the poor experience not enough stable work opportunities, with growing precariousness in their work lives and inadequate resources and support to manage their personal care work. As such, work–family balance issues are dramatically different in these two communities.
2. Studies of time use and unpaid care work have revealed interesting trends in family–work relationships. Over the past four decades, research has revealed that married women are spending about the same amount of time with their children that they did before the major shift of women into the marketplace. This finding suggests some sort of statistical glitch in that there are only 24 hours in a day. What emerges from a close examination of this body of research is that married women are spending less time on personal care and on household chores.
3. These time use studies also revealed that men and women spend about the same amount of time on work, considering both market work and personal care work. The difference is that men devote more time to marketplace work and women are more engaged in personal care work.

4. A promising finding is that men are in fact doing more caregiving work, primarily in feeding and bathing their children.
5. The time use results for single mothers were very disheartening. The burdens of developing a sustainable livelihood coupled with personal care work are daunting, and the social safety net in the United States has made survival questionable without considerable support from family and kin.
6. The major conclusion from these analyses by Richardson and Schaeffer is revealing: Families have changed far more than the labor market to accommodate shifting opportunities, resources, and barriers.

In the face of these trends, Richardson and Schaeffer developed a dual working model as a way of framing work and family intersections in contemporary American culture. The dual working model is based on an acceptance of the current reality in which women are increasingly taking on roles in marketplace work. According to Richardson and Schaeffer, the dual working model is based on the expectation that men and women will engage in marketplace work and in unpaid care work. Underlying the reality of caring and work currently in the United States is the affirmation of the importance of economic productivity, which also functions to diminish the value of care work. As an example, the welfare reform of the mid-1990s in the United States sent a message to women that they had to engage in market work, even though the social and economic supports for market work were (and remain) inadequate. While on the surface, having women enter the marketplace makes eminent sense, as so compellingly argued by feminist scholars and vocational psychologists for decades, the question remains about how we manage our caregiving tasks. Of course, one solution is for men to carry more of the burden of care work; fortunately, we are witnessing some modest progress in this area.[39] However, the marginalization of personal care work and marketplace care work continues unabated.

The solution, according to Richardson and Schaeffer, is to create major policy changes in how we understand and reward care work. Care work is clearly not consistent with the current focus in our neoliberal economic context on maximizing profits and enhancing productivity.[40] A number of scholars of work, feminist studies, and psychology are now arguing that we need to create a culture that affirms the need to care and to be cared for as a human right, much as we increasingly view access to decent work in the marketplace as a human right.[41] As Richardson and Schaeffer noted, caregiving work is a form of work, but it does not translate into the sort of productivity indices that are affirmed by leading economists and policy leaders. What Richardson and Schaeffer proposed is that caregiving feeds society's need for social productivity; in effect, caregiving provides the social glue that is needed to create cohering and kind communities.

The dual working model does provide a counterbalance to models that differentiated work roles based on gender. The current discourse about work, family, and caregiving is based on the need to unpack gender stereotypes that have long fostered a culture of domesticity for women and market work for men. While changing this dynamic is not easy, shifts in the psychological conversation can impact the public dialogue to optimally create a case for affirming care work in ways that are both economically feasible yet not degrading or detracting from the efforts that we make in caring for others into strictly economic terms. Another critical issue raised by Richardson and Schaeffer is the need to elevate paid care work to a status that befits its importance in society as a critical means by which we take care of those who need our better angels in order to survive and thrive.

Conclusion

This chapter has provided an important perspective on an issue that is very much on the margins of current conversations and debates about the nature of work in our lives and in our broader social and economic interactions. Caring, caregiving, and care work are all central parts of the human experience, much as they have been since we evolved out of the savannah of Africa. The literature in psychology, social sciences, and the detailed and evocative vignettes from the participants conveys that issues around caring and working are never far from the lived experience of people. So, what are the takeaways from this chapter? A number of ideas emerge that merit closer attention.

First, the question of whether caring is a form of work is probably best answered in a complex and nuanced fashion. As the participants from the Boston College Working project suggested, the answer to this question really depends on the situation and the demands that people face in a given context. Second, the gendered nature of caregiving has been and remains a major cause of concern. Clearly, scholars who have informed this work (such as Mary Sue Richardson and Nancy Folbre, among others) have made very compelling arguments in favor of reducing the impact of sexism and marginalization in how we manage caring and care work. However, the hard reality is that, at least within the United States, the deep commitment to the free market economy and its highly questionable capacity to equalize the playing field has resulted in a harsh and inadequate social safety net for women, particularly for poor and working-class women, who also carry the burden for many well-off families who easily outsource their care work.

In short, government policies, such as unfunded preschools, lack of mandated financial support for family leaves, and very low wages for marketplace care work, collude to create a culture that continues to reify market work at the expense of care work. The failure to reduce the impact of sexism and gender role socialization has created a significant barrier in any concerted attempts to provide reasonable supports for women, families, and communities who are seeking meaning and dignity in both their care work and their marketplace work.

A number of scholars, most notably Guy Standing, an inspiring British social scientist, have argued that we need to provide some ways of compensating care work.[42] As I have read these suggestions, I come away with some hope that major shifts may occur in our economic systems that will function to affirm care work. One of the major drivers of these changes may be the growth in precarious work and the increased role of automation in the workplace. As many experts predict (as summarized in the first chapter and again in Chapter 8), stable and decent work may be increasingly less available, especially for individuals without very high levels of marketable skills. Into this mix will soon emerge a renewed debate about the universal basic income. The universal basic income (UBI) is a proposal (emerging now from the left and right in the United States, and indeed, globally) to provide a foundational set of resources to all citizens that may be detached from marketplace work. One of the driving forces of this movement is certainly based on justice and equity, ensuring that people have access to the basic necessities of life. However, another objective is to reduce the potential for social and economic disruption. (Further details on basic income guarantees will be provided in Chapter 9.) An option of enhancing the viability of work in an era of declining options in the marketplace may be to reward and affirm care work via payments that are guaranteed to people who are in need of financial support. Many complications exist in this sort of plan, which are probably best summarized by economists (see Standing, for example).[43] However, there may be ways of economically validating care work, without necessarily making it part of the marketplace system, which will clearly require careful planning and consideration of various intended and unintended consequences.

In closing, I propose that we may need to think outside the box about caregiving in relation to marketplace work and concerns about the future of work. Caring is an essential part of life, and in many important ways, it is an important part of our work lives, resulting in what Richardson and others call social reproduction. In contrast to economic production, which is the coin of the realm in the United States, and many Western societies, caring feeds our needs to be connected and to nurture others and ourselves with a very human capacity to be kind and gentle with others who need our services and support. My vision of a society that fully rewards and values caregiving may not be that far off—as I propose in the conclusion of this book, the changes in the labor market may provide us with opportunities to create more humane systems of support and care as well as more nurturing workplaces. The bottom line, for me, is that these decisions will require a deep critique of existing assumptions about work and an equally deep openness to new ideas and paradigms. The time is right for a caring revolution that can remake our work lives and our relational lives.

7

Being Able to Work Without
Oppression and Harassment

The Boston Public Schools (BPS) system is a storied school district that includes some of the most prestigious high schools in the United States. For example, Boston Latin High School, an examination school (i.e., students compete for positions via a comprehensive test), has alumni that include eight governors of Massachusetts and four presidents of Harvard University, among other notables.[1] However, many of the high schools in BPS currently struggle to educate students who are confronted with poverty, poor housing conditions, and other social and economic barriers. Most of the high schools do not require an examination for entering students and are open to any and all students. These schools were the ones that I found compelling and that I turned my attention to when I moved to join the counseling psychology faculty at Boston College in 1999 after 14 years at the University at Albany. At that point in my life, I was eager to enact my passion for those on the margins by designing a career development program tailored for high school students from poor urban communities. My colleagues and I, working closely with professionals from BPS, developed a career development intervention (called Tools for Tomorrow) to pilot in a few of the more challenged schools in the BPS system. To ensure that I, as one of the developers of this program, would have an empathic connection to the process of delivering our curriculum, I committed to teaching a section within the ninth-grade cohort. A particular incident in this class provides a powerful introduction to this chapter, which focuses on how work interfaces with marginalization and oppression.

I walked into my assigned high school class one Wednesday with handouts of an exercise that we had developed called "What Is Work?" This exercise was designed to help students understand the broader personal and historical terrain of work. We asked the students to define work and career and also to reflect on how their families and communities defined these terms. I then followed this exercise with a career and work timeline; we asked the students to speculate about the most common occupations in 1900, 1950, currently (2000 at the time), and 2050. The goal of this exercise was to help the students internalize how much the world of work has changed and to relate to education as a means of enhancing their options in life. Nearly all of the students in the class were of color; most were Latino, African American, or Caribbean American, and many were either immigrants themselves or the children of immigrants, often living in the poorest neighborhoods in Boston.

During the exercise, I asked the students to call out occupations for each of the aforementioned time periods, which I then wrote on the blackboard. As we got to the present era, a student called out doctor and another called lawyer. At that point, a student then chimed in that these jobs "are available only if you're White." This comment silenced the class. I then began to discuss this experience but was met with continued silence as the class shut down, perhaps reflecting a sense of psychic pain that could not be discussed openly or a reluctance to share their views with a middle-aged, White college professor. After a few earnest attempts on my part to affirm this comment and to generate a conversation about the role of race and racism in the workplace, I finally forged ahead without being able to support the students as they all mulled over the elephant in the room. In this case, this elephant was the pervasive impact of racism, which had no doubt affected their parents, most of whom were excluded from the best schools and neighborhoods growing up and was continuing to affect all of the students of color in this class.

I walked out of the school that day feeling humbled by the limitations that I had experienced in the classroom. Despite my diverse experiences as a therapist and, in particular, the deep immersion that I had as a counselor in a program for first-generation college students of color from the South Bronx and Yonkers early in my career, I came away with a deepened awareness that my White male privilege and my role as a professor from Boston College may have created an unsurmountable barrier at that moment. Once the issue of race came up in the discussion, the classroom, which had been full of excitement and engagement, became silent. I was treading into a space that felt full of intense emotions, but these feelings were not easily shared with relative strangers, especially with someone who was not part of the students' community. What moved me so powerfully that day was not just the knowledge that racism is indeed very alive in our schools, communities, and workplaces, but that this pernicious human virus seeps into the consciousness of all of us, including children and adolescents. Another takeaway from this experience was that the feelings evoked by marginalization are not always easy to talk about because they tap into a deep emotional well that may feel too painful to discuss. As I left the school that memorable day, I was acutely aware of my social identity, which was evident in my appearance, language, and overall presence. This experience underscored my knowledge that I benefited from being a White male in a society that gave us not only one leg up but also many legs up. And, this privilege created a gulf between the students and me that was not easily navigable even with my attempts at reaching out with empathy and warmth.

The incident in this high school, of course, is the tip of the iceberg of a society that has created boundaries and categories for people in a way that serves no essential function at the present time, except to marginalize some people and privilege others. In this chapter, I explore the impact of oppression and marginalization in relation to work from the unique perspective that I have adopted in this book. In contrast to the extensive body of knowledge about race, gender, disability status, sexual orientation, and other marginalized identities that exist in our public and intellectual spaces, I seek to chart an intentionally psychological view that builds on the experiences of people as they confront oppressive forces in their work lives. Because of space limitations, I am not able to go into the depth that these issues merit; in fact, entire books have been written about nearly each of these marginalized identities in relation to the full array of social contexts, including work.[2] Throughout this chapter, I make a case for considering the workplace as a central location for much of what the social and economic world has to offer; yet, it is the same social and economic space that confronts us with very real barriers that continue to plague our society as we still wrestle with our collective demons of social oppression and marginalization.

Being Able to Work Without Oppression and Marginalization: An Introductory Journey

The depth and scope of marginalization at work is quite diverse and complex. In this chapter, I focus on the most obvious culprits: racism, sexism, social class, heterosexism, and disability status, which were the prevailing themes in the Boston College Working Project narratives. I initially review the prevalence and psychological meaning of marginalization currently in the American workplace to create a context for the very moving and illuminating narratives that follow.

Prevalence of Oppression and Marginalization at Work

The entire process of preparing for work, adjusting to work, and managing work brings us into contact with the social world. Once we enter the labor market, we are exposed to interactions with others and the broader social and economic world. In addition, preparing to enter the marketplace places us into the educational system, which has many parallels to work; in many ways, it is also infused with oppressive practices and norms. As reflected in previous chapters, people have the potential to gain a great deal from work, including access to survival, relationships, and the capacity to contribute and create. However, the world of work contains a dark side (as in life) in that people are not always kind, and the institutions that undergird our interactions with others are not always benef-icent. In the material that follows, I map the ways in which social oppression and marginalization play a role in the work lives of nearly everyone who enters the marketplace.

As a means of encapsulating the impact of oppression at the workplace, I begin by summarizing the conclusions from a very thoughtful chapter on race and working by Lisa Flores, a highly respected counseling and vocational psy-chologist. Flores presented a wealth of data that, taken together, present a pic-ture of a world of work that is far from equal.[3] (It is important to note that race is currently understood not as a biological construct but as a social con-struct, one that has meaning only in a context where one's physical attributes are identified, categorized, and evaluated.[4]) Although some remnants of biolog-ically based theories about race are scattered about in the social sciences, they are, thankfully, marginalized themselves as the final gasps of a racist ideology that belongs in the dustbin of history.[5] Some of the noteworthy points made by Flores include the following:

1. Poverty is intertwined with race in the United States in a very pronounced way. African Americans have the lowest median incomes of all racial and ethnic groups, followed by Native Americans and Latinos. Whites have the highest median income, although much variability exists within all of these groups.
2. Whites continue to be more likely to complete high school and college, in comparison to communities of color.
3. Racism in the workplace is pervasive. At times, it is overt, and at other times, it is more subtle, expressed as microaggressions, which refer to episodic, yet quite aversive, messages that people of color receive, denigrating them and their cultural experiences.[6] Considerable evi-dence attests to the role of the work context essentially replicating other social situations, particularly in relation to power hierarchies. Because the world of work often has fairly regimented organizations with some people having more power over others, there is a built-in infrastructure that can authorize and legitimize racism.[7]

A similarly depressing picture emerges as we consider gender and work. As reflected in Chapter 6, many women continue to be expected to engage in both caregiving work and marketplace work, leaving them feeling overwhelmed, ex-hausted, and often disconnected from their dreams. Women continue to earn about 80% of the earnings of men with the same training and experience.[8] In a wonderful synthesis of the literature, Neeta Kantamneni, a rising scholar of vocational psychology, painted an informative and disconcerting picture of women at work, summarized by the following points[9]:

1. On the plus side, women have entered the marketplace in large numbers, particularly during and after World War II. This dramatic shift in labor market participation has been viewed as a major impetus for the feminist movement and has helped women to free themselves from the very real barrier of lacking agency and choice in their lives.[10]

2. Women continue to experience constraints in their career choices, with many women feeling that they should enter fields that are considered traditionally female (e.g., helping professions; nursing; child care work). The complex factors that play a role in this process have been detailed by vocational psychologists for many decades and include the forces of socialization about where women belong in the workplace, which are internalized into women's views and aspirations.[11] In addition, sexism in the marketplace continues to play a prominent role in limiting access for women, particularly in fields that are dominated by men.[12] Some movement toward a more expansive array of career choices is emerging, in part due to the efforts of psychologists and educators who are developing programs and interventions that diminish the aversive impact of social forces that have curtailed women's preferences.[13] However, despite shifts in women's career aspirations, they still face overt and covert forces in education and the workplace that sharply limit their options.

3. Women are vulnerable to sexual harassment at work, particularly when they are in positions where men have greater power over them.[14] The continued prevalence of sexual harassment represents the tip of the iceberg of sexism in the workplace, which has a wide array of manifestations, including overt hostility, isolation, marginalization, and discrimination.

Other social identities present with equally complex challenges for people engaged in marketplace work. Diversity in sexual orientation has generated a great deal of attention in recent years, with some very promising trends, such as access to marriage for gay and lesbian couples in the United States. However, discrimination at work continues, as reflected in an excellent chapter by Mary Anderson and James Croteau, two well-known scholars of LGBT (lesbian, gay, bisexual, transgender) issues at the workplace.[15] In their view, men and women of diverse sexual orientations struggle at work with discrimination and marginalization. In summaries of recent studies, the percentage of LGBT workers who reported workplace discrimination ranged from 15% to 43%.[16] Moreover, the entire process of considering whether to disclose one's sexual orientation at work or conceal it is replete with complications and ambivalence.

Disability status is a major source of oppression, evoking stigma and intolerance in social interactions and in the workplace. Ellen Fabian, a well-regarded rehabilitation psychologist, has written a number of thoughtful contributions on the work lives of individuals with disabling conditions. Interestingly, in the United States, disability status is inextricably linked to work in the marketplace.[17] Disability is generally defined as encompassing a physical, mental, or emotional impairment that has an impact on an individual's functioning, particularly their capacity to work.[18] In addition, those individuals whose disabling condition impairs their capacity to work may be able to access government-sponsored supports for healthcare, training, education, and survival needs.

While there are legal protections in the marketplace to support individuals with disabling conditions, the reality is that the labor market participation rate for individuals with disabling conditions is modest, at best. Currently, the percentage of individuals with disabilities who are engaged in the marketplace is 17.9%, which reflects a dramatic difference from the overall rate of 65.3% for the population of working-age adults.[19] A complex feature of disability is that it is often not visible and may require that individuals advocate for themselves to be defined as disabled. Although the legal definition of disability offers some access to a safety net, it also opens people up to a pronounced sense of marginalization—treated as if they are so different from others that they exist in a sort of limbo state.[20]

Poverty presents yet another source of marginalization and oppression. In the United States, the division between the affluent and the poor is growing rapidly, creating a vast chasm in our society. Poverty itself has dramatic impacts on people and communities.[21] The lack of resources that define the lives of the poor is seemingly endless: inadequate healthcare; an educational system for poor and working-class students that pales in comparison to the opportunities offered to the middle class and wealthy; insufficient childcare; housing deficits; and an overall lack of financial resources to manage any of these challenges.[22] The social science literature on poverty is rich and compelling: In short, poverty creates multiple dimensions of problems for people that tear at the fabric of their lives.

As reflected in Chapter 2, survival needs, when they are not fulfilled, become omnipresent in our lives. From the cold-water residences that people inhabit in cities and rural areas to the schools that lack resources and skilled teachers to a job market that excludes poor and working-class people at nearly every turn, the experience of life without adequate resources is often brutal. In addition to the very real impact of poverty, the lack of resources leads to marginalization via membership in a less-than-privileged group, as reflected in our language, accents, mode of dress, and a host of other features of our daily lives. The experience of being cast aside due to poverty is reflected in a sense of feeling less than others due to lack of access to resources; as demonstrated in considerable research in psychology, the consequences of such starkly differentiated social classes leads to classism, which has a profound impact on the inner psyches of people and communities.[23]

Ageism is yet another form of social oppression that has a particularly aversive impact on people, with significant implications in the world of work. Considerable research evidence has been gathered that underscores that ageism is alive and well in our society, with older people experiencing many challenges as they seek to sustain their livelihoods.[24] The new reality at the workplace is that many older individuals are increasingly a marginalized group who are stigmatized in their job searches, pay, and overall access to resources.[25]

When considering these various social identities collectively, a stark picture emerges. Although social categories may have made sense in prehistoric times when clans and tribes felt that they needed to differentiate people to sustain their own survival, these categories are now vestiges that serve to separate and marginalize some groups of people and privilege others. Of course, there are some inherent advantages to sharing cultures and social mores with people from similar regions and background. In this context, I am not advocating for the destruction of these culturally-rich communities per se. I am concerned, though, with the continued investment in marginalizing some people while others are privileged in ways that have enormous implications for work and well-being. In the next section, I review the internal and psychological aspects of marginalization and oppression, linking important insights from psychology to the work context.

The Internal Space: Psychological Implications of Marginalization and Oppression

The history of marginalized identities and work provides a glimpse into some of the most horrific episodes in the history of Western civilization. For example, understanding race and race-based trauma at work cannot be divorced from slavery in the United States, which has cast a long, dark shadow on this country, with profound implications in the work lives of African Americans and many other communities of color. As is well documented in American history and in current discussions of work, slavery created a culture of oppression for African Americans that has reached over the span of 150 years since emancipation to continue to plague American society.[26] In a similar vein, women have been oppressed throughout recent history in the workplace, often having to engage in physically arduous tasks in both the marketplace and their care work for their families. At the same time, women have been subjected to untold abuses by men, who generally have held the powerful positions in many work environments and at home. These experiences naturally evoke complex psychological reactions, which have been described by gifted scholars who have sought to name and describe the impact of racism, sexism, classism, and other forms of oppression.

People develop internalizations in relation to oppression, often in ways that can be even more painful and often in ways that help them to resist and transcend the marginalization. As described in Chapter 3, Being With Others, people develop internalizations about a wide array of experiences, including their social interactions and their exposure to inclusion and exclusion. In general, the internalization process is complex and has many pathways, including early childhood experience, relationship patterns throughout life, and the social interactions that one has with people and communities in various contexts.[27] In this section, I explore how psychologists have employed internalization processes to explain individual differences in how people respond to similar challenges.

Scholars studying race have been at the forefront of understanding the construction of internalizations that structure how people manage race-based interactions and internal feelings. Janet Helms, my valued colleague at Boston College and one of the leading voices in race and culture studies in psychology, has developed a widely used concept known as *racial identity statuses*.[28] In short, people construct their racial identities via specific statuses (or lenses) that frame how they view themselves and others in relation to race and culture. The statuses vary in terms of how one views the dominant culture, one's own culture, and the ways in which the racial aspect of one's identity is constructed (i.e., a person whose identity is shaped to varying extents by their culture and race). The statuses are somewhat fluid in that people can shift among them depending on the demands of their specific social situation. Considerable research in psychology has identified predictable relationships between racial identity statuses and various aspects of work-related functioning.[29]

Social class identities are also internalized and become part of our self-concepts, as reflected in the fascinating research by William Liu, who has devoted considerable attention to understanding the nature and impact of social class, poverty, and marginalization. Liu has proposed that people develop internalized ideas about their social class identities that impact various aspects of their psychosocial functioning.[30] Social class worldview refers to the lenses that people use to make sense of how economic resources are distributed, reflecting both the messages that we receive as we grow up in very class-oriented societies and our internalized consciousness about our past and current social class identities. Liu aptly noted that differences in social class worldviews would not exist without the oppressive nature of classism, which is a similar feature of racial identity theory. As an example, individuals learn early in their lives about the communities that they belong to and those to which they are excluded. These experiences, according to Liu and his colleagues, can lead to intense psychological distress, despair, and disengagement.[31]

In research on race, gender, and social class, psychologists have observed that trauma is a potential outcome of social oppression, reflecting the deep and painful psychological consequences of being dismissed, diminished, and often hated due to attributes that are social constructions and not inherent to our being.[32] When people are viewed primarily via their social identities and not seen as individuals with a core being, the experience can be profoundly painful. Moreover, American society exposes people from marginalized communities to even more pronounced difficulties, such as physical violence, harassment, teasing, bullying, and abuse.[33] When considered collectively, the impact of these oppressive practices can be traumatic, causing extensive psychological pain and anguish that can negatively affect people for decades.[34] We return to these observations after reviewing the narratives, which reflect both the complexity of the internalized identities that people construct as well as the traumatic reactions that are a natural outcome of being so harshly and, at times, violently treated.

The Pushback

The material that I summarized previously in this chapter is certainly daunting. Continued racism, sexism, heterosexism, and other sources of oppression are prevalent in many workspaces as well as in the pipeline of education and training that prepares people for work. However, both social scientists and working people themselves have pushed back to tear down the walls that separate people and that create vast pockets of inequity and despair. Within psychological studies and practices about work, brave colleagues throughout the past century have stood up to the existing power structures and norms that had reified racist and sexist practices at the workplace. For example, when prevailing theories of career choice and development after World War II emerged that assumed that many people had extensive options, scholars who were examining racism, classism, and sexism began to question the increasingly marginalizing discourse, which had been focused primarily on the lives of privileged White men.[35] Similar movements occurred throughout the social sciences, education, and counseling professions as our society began to openly question the limited focus on middle-class populations in nearly all aspects of working life in America.[36]

Another major pushback came from the feminist movements, which emerged in full force in the 1960s, in part as a revolt against the oppressive expectations that women would primarily focus on unpaid care work. The flipside of these expectations, of course, was that women ignored themselves and cut off part of their own dreams to fit into society's narrow boundaries. Here, again, brave pioneers took on the overwhelmingly male work contexts that had dominated the American culture and raised the stakes in the social justice movement to embrace the need to combat sexism.[37]

In addition, a major pushback against discrimination occurred within the disability community, which has a remarkable record of being quite effective in its social and political advocacy. Perhaps the best exemplar of this movement is the 1990 passage of the Americans With Disabilities Act (ADA), which dramatically changed American culture with respect to disabilities. These changes range from the redesign of bathrooms to the use of curb cuts (to accommodate wheelchairs on sidewalks) to major shifts in the workplace that are still transforming the landscape.[38] Of course, it has been hard to root out discriminatory hiring practices with respect to disabilities (as well as other marginalized identities); however, the ADA remains a touchstone of advocacy and policy shift that has resulted in major social change against the harsh climate that has characterized the work lives of so many people in the United States.

The need for further pushback to ensure that all people who work and who want to work are provided with access to jobs with dignity and meaning remains paramount for our society. The need is even more pronounced as we face a future of work that is very much uncertain given the potential impact of automation in the workplace, outsourcing, and other macro-level forces that are rapidly changing the world of work. In this context, many scholars and policy analysts believe that the most vulnerable workers will be those who are most marginalized, including women, individuals from poor and working-class backgrounds (whose educational affordances have often left them ill-equipped to compete in the labor market, especially one that is shedding less skilled jobs). In the material that follows, the participants from the Boston College Working Project contributed to this discussion with some very insightful passages that further illuminate the complex issues that we are grappling with in this chapter.

Marginalization and Oppression: Lived Experiences

Introducing this section provides an opportunity to reflect on the organization of the narratives, which represents an intentional decision on how to present marginalized social identities, many of which intersect with each other in important ways. Although I have considered all sorts of options, I decided to use the natural categories of each social identity, which seemed to be how the narratives organized themselves. This structure does not imply my belief that these social identities are clearly demarcated or circumscribed. In reality, social identities inhabit intersecting spaces that are often unique for each individual, thereby defying the categories that characterize our inadequate attempts to understand our complex social and psychological interactions.[39] In the passages that follow, these overlapping identities intrude, creating a close approximation of the lived experiences of people navigating their work lives.

Race and Work

The topic of race and work evoked extensive comments by the participants, often in ways that have defied easy interpretation or understanding. In the next passage, Vicente, the Latino man who worked as a banker prior to becoming a career coach, reflected in a deep, emotional way about his experiences in the banking industry.

> So race and ethnicity . . . it has been a challenge, one that I learned to work with fortunately because I had good mentors along the way. I can tell you right now that when I first applied to become a branch manager even though my numbers were there and my credibility was there, it took me . . . , oh my God this is flashing me back. . . . It took me interviewing like 11 times before they even considered me for the position. You just flashed me back to the point. How mad I was! It didn't really dawn on me that I was, I was naïve in the sense that I, why would you even consider not hiring me because I'm Latino since I had the numbers. I know how to do it. Now it wasn't until the bank realized that the Hispanic community was growing in the community in which the bank was and that they could capitalize on me, they then said, well we need to open up the door and they did.

Vicente's comments seemed to evoke some trauma and flashbacks about the very difficult process of interviewing for a promotion in the banking industry, which seemed to reach a dead end until the corporation realized that his Latino background could be an asset to the organization. In the next passage, Vicente replied openly to a question about his experiences of direct racism at work:

> Oh yeah, absolutely. I mean I experienced racism all of the time. I think in my case I learned just to move forward and kind of not pay attention to it.

We kind of wear this mask that they want us to wear and that's what you do in corporate America.

Vicente's comments are poignant and rich with pain and insights. He did seem to experience considerable psychological anguish as a result of his frustrating struggle to move into the position of branch manager, which he seemed eminently qualified to assume. At the same time, he described the use of adopting an inauthentic persona to deal with racist comments and actions at work. Even in this short passage, the overwhelming personal cost that racism exacts in the life of this one individual, Vicente, is compelling and heartbreaking.

In contrast to Vicente, Betsy, the African American dental hygienist, took a somewhat different approach to direct questions about her experience of racism at work:

Oh yes, I have experienced racism at work. I'm trying to think because I guess I block out things that are uncomfortable and try to focus on the things that are good. But I do remember like maybe someone didn't want to see me, or maybe their attitudes were harsh. I feel like I can pick up on people's vibes. I've always been very professional at work, so I'm able to deal with all kinds of people, which I've learned through almost 20 years of working as a hygienist. It's amazing that you learn to deal with all kinds of people.

Betsy's comments seem to dance around the issue of how racism was expressed and manifested. In response to a question about racism from her supervisors, Betsy commented as follows:

Yeah! There's been racism from my supervisors. Again I try to not focus on those things, but there has been a little bit of everything.

Interestingly, Betsy's seemingly distanced comments were not atypical when considering the full array of narratives about race. Some of the participants may have struggled to open up with an interviewer that they did not know or may have felt some distance because of cross-race dyads (e.g., a white interviewer and a participant of color).

In the next passage, Jamal, the African American higher education professional, described his struggle to obtain a secure position in the student services departments of a community college system in a state in the western United States:

And so all of these things impacted me as far as being able to being hired and I saw people who were White, who were Latino being hired straight out of college without any experience, when I had more experience. And also I didn't have the social capital too, so I never had anyone that took me under their wing and mentored me and taught me the ropes about networking, about those types of things to build relationships so I could get hired. I had to really figure all of this out myself, and because I am an African American male, I wasn't seen as someone that was of value to invest in me. So no one ever really took the time out to mentor me and help me out along the way. But I saw that happening with people who were White and people who were Latino. There was a time where I was very angry and I thought maybe this is not what I should be doing, and I am going to throw in the towel and maybe I need to think about doing something else, because this is not working and it's taking so long to get a tenure track position. And finally I kept at it. I almost gave up several times, but in 2007, and this is where my spirituality comes in because I believe everything happens when it is supposed to. . . . It has been a journey.

Jamal's comments were complex and honest. He clearly named the racism that he felt and also identified another marginalized community (Latino professionals) who he perceived as having an advantage in his community. His full interview is very insightful about the process of being an African American man in an organization that ostensibly is inclusive, but in reality creates both overt and covert barriers that result in people competing with each other.

While many other participants described the complexity of race at work in their interviews, these three participants each gave voice to very specific aspects of the experience that foreshadow themes that conclude this chapter.

Gender and Work

The relationship between gender and work also evoked an expansive diversity of comments. In this section, I present a number of vignettes that highlight some of the most salient issues that were discussed by the participants. In this first passage, the impact of gender on people's choices about work and career was conveyed by Mary, a social worker, who commented about her decision to pursue her career in the helping professions:

I thought I was stupid at science and math. I have really found out that I like science a lot, but I was terrified of it when I was younger and that I could ever be successful in anything like that. My dad was an engineer, his dad was an engineer, and his dad was an engineer. It never even occurred to me that I could do that, that I was capable of anything like that. I think definitely my gender totally impacted my decisions, my gender and my age, where I was in society, and the years I was coming up, and where society was. So teacher, social worker, nurse—these were the options open to me.

Mary described the ways in which social pressures affect the career decision-making of women, who are given messages throughout their lives about their place in the world of work. Despite the influence of her family and her love of science, she restricted her options so that they were more consistent with the expectations of women from her generation.

Another disconcerting theme in the narratives about gender and work is sexual harassment; a troubling example of this all-too-common problem was presented by Patricia, a 27-year-old woman who recounted her experience in the food service industry:

At the bakery and the restaurant I've had issues with some of the staff in the kitchen. Sometimes they act like pervs, and they do really kind of perverted things. A couple weeks ago I was . . . I was like kneeling down to get something out of the dessert fridge, and the head chef kind of grabbed my head and pulled it towards his groin a little bit. And I don't . . . I was like, freaking out a little bit, and I was just like, "WTF was that about!?" And I kind of just walked away. And I kind of felt all week like: I feel like I was sexually assaulted at work. I don't really feel comfortable. And so, next time I saw him . . . I took him outside and I was like, "You can't do shit like that to me!" He's like, "No, I was just playing around. I didn't mean to hurt your feelings." I'm like, "Yeah, but I can't be afraid to come to work . . . because you might do that again. So you need to know not to do stuff like that again!" So, you know, we had that talk and it was super awkward, and . . . I didn't want to involve my boss because I feel like on some level, he wouldn't take me seriously.

Patricia's comments are achingly painful to read. Although she was able to set limits, people who are frightened about their job security or in powerless positions may not feel that they can speak up for themselves. The level of terror that Patricia described underscores the vulnerability that many women feel at work and in their lives as men exploit their positions and power to meet their own needs. A full review of Patricia's interview indicated that she had considerable inner strength and social skills that may have provided her with the tools to push back against a sexual perpetrator. Of course, that she had to muster the resources to counter sexual harassment of this nature underscores the abuse that women face in the workplace, interacting with men who may exploit the power of their positions.

Another theme that emerged in the discussions about gender and work was the sense of competition between women. This theme, while not common in our interviews, was nevertheless more common than I had expected. In the next quotation by Joyce, a 31-year-old woman who was unemployed at the time of the interview, a particularly awkward scenario is described:

> I've had so many bad experiences at work. I'm the kind of female that, and it's typical, a female can't work with another female boss. And it's been happening a lot with me because all I seem to get is female bosses that just don't like to see another one at least succeed. If they've been in the position like 15, 20 years, and this is your boss, or somebody's coming in as a new person, for like a month, if this person is looking good on a job, and the boss is insecure, what is the next step the boss is going to take? Just find a way to keep their job by doing undercover things, that's not even really relevant. I had a boss who actually was in cahoots with the HR [human resources] member to just set me up because she didn't like the fact that I was getting along with everybody in the department. . . . And this is where it gets hard for me to stay on the job. And I know there's a lot more women that feel like that but they don't know where to go for their outlet, because it's a lot of women that are in battle with each other on these jobs. And once they do work, there's always somebody who don't, or a boss that don't want them there.

Joyce's description is painful to read, reflecting a similar type of competition among marginalized communities of workers that Jamal described in the previous section. Taken together, the three contributions on gender and work tap the most prevalent themes that emerged in the interviews. The overriding theme in the narratives reflected the aversive impact that work can create in the lives of women.

Sexual Orientation and Work

Although American society has become more welcoming to individuals from diverse sexual orientation communities (albeit with considerable ambivalence in some sectors of our society), the working context has the capacity to provide a bit more resistance to the movement toward inclusion and affirmation. One of the attributes of work is that power-based hierarchies remain entrenched, often privileging groups that can continue to marginalize and stigmatize those who seemingly fall outside the boundaries of what some consider to be acceptable social and relational behavior. Into this murky mix, a number of the participants from the Boston College Working Project discussed this complex issue with insight and passion. In the first passage, Dick, the 53-year-old instructional aide, opened up about his sexual orientation in his work life in education:

> I would classify myself as gay/bisexual, so that social dynamic, especially considering I am a bit older—younger people have grown up in a time where there are more rights. When I was growing up, there was no acknowledgment that it even existed outside of it being a slur, outside of it being an abnormality. Now there is the social base and there is the social acceptance, but there is still the struggle. . . . I would say there is a lot of hatred, there's a lot of obstacles. . . . A lot of people at work are aware of my sexuality. So this is why I am not even sure because I know people talk a lot, but I was pretty open with it in my classroom to the classroom teacher that I'm assigned to. Now when I go to different classrooms, which are the mixed classes where I would accompany a student, it really depends on how I feel the level of acceptance is going to be. There are some people who seem to be socially aware, and they will just sort of pick up on things, and so they might say something that would make me feel comfortable to respond in a manner that would be the identification that I'm gay, and generally that's been very positive. And in some cases, there are people who have said some very disparaging remarks, in which case I generally feel sorry for them, more than anger, because they have such a narrow view of life. . . . But I've definitely experienced in different jobs disparaging remarks, either directly or around me.

Dick's powerful comments underscore the pervasive struggle that exists for many individuals who are members of a sexual orientation minority. Despite his insight and his capacity to take a broader perspective, the sheer level of energy that Dick needs to devote to this issue is striking, reflecting a working context where it seems likely that coworkers or supervisors can say hurtful or marginalizing comments with impunity. In the next example, Paolo, a 37-year-old gay immigrant man from Brazil who was working as a mental health counselor, described his struggles with marginalization due to his sexual orientation:

> I worked with a person who would blatantly claim ownership of work that I had done. The same person was very overtly prejudiced because of my sexuality and I think that it also had something to do with gender. Not necessarily sexuality; it was very disappointing because it was my first job at a university. That's not what I thought of when I aspired to work for

an educational, postsecondary educational institution. Those were some pretty rough years there working under such persons who would do such things. Even today, I have to deal with fear of retaliation due to sexuality. So I work and I like my job very much, but I'm not necessarily out at work. I'm not in the closet at work because if people ask me I say it. For instance, there was an end of work party yesterday and I chose to go for drinks and not stay for dinner because I'm not out at work. I wouldn't take my partner for instance. The reason why I made the choice to keep it that way was because when I first started working this job, I advocated so that we would be a little more inclusive in terms of sexuality and I was told by one of the persons that I work for that we couldn't put rainbow stickers on our windows for instance because that would make some therapists uncomfortable. . . . My goal is to continue looking for an opportunity where my partner would be included in my professional life too even if it's just in terms of having the same benefits if I were married.

Paolo's comments resonate with Dick's narrative in his compelling description of prejudice and a sense of being on the outside at work. In Paolo's full narrative, he described that he had felt profoundly hurt that he experienced such homophobic experiences in a professional counseling job, which he had expected would be a comfortable and accepting home for his work and his overall personal life.

Disability and Work

Only a few of the participants described disability status as an issue in their lives and in their capacity to engage in work. Jim, a 51-year-old White career counseling intern who had been through both active duty service in war zones and then a period of unemployment, described his struggle with post-traumatic stress disorder (PTSD):

I'm someone suffering from PTSD. Sometimes people don't really understand what a veteran goes through. And that is hard to deal with. And over the years, I've had people ask me some ridiculous questions. They don't understand their boundaries. I mean I've literally had people say when you were overseas, how many people did you kill? I mean really? You really want to ask me that? I didn't personally kill anybody, but what are you going to do, go ask a kid who just came back from Afghanistan that? Are you out of your mind? People just don't use a whole lot of insight sometimes. And that's really frustrating. If somebody asked me something like that today, I would just shake my head and, say, dude listen pal just you need to rethink what you just asked me. Think really long and hard about what you just asked me and then go away. That's pretty much it. It's frustrating. But you deal with it. And that's happened to me in the past at work.

Jim's comments were particularly important in this project because he was one of the only participants who spoke directly about his own experiences with a disabling condition. Other participants spoke about disability in a more distant way, yet their comments are relevant to our discussion. In the first passage, Fae, a 24-year-old White graduate student in counseling psychology, shared her perceptions of the role of disability as playing a constraining role in attaining the American dream. Fae had a number of profoundly meaningful interactions with clients with disabling conditions, which helped her to attain a deep empathic connection to this very challenging source of marginalization.

The catch phrase in my work is that the American dream and the pull yourself up by your bootstraps is a myth. I have seen hundreds of people work as hard as they can and it's just not enough. Without the right look—a client with disabilities because she has pain—it's easier for them to deny her application than make accommodations for her, whether or not the American with Disabilities Act is in place or not—they can say they chose another applicant for a thousand other reasons. There aren't enough protections in place for those who are not White middle-upper class individuals that have connections to make it. It's not about what you do it's about who you know.

Rich, the 63-year-old retired teacher who was receiving disability payments because of his cancer diagnosis, also commented on the concept of the American dream by discussing disability in a more generic sense:

I think there are certain limitations on the American dream statement [i.e., you can achieve your dreams in the United States if you work hard enough] because. . . . Yeah, if you work hard, but . . . let's say you have a disability. It doesn't matter how hard you're going to work if your disability will prevent you from achieving what you want to achieve. Or, let's say you don't have the intellect that you need to be something or that you just don't have the skills for—it's not going to matter how hard you work, you're not going to succeed in that area, because you don't have the basic skills. So it can be a detriment in that respect, whereas people think: Well, I'm an American and all I have to do is work really hard and I'll succeed.

But there are a lot of people that don't have the basic skills necessary to. . . . Also . . . I think that there's a set of basic skills that all people who succeed have.

A close examination of Rich's full narrative suggests that some of his insights may have been a function of his own disability, with Rich having to leave his job earlier than he had planned. He was recently tenured as a special education teacher but because of the intense fatigue of the multiple myeloma cancer that he had, he could not stand up in the classroom. At that point, he had to go on disability because his school system required that teachers stand during their lessons, which he could not sustain on a daily basis. In addition, his work in special education gave him a close connection to many young people whose dreams for a life of meaningful work were dashed or severely compromised because of their disabling conditions.

All three of these participants approached disability from somewhat distinct perspectives but were able to provide a broad perspective on the various challenges and consequences of that people experience as they approached a work context that takes the measure of people in often very harsh and judgmental ways.

Social Class, Poverty, and Work

Discussions about social class among the participants generally focused on poverty and other experiences of inadequate resources. The sample included numerous individuals who were quite impoverished and, at times, homeless, as well as others whose standard of living declined sharply in their adult years due to disappointments in life and at work. Often, the discussions of poverty intersected with other social identities, such as the need for survival and unemployment, both of which are covered in separate chapters (Chapters 2 and 8, respectively). In the first passage, Robert, a 51-year-old unemployed man, took a somewhat distant perspective in describing class struggles that he likely was experiencing in a more direct and personal way:

I mean all this fighting over benefits and minimum wages and you know tax breaks. . . . It's definitely class warfare that's going on now. I don't think people want to accept it but. You know, it's greed, it's all greed. I look at what happened in the Middle East with all these are countries I thought would never overthrow their rulers. Or try to overthrow their rulers. And sure enough, people were pressed enough and go to the breaking point. And they weren't overthrowing these rulers because they wanted to be

Christian or democracies, or wanted democratic society. They just didn't want to be oppressed. And I don't know how long I'm going to live, but I would be very surprised if I don't see something like that here. We're getting to the point where you can only push the masses so much. You can only deny them so much. Neither Democrats nor Republicans seem to understand that. They're kind of living in the fantasy world. And the richer are getting richer and the poorer are getting poorer. I mean I don't have a family and I thank my God, thank God I don't have a family. If I believed in God I would thank God for that. Because nothing good is going come from it—I mean, we live in a society, I don't know if socialism is the way, but we live in a society and if we don't start to treat people with decency, then bad things are going to happen.

In the next passage, Kim, a 26-year-old customer service representative, described her life from the context of inadequate resources:

Jobwise here, it's not the greatest. I mean unless you're a doctor, you're a nurse, or some kind . . . in that career wise. I think that money, money has become our biggest issue. Yeah, we don't have the money. And recently my husband got demoted from his job too. He was doing really good, but another manager took over his position so he got demoted from his job too because it was . . . it is about who you know and I think that just what I hear from him. I believe in his work environment it's really racism. I think the majority of them [his supervisors and coworkers] are Hispanic. And the main boss, the head boss, you know are friends with the new boss that took over, that became his boss.

Like other participants quoted previously in this chapter, Kim reported struggles with other groups who are also marginalized, underscoring a disconcerting theme in these narratives wherein people feel competitive with other communities that are also striving for security and success. In the final contribution in this section, we return to Paolo to learn about his insights about poverty, which he lived through in his immigration to the United States and once again connected to in his counseling work with impoverished clients:

The whole notion of people working hard . . . the people who are the poorest of the poor that I work with, are people who have . . . oh my god, life is so difficult for them. For me to say that they aren't working hard. They are complying with all of these government things just to get their food stamps. It's just sad. People work hard. It's that the whole notion of privilege. If you came in with a lot more on your plate already, it's going to be easier for you to succeed. Those that come in without nutrition, it's very hard for us to say you aren't working hard enough and that's why your life sucks. These people have had to fight for food in their own house.

The three vignettes in this section underscore a hard truth about life in America. Considerable inequality exists, which seems less amenable to upward mobility via work than it was many decades ago (especially right after World War II).[40] The American dream, which has consumed so much of our political and personal discourse, has been battered in this age of uncertainty as stable work that is financially viable becomes less available, particularly to those in marginalized communities.

Immigration and Work

The challenges of being an immigrant in the United States are well documented and seem to be even more intense during political eras that tend to marginalize and blame people from other countries and cultures. In the first passage, Suba, a 29-year-old Asian migrant who came to the United States from India for graduate school, described the intersecting space shared by racism and discrimination against immigrants in his powerful recollection of the hierarchy that was established by his graduate professor:

The Chinese guy [in our lab] was a really smart person. You know, he was really very intelligent and he fulfilled his expectations but even then I felt that the professor was more favorable toward the American students—the White American students—than both of us. So, there were like two White Americans, there was the Chinese guy, and then there was me. I felt that I was number four. And the Chinese guy was number three. And then the two American guys were number one and two. Even this one American guy actually didn't have a lot of results. I mean one guy was really smart and this other guy did not have a lot of results, but he was always treated nice and, I mean, the Chinese guy was probably the smartest, but he didn't get the first priority or his most favor.

Suba's comments are telling in the way in which the two immigrant students were treated as second-class citizens, despite their performance. In this brief vignette, the advantages of being a native-born White American are apparent as the two immigrants seemed to struggle for recognition and affirmation. In the next vignette, Donald, a 58-year-old Chinese immigrant, described his major challenges in his life both at work and in his social life:

Well, I think the biggest challenge for me is the cultural gap, if I have to say that. I'm from China, from Asia, and the kids grew up in the United States and the east and west have totally different cultures, especially on how to raise the kids and how to educate the kids. In China, we usually push kids hard and always educate kids to study more and study hard and sometimes we intervene in their personal lives quite a lot. But here, there is a totally different way to educate the boys and girls. So we should find a balance between the Oriental way and the Western way. It is pretty hard, you know. I should say a strong Asian way can give the kids a pretty tough time when we try to educate the kids here. . . . Most of my social circle is still among Chinese or Asian people. Of course, that limits my social life and my relationship with the whole community. In work, it limits the opportunity of getting promoted and exposing myself to different people. I think the impact is pretty strong.

These two vignettes provide a glimpse into the complexity of managing the immigration process at work. Both of these individuals described the challenges of transitioning to the United States for work in light of fairly obvious differences with respect to appearance, language, and culture. In addition, several other participants described the intersecting nature of their struggles, which encompassed race, culture, immigration status, and, for some, sexual orientation.

In the next section, other forms of marginalization are described that often elude specific social identities, but nevertheless are pernicious aspects of life in America.

Marginalization as a Social Identity

As we have seen in some of the narratives, the experience of being marginalized was often due not to some designated social identity but life experience. For example, a few of the participants described the burden of having to obtain and sustain work with prison records. In the first passage, Matteo, the 45-year-old musician and audiovisual technician, described his views on the struggles of people with prison records to gain a foothold in the world of work:

Give guys a second chance. Business leaders need to give guys that have criminal records . . . the benefit of the doubt. Especially if they've only been in once, and they don't have any other criminal history—they haven't demonstrated a whole lifestyle. . . . And they just made a mistake. . . . Because the background checks are huge. I mean you're applying online now. It's a different world. And they have 300 or 400 applicants in a day that they got to go through them. And before they even meet you, they're looking at . . . googling a person's name or whatever, just to eliminate. Eliminate, eliminate, eliminate. . . . You know, those of us that have that on our record. . . . Don't put so much weight on the background checks. Let guys have a chance to present themselves to you, because I really do think that a lot of us . . . have a lot to offer a company.

Matteo was able to get back into the workforce owing to his technical skills and his musical ability, both of which led to meaningful and satisfying work experiences. Matteo's experience was infused with both frustration and resilience; he struggled considerably in getting back into the marketplace, yet he did have some advantages based on his education, gender, and race.

In the next passage, Milo, the 38-year-old African American career counselor, recounted his inner theory about marginalization, which for him included his exposure to racism and growing up working class in a dangerous urban community:

I usually have this theory in my head—and I relate it to me—is that I try to carry myself in such a manner, that there is no way that you can aspire to structurally discriminate against me. That's part true, and part naiveté. And, for what it's worth, I think that some of that has stuck with me. . . . I make it a point to carry myself in a manner that creates no questions. Because in our society, I think people can look at you as a person of color . . . and create a stereotype if they see one iota of you lacking somewhere. No matter how many degrees or PhDs you have by your name . . . do a couple of things—show up late for work a couple of times—and you'll be connected to a larger sentiment about that group. . . . Not that individual: that group. And that's just my observation. That's my understanding. . . . I've seen stories of administrators of color in other complex situations, where they felt that structurally speaking, that there should have been no question why they shouldn't have moved to the next step. The other thing I can surmise is that maybe I haven't had the opportunity to be in that situation yet, where there's a question of me versus the next guy . . . or the next woman, as it were. So . . . it's something that I think about too, because as the world becomes more polarized around issues of race, ethnicity, sex, gender, and so forth. . . . Up to this point, I've been lucky. I've haven't seen a lot that impugns me personally. I've just seen people that, sometimes they're just cranky . . . they behave a certain way. . . . They have a reputation. . . . Sometimes if you grow up, and even if you're a person of color, that can be interpreted as: "Well, are they just doing that towards me?" That's a fair question, especially given the experiences in this country. So my assessment of people is like that? That's just how they are. Are they more rough towards me because I'm a person of color? I don't know! You can see where the complexity forms.

Milo's comments were indeed complex and conveyed the struggles that he went through to make his way in a world of work that clearly and quickly identified his social and external characteristics, forcing him to reckon with a set of expectations and experiences that were not required of White men in similar circumstances. He also noted that he felt that he had to work extra hard in both his social interactions and his work itself to ensure that he did not evoke in any way stereotypes that existed about his particular community. In a sense, Milo's comments (and indeed, his entire interview) reflect the intersecting spaces of marginalization and the overwhelming sense of effort that is required to be a visible racial and ethnic group member in a society that so quickly defines people in ways that function to separate and marginalize some groups while privileging others.

In addition to these notable experiences so courageously shared by our participants, the next chapter on unemployment describes the sense of being marginalized due to the inability to access marketplace work. Reviewing Chapter 8 in light of the observations and inferences culled in this chapter provides an important theme about the ways that society functions with respect to work, inclusion, and diversity. Being without work and lacking access to work is, in of itself, a form of being forced outside mainstream society, leaving people lost and disheartened.

The following section explores recent psychological research on marginalization and oppression that builds and deepens the insights that have been gleaned thus far in this chapter.

Being Able to Work Without Oppression and Harassment: A Psychological View

In exploring new psychological research on work and marginalization, the findings from the Boston College Working Project participants emerged as vitally important to discuss in further depth. Following this discussion, I have decided to include two very innovative and compelling bodies of research that collectively offer explanations about the sad state of our working lives and a potential way forward for individuals and communities: race-based color-blindness and critical consciousness.

The Erosion of the Social Foundations of Work

The narrative vignettes that are presented in this chapter coupled with my review of the full interviews tell a powerful story that may reflect an emerging reality across many sectors of the workplace. One of the common themes in a fairly diverse array of responses was the sense that people did not feel safe at work and very often were not confident or comfortable looking for work. Even more disconcerting was the discussion of infighting among groups of marginalized people, seemingly struggling to feel secure in a working environment that was described as fragmented and, at times, dangerous.

The sense of there being an eroding foundation for work was particularly pronounced where people described conflicts between groups that had already been marginalized. For example, Jamal and Kim both discussed competing with other marginalized communities for work, while Joyce discussed the infighting among women at work; each of these stories showed a working context that seemed to be pitting one group against another. What is striking about this observation is that it was not isolated to these three individuals. Other individuals in the sample also described conflicts that became charged with emotion and bitterness, reflecting perceived or real battles among groups that have already been isolated and oppressed. While these vignettes were not the majority, they reflect a notable minority of participants, underscoring a reality about social marginalization and work that needs to be openly discussed here.

What would lead well-meaning people, many of whom openly expressed their commitment to equality and justice, to openly critique other groups (or their own social group)? In my view, this chapter's responses reflect a troubling trend about the workplace, where access to stable and decent work is increasingly constrained and people feel that they need to call out other social groups, even as they themselves are marginalized by race, gender, sexual orientation, or other marginalized identities. I believe that these narratives reflect the erosion of social cohesion at work for many people, who are caught in a battle of competitiveness that often seems to take on personal tones.

From a psychological perspective, the narratives do not inherently represent shortcomings in our participants; rather, they seem to reflect a social and economic system that is dysfunctional and, at times, abusive in its treatment of people. While I am not trying to diminish individual responsibility for understanding and discerning the social and economic world, I do believe that the impact of a working world that is so disruptive is a stressful and, for some, a traumatic experience. As Jamal noted in his very thoughtful interview, he trained for years to be a higher education professional, working very hard to move out of an impoverished community, only to be met with resistance and rejection at nearly every turn. He was able to identify the role of White people as the privileged "others" as well, which reflects the sort of critical thinking that I discuss in the next section.

The emergence of these disconcerting narratives, therefore, needs to be examined in light of a context that has narrowed access to opportunity to a point that feels like it is crushing people as they try to enter the work world. The experience of feeling crushed and cast aside very likely evokes the sense that people focus on the most proximal perceived barrier that exists between themselves and their dreams. As we discuss further in the chapter, helping people to look beyond the folks on the next rung of the ladder is a critical task for educators, psychologists, and, more broadly, our society moving forward.

In addition to the notable episodes of blaming other groups for one's struggles, the narratives conveyed profoundly painful experiences of being marginalized at work due to social identities, past life experiences, or not being able to access stable, decent work. As I stated previously, the workplace is the most obvious, and often most painful, venue for people to interact with others within an often highly charged social and economic space. The full picture of the interviews, taken together, attests to the concerns that have been noted in the overwhelmingly depressing statistics and research about oppression and marginalization at work. People are being judged at nearly every turn and are feeling vulnerable, exposed, and very anxious about their capacity to survive in a world that categorizes and diminishes people based on appearance, cultural background, or other extraneous factors. In the next section, a new set of ideas about the pernicious existence of racism and oppression is introduced and integrated with the material presented thus far.

Racial Color-Blindness: The Workplace Default

The prevalence of racial disparities in employment across many dimensions (including access to work, salary, promotion opportunities, and the like) between various groups within the United States (and in many other nations as well) is certainly troubling and has clearly affected individuals and communities in very profound ways. These disparities are an integral part of American history and have survived to this day, as reflected in the narratives presented previously in this chapter and in an extensive literature on employment and disparities.[41] A question that emerges is why these differences exist and persist, especially in light of very strong scientific evidence that clearly contradicts notions that abilities and talents vary based on gender, race, social class, or other external social identities.[42]

Recent research by Helene Neville, a highly talented counseling psychologist from the University of Illinois, provides a thoughtful perspective that can

help us to understand how organizations and institutions in our society collude to sustain inequality in the workplace. Neville and her colleagues have
elaborated on the commonly used term of color-blindness in their notion of
color-blind racial ideology (CBRI), which they very thoughtfully embedded
in a critical body of psychological theory and research.[43] According to Neville
and her associates, CBRI refers to a very common tendency for individuals
and institutions to assume that racial issues are no longer pertinent, and that
people's behavior, attainment in life, and other aspects of their psychosocial and
economic functioning are determined by effort or ability. CBRI was particularly
popular after Barack Obama's two election victories, which, for some, promised a postracial society, one where skin color and race no longer mattered.
However, as we have seen in statistics about employment discrimination, earnings, and the full array of indices of social and economic functioning, African
Americans, Latinos, and Asian Americans consistently struggle in nearly all
sectors of life.[44]

The work by Neville and her colleagues on CBRI explored the nature of
explanations for these disparities in a richly illuminating way. In their original
statement about this perspective in an often-cited article from the *American
Psychologist*, Neville and her associates described two ways in which color-
blindness is manifested in racial contexts.[45] The first of these is color evasion,
which is reflected in the avoidance of acknowledging that racial differences produce meaningful implications in people's lives. This approach, which does reject
White superiority, nevertheless avoids the reality that race in the United States
is rife with problems for people who are born on the wrong side of the pernicious racial divide. A more critical view would be to maintain the rejection of
White supremacy, affirm that racism is alive, and that it has created differen-
tial access to the institutions and support systems that nurture people and help
them to realize their dreams. The second way in which CBRI is expressed is via
power evasion, which assumes that people all have the same level of access to
the power levers that provide access to opportunity and well-being. Here again,
a more critical view would encompass a clear affirmation that power is differ-
entially allocated, and that people of color in the United States are very often
denied access to the resources that would promote their power and agency
in life.

As summarized in a thoughtful application of CBRI research to the world of
work, Caryn Block described how CBRI creates some insidious explanations
for disparities in the workplace that are very troubling.[46] In Block's analysis,
when CBRI is the prevailing way for people to understand racial differences, a
host of implications ensue, some of which are damaging to people of color. In
this discussion, the linkage between CBRI and the stereotype threat, a psychological perspective that has transformed our understanding of the performance

of marginalized groups, merits further exploration. According to the work of Claude Steele, a prominent social psychologist from Stanford University, people who are in the margins (including women, African Americans, Latinos, and other oppressed groups) are likely to experience stereotype threat when they learn that the performance of members of their particular group on an educational or work-based task is likely a function of inherent ability. For example, African American students who learn that their racial group membership is associated with poorer performance on cognitive tasks (such as an aptitude test) due to inherent and unchangeable biological attributes will perform less effectively on cognitive tests than a similar group that learns that these differences are due to social and economic factors.[47] Block's thoughtful analysis of CBRI suggested that the prevalence of this ideology may promote views that would result in explanations of disparities based on racist and sexist ideas. If organizations are ostensibly color-blind and do not acknowledge the impact of slavery historically, racism currently, and vast differences in resources and affordances, the continuation of racist ideas based on inferiority of some groups is likely to continue.

In relation to the powerful vignettes that we reviewed previously, an understanding of CBRI may help to explain the battles between marginalized communities. If people are internalizing the view that race no longer affects attainment at work, frustrations and disappointments that occur may not be easily understood or explained. As human history regrettably demonstrates, people often look for someone or some group to blame as a way of explaining their pain and as an outlet for unpleasant emotions. In effect, the CBRI may be the default mode in many communities and institutions that creates the framework for pain and marginalization. In the section that follows, I explore an educational and psychological tool that offers people and communities a way to think more critically (and accurately) about the complexities of work, oppression, and marginalization.

Thinking and Acting Critically for a Just Work World: Critical Consciousness

One reading of this chapter to this point is that people are passive recipients of racism or sexism and are very vulnerable to overt and covert messages about where they are located in the social and economic hierarchy of our society. And, while I have continually sought to hold the context and the broader world responsible for many of the painful experiences that we have read about in this chapter (and, indeed, throughout this book), as a psychologist, I do believe that people can take action to improve their situation and to enhance the responsiveness of our communities to protect people from the brutality of oppression. I also believe that individuals can accomplish a great deal in reaching their own goals and changing the world by joining together in meaningful communities and collaborations. One of the tools that has attracted a lot of attention is critical consciousness, which captures a capacity to reflect on the causes of social injustice and inequity coupled with a commitment to engage in actions to eradicate these sources of oppression.[48] In my view, critical consciousness offers a powerful set of ideas and tools that can help mobilize people and communities for a more equitable and humane world and, in our case, a more dignified and caring workplace.

Perhaps the best way to describe critical consciousness is to briefly outline its history, which is moving and informative. Back in the 1960s, a well-known Brazilian educator and activist, Paolo Freire, was focused on helping working class and poor people in Brazil's diverse communities learn to read and become literate. As Freire engaged with the peasants within Brazil, he realized that learning to read also involved learning to read the world, in effect, learning to discern the root causes of injustice and to hold social, corporate, and economic interests responsible for creating a world where some people have privilege and many others are left outside, looking in.[49]

This focus on becoming a broad and critical thinker has transformed scholarship and practice in pedagogy and, over time, has seeped into psychology and other social sciences. Freire's passionate call to integrate literacy training with education on the sources of inequality and the role of political power in the lives of individuals and communities has had a major impact in many sectors of the world. Within the past two decades, research on critical consciousness has blossomed, with a particular focus on education and work.

A particularly compelling finding by Matt Diemer, a talented psychologist from the University of Michigan (and a former doctoral student of mine), is very telling. Diemer found that a robust level of critical consciousness in high school was associated with high levels of occupational expectations and was predictive of occupational attainment 8 years later.[50] In an integrative summary of the literature on critical consciousness by Diemer and his colleagues, the importance of this attribute emerged with clarity; among young people and emerging adults, critical consciousness has been associated with school engagement, academic achievement, higher levels of mental health, and more adaptive relationship decisions.[51] Although critical consciousness is not a panacea for all of our ills, it is a particularly robust set of attitudes and knowledge that can help people manage and take action on inequality and injustice.

When considering the contributions by Freire in conjunction with the work by Diemer and his colleagues, an emerging bright spot is evident in relation to the problems documented in this chapter. Critical consciousness can serve as a preventive factor in life by helping people not blame themselves for their experiences of marginalization and by providing some important life skills, including strategic thinking, critical decision-making, the capacity to seek like-minded people for support, and a sense of agency and direction about making changes in one's life and in the world.[52] In addition, critical consciousness can serve as a major source of transformative change for our society. If we help students and adults learn about the nature of inequality, the impact of social marginalization on individuals and families, and the role of institutions that delegate privilege to some and not others, people may be able to mobilize and take action instead of feeling passive.

In the world of education, considerable progress has been made in infusing critical consciousness into various part of the academic and socioemotional curriculum. Some promising approaches include direct instruction on the causes of race, class, and gender-based inequality as well as more experiential approaches that involve students doing research on marginalization and participating in psychoeducational exercises that highlight the etiology and impact of oppression.[53] In my own counseling work, I have outlined ways of incorporating a critical consciousness approach to working with students and adults who have been cut off from the marketplace.[54] From a broader perspective, critical consciousness can form the core of social interventions designed to help workers advocate for access to decent work, the infusion of human rights at work, and other critical attributes of a fair and dignified society.

Conclusion

When considering the big picture about oppression and harassment that has been presented in this chapter, the main points do connect to provide some clarity about what is happening to people as they make their way in the world of work. One of the major issues that emerged with clarity is the continued prevalence of marginalization in systems that prepare people for work and in the actual workplace. If individuals are part of a social group that is the target of discrimination or prejudice, it is very likely that they will be confronted with challenges and barriers that can be devastating and psychologically damaging. Combining the stubborn tendency that people have to categorize and oppress some people with an economy that is increasingly valuing more highly skilled and privileged workers is leading to a situation that is tearing people and communities apart. The end result is that racism, sexism, heterosexism, classism, and other forms of oppression continue in the workplace, despite noble efforts to protect people from these offensive and horrific experiences.

Another major point in this picture is the disconcerting emergence of erosion of the social contract within the workplace and, more broadly, within our society. The constriction of the labor market, which many participants spoke about in depth, has left some people feeling terrified about their capacity to survive, let alone find meaning and purpose in their lives. One manifestation of this phenomenon was the troubling tendency by some of the participants to blame other similarly marginalized groups for their struggles. However, a broader and more subtle, but equally disconcerting, trend emerged in both the narratives and the literature that was reviewed.

It seems that American society is sort of settling into a default pattern where membership in various social groups remains paramount in how we are viewed and treated. While many thought that the tendency to use these social group memberships as a way to classify and marginalize people would diminish over time, this disconcerting tendency seems rather resistant and to change and continues to impact the world of work. I can imagine some readers responding to this by arguing that I am viewing the glass as half empty. Yes, there has been some progress in the world of work, particularly for people who have access to high levels of education and the corresponding social capital that comes with elite education. However, this observation is mitigated by the deep immersion that I have had in this issue for many decades in working with women, people of color, immigrants, and others who have recounted some horrific abuses, many of which were simply absorbed by my clients so that they did not jeopardize their jobs and livelihoods.

So, where does this leave us? It seems clear that our society needs to take action to reduce the impact of social oppression, harassment, and marginalization. One option is to build on the work of scholars and activists who are infusing critical consciousness into our education and training systems. If we help people to mobilize and become actively engaged in the struggle for decent work for all, they may be less prone to accept the harsh climate that exists in our society. However, a more compelling problem exists: The challenge of achieving social and racial justice at work will involve shared sacrifices by those who are in privileged positions. How do we educate those who are in power to share their power and resources? This is obviously a major challenge, especially in an economy and social system that so deeply values hard work, meritocracy, and individual responsibility. As noted in the discussion of CBRI, people in power have developed elaborate causal systems to explain disparities.

Clearly, these ideologies need to be confronted with solid facts and data from the social sciences, which is quite evident and very compelling. Developing the tools to talk with those in power about the need for shared sacrifices (such as owning the impact of one's historic privilege) is complex, but it is clearly doable;

indeed, some of the scholars within the critical consciousness world have developed some effective tools that can be replicated and expanded.[55]

As we consider the world of work in the face of automation and other massive transformations, it may be useful to infuse a focus on the issues raised in this chapter into the debates and dialogue about the future of work. As I have noted elsewhere in this book, the impact of the diminishing labor market is likely to be most pronounced in communities that are already hit hard with unemployment and precarious work. Rethinking work, as we do in Chapter 9, ought to involve serious conversations about infusing justice in how we think about access to opportunity.

Revisiting the chapter title provides an appropriate way to conclude this very powerful discussion, which has covered some painful material that has demonstrated the capacity that people have to hurt and harass their fellow citizens and the robust human strength that allows people to fight this abuse situation. So, how do we ensure that people can work without oppression and harassment? First, we need to acknowledge that these problems exist and, indeed, are quite resistant to efforts to change this very disturbing status quo. Denial is not an option here—the narratives and the research converge in describing a painful situation that requires a full and comprehensive plan of action. Second, we need to explore the ways in which people with privilege collude to sustain inequities in education and work. This will involve serious deliberation and a shared commitment to identifying how those with privilege are benefiting from marginalization and oppression.

Finally, we need to take the concerns that arose in this chapter and that have been so profoundly shared by the participants of the Boston College Working Project seriously. The workplace is particularly complex because of the built-in hierarchies, many of which are clearly sanctioned by employers and by society. People deserve to be able to work and to be treated with dignity at work and in preparing for work. The stories that were shared in this chapter need to be heard and responded to as we seek to create a society that will affirm everyone's right to decent work without oppression, harassment, and marginalization.

8

Being Without Work

Walking into the Sloan School of Management at the Massachusetts Institute of Technology is a stirring experience: The building is stunning, reflecting the sleek and modern architecture that befits one of the best business schools in the world. I entered the Sloan School to speak at a workshop for long-term unemployed adults who were participating in a program sponsored by a collaborative of employment scholars, activists, and career counseling practitioners, known as the Institute of Career Transitions.[1] The workshop, which was called a boot camp, was designed as an intensive 2-day conference to help invigorate long-term unemployed individuals to continue their frustrating, and even painful, search for stable and decent work. Once I was in the building, I noticed small groups of men and women talking, often in hushed tones, about their shared experience: being unemployed or underemployed, often for years, and facing the harsh reality of looking for a job in a labor market that seems to have forgotten that they exist.

My role at the boot camp was to give a presentation to the 120 participants and Institute of Career Transitions volunteers on shoring up their mental health as a job search continued. I felt that the talk went well as I shared best practices from counseling and vocational psychology along with some wisdom gleaned from my own work with unemployed clients throughout my career. What was even more powerful for me, though, was the reaction that I received and the conversations that I had with the participants. Right after my presentation, some of the audience members came up to talk with me, sharing relevant snippets from their life stories and highlighting the devastating impact that unemployment has had in their lives. Some reached out to me for advice, evoking my natural tendency to help people solve their work-related problems in ways that would yield dignified outcomes. Despite my hesitation about starting a conversation that I could not complete, I did offer some input to the participants, who shared their dilemmas and asked for ideas about next steps.

Participating in two of the boot camps had a profound impact on me. While I have been working with long-term unemployed clients in my psychology practice for many decades, somehow the experience of witnessing the collective anguish of so many people at the same time had a more intense effect. Many people's lives were in complete shambles. Quite a few of the participants who reached out to me had been without a stable job for years; some had started out in professional positions, were laid off during the height of the Great Recession, and were finding the job search process increasingly less viable. A number were working in short-term contract jobs or were finding some source of sustenance in the gig economy (e.g., driving for Lyft or Uber or opening their homes up to Airbnb guests). I felt like someone who enters a room with people who are starving and that I held the key to food and security; in fact, for many, as we addressed further in this chapter, being without work was resulting in food and housing insecurity. I ended up giving some of the members job leads that I was aware of, but for many, all I could offer was some encouragement and admiration for their tenacity and courage.

As I walked out of the Sloan School, I reflected deeply on my experience. What had gone wrong in our society to lead to such devastating experiences for so many people? How could I, as a psychologist, professor, and author, hope to do anything substantial to change the system that had dealt so many people such a hard hand? Some of the impetus for this book emerged from the boot camp experiences and from other conversations, both in my therapy office and in my research interviews with participants in the Boston College Working Project, with long-term unemployed young adults, middle-aged adults, and older people who have been either cast aside or never fully integrated into marketplace work.

One way of responding to the feelings that I experienced during my many interactions with long-term unemployed people is to give their voice the dignity and authority that it deserves. In this chapter, we hear from many of the participants interviewed who had been marginalized in the marketplace by unemployment and underemployment. Their pain, ideas about what to do both individually and collectively as a nation, and search for a meaningful and dignified way out of their dilemma are infused with strength and wisdom. In addition, I explore some new research findings that further embellish the messages that conclude the chapter about the centrality of work in people's lives. Throughout this chapter, I focus on the inner experience of unemployment, which complements the material that I presented in Chapter 2 on survival that focused more on the external struggles to sustain a livelihood.

Being Able to Work: An Introductory Journey

In the early part of the twentieth century, psychology moved from the laboratory and clinic to the actual contexts where people lived and worked; a key question that emerged for psychologists and others in mental health and employment/vocational counseling services is how people manage during periods of unemployment. An added impetus was the advent of the Great Depression of the 1930s, which devastated North America, Europe, and many other parts of the world with unprecedented unemployment, often in nations without a reasonable safety net, leading to poverty, starvation, homelessness, and pervasive despair. The movement of psychology toward the environments in which people created their lives coupled with the devastation of the Great Depression led to important research on unemployment and mental health that continues to inform our thinking about this very difficult part of life: living life without access to decent work.

The Nature of Unemployment

Before we can explore the psychological meaning of unemployment, we first need to identify the prevalence and impact of not being able to attain work in the marketplace. In the United States as well as many other countries, unemployment statistics have been considered one of the primary indicators of the vigor of the economy as well as an overall measure of how well people are doing in accessing work. Moreover, some economists have viewed a modest degree of unemployment as an expected and tolerable byproduct of a free-market economy, reflecting what is known as "churning" in the labor market, wherein people would often be without work during short-term transitions (both voluntary and involuntary). The prevailing view among some economists is that some modest level of unemployment is needed to provide employers with an accessible labor pool.[2] This position, which has often seemed rather callous to me, is not endorsed by all economists. Indeed, many important books written by economists about inequality and unemployment are now taking issue with the position that unemployment is a necessary feature of free-market economies.[3]

To help make this churning process more humane, the US government provides unemployment insurance, typically for a short term (6 months on average currently), which affords a very modest level of financial support. (During the Great Recession, unemployment insurance in the United States was provided for up to 99 weeks, which was certainly a critical resource for many who had been fired or laid off during the peak of the downturn. Yet, as we shall see, even a 99-week level of support was not sufficient for people to find stable work; for some, their layoffs meant an early retirement or disengagement from marketplace work.)

This economics-based approach to understanding unemployment is complicated by many factors that are often elusive in aggregate data reports. One of the most difficult statistics to identify accurately is the actual number of people who are not working in the marketplace and who want to work. Current measures of unemployment in the United States are generally based on people who are actively looking. During the Great Recession, many people gradually left the marketplace, giving up on looking for work, entering a forced early retirement, or, when possible, obtaining disability payments to provide some financial support. Another statistic, known as labor market participation, emerged as a more sensitive index of access to the world of marketplace work; this statistic includes people who are working as well as people who are not working but seeking to enter the labor force.

Another interesting trend in long-term unemployment is the increase in the proportion of white-collar workers who are struggling in getting back into the labor force. Ofer Sharone, a highly respected sociologist who has dedicated his career to understanding and improving the lives of the long-term unemployed, provided a very insightful analysis of the class-related distinctions that are reshaping our views of employment and unemployment.[4] While white-collar workers have historically been considered to be more securely attached to the marketplace, in large measure due to their education and related resources, recent trends have caused a major shift in these assumptions. During the Great Recession, the longest duration of long-term unemployment (defined as 27 weeks or more) was found among white-collar workers and not blue-collar workers.[5]

Sharone proposed that the growth of white-collar unemployment is due to several factors, which have shifted the labor market context markedly. One set of reasons has to do with globalization and technology, which has replaced the functions of many white-collar workers.[6] For example, a few decades ago, midlevel managers often focused their efforts on communicating policies and information from upper level managers and technical experts to less skilled workers. Now, many of these functions are handled by computers, which offer seemingly endless sources of information for all workers via the click of a mouse.[7] Another set of reasons is related to shifts in political, corporate, and other institutions, which increasingly have reduced supports for workers (such as unions) and created policies that buttress neoliberal economic systems (such as flexible employment policies and lower taxes for corporations and wealthy investors).[8]

As I reviewed the data available on unemployment, it became clear to me that people can parse the statistics in a variety of ways, often in the service of a specific point or agenda. I do believe that labor market data are important; however, examining these data divorced of the inner experience and psychological meaning of unemployment in people's lives is risky at best and perhaps even dangerous for the coherence and vigor of our nation's welfare.[9] The danger lies in not knowing what the process of churning (short-term unemployment) or long-term unemployment is really like for people. Simply referring to statistics and data removes us from having to deal with the reality of the lived experience of those without access to work. Our failure to understand this process is particularly problematic from the perspective of those who are left on the margins of a "full-employment economy" currently and for our considerations of the meaning of being without work in relation to the near future, when work may in fact disappear for many sectors of the American population.[10] As an example, the surprising results in the U.S. 2016 presidential election may reflect some of the deep-seated anxiety about work and the striving for stability, along with many other factors. In the sections that follow, I pursue the psychological angle, focusing on the impact of unemployment in relation to mental health, well-being, and the welfare of our communities.

Unemployment and Mental Health: A Historical View

Early in the twentieth century, different ideas were debated about the causes and impact of unemployment from both economic and psychological perspectives. Some scholars thought that unemployment was due to personal deficits: People could obtain work if only they tried harder or were more flexible, adaptive, smarter, or somehow better than their counterparts who were competing for the same jobs.[11] Indeed, a theory evolved, known as the downward drift hypothesis, that proposed that people who struggled in finding and holding jobs were more likely to be on a negative spiral in their lives due to mental health problems or other internal deficits.[12]

Into this intellectual stew emerged a brilliant young Austrian psychologist, Marie Jahoda, who collaborated with two other colleagues (Paul Lazerfeld and Hans Zeisel) in conducting an in-depth study of a town named Marienthal in Austria during the early 1930s.[13] Marienthal is a small town near Vienna that was shattered by the Great Depression, resulting in overwhelming unemployment and financial ruin for many of its citizens. Jahoda was a passionate socialist at the time and was also deeply committed to the young field of psychology, which she felt could provide important answers about the impact of work (and its absence: unemployment) on well-being and on the development of political and class consciousness. Jahoda's research, which used a combination of qualitative and quantitative methods, identified some intriguing findings that have shaped our thinking about work and unemployment currently.

Because the Marienthal project involved very intensive studies of the families who had been hit so hard by unemployment, Jahoda and her colleagues were deeply committed to exploring the meaning of the job loss for the entire family. She identified the manifest or overt function of work, financial stability, which was clearly core to the experience of the workers who lost their livelihoods. The unemployed citizens of Marienthal, like their peers across Europe and North America, had to rely on modest unemployment benefits or the kindness of their families and communities. However, Jahoda also identified five covert or latent functions of work that were most obvious when they were no longer available. The in-depth interviews that Jahoda and her colleagues conducted with the unemployed individuals in Marienthal revealed that work functioned to provide the following attributes, which were central to the overall well-being of the residents of this deeply wounded community:

1. *Time structure:* Without the formal organization of one's time that work provides, many of the residents of Marienthal struggled to structure their days and weeks into manageable time frames.

2. *Collective purpose:* The notion of collective purpose is similar to the ideas that were presented in Chapter 5, which focused on how work links people to the broader social and economic world in purposeful and meaningful activities.

3. *Social contact:* The interpersonal connections that are made at work, reviewed in Chapter 3, are central to the well-being of individuals and communities. The residents in Marienthal, most of whom worked in the town's textile plants, seemed lost and disconnected after they lost their jobs.

4. *Status:* Work provides people with a sense of identity and a clearly understood role within their families and communities. The unavailability of work produced a corresponding loss of status, leading to many of the people in Marienthal feeling alienated and disengaged.

5. *Activity:* The basic tasks of work offered people a structured means of being active in their lives; the inverse of this activity, passivity, led people in Marienthal to feel a sense of apathy and disengagement in their lives.

The Marienthal study was a game changer in how people thought about the impact of unemployment in people's lives. While the downward drift hypothesis remained vibrant for many more decades, the view that unemployment itself functions to remove people from their natural striving to create, contribute, and connect through work (in both the marketplace and caring contexts) gained increasing prominence in psychological studies of working.[14] Moreover, considerable research evidence has supported the centrality of what Jahoda so aptly called the latent functions of work, which I argue throughout this book are central to a life fully lived.[15]

Unemployment and Psychological Well-Being: The Current View

Fast forwarding from the early 1930s to our current era brings us to a large number of empirical studies that flesh out the inferences that Marie Jahoda and her colleagues developed in their very creative study of Marienthal. A particularly relevant project for our discussion is a large-scale meta-analysis of 324 individual research studies across 26 countries on unemployment and mental health. A meta-analysis is a mathematical summary of individual research projects, based on averages of statistics that assess the relationships between specific variables or the outcomes of experiments and treatment studies. (Think of a meta-analysis as a baseball batting average for aggregating research findings.) The meta-analysis conducted by Karsten Paul and Klaus Moser, two German psychologists, since its publication in 2009 has become a classic.[16] Paul and Moser conducted their extensive research prior to the onset of the Great Recession; however, their findings are striking and have been replicated in subsequent research reviews conducted during the height of the recent economic crisis.[17]

Integrating the findings from research studies conducted mostly in Western countries and a few Pacific Rim nations, Paul and Moser came to some essential conclusions about the relationship between unemployment and mental health. While mental health problems, on average, occur in approximately 16% of the general population, the integrated findings from these studies, which included over 500,000 participants in total, indicated that 34% of the unemployed participants were experiencing mental health problems (defined by the experience of distress, depression, anxiety, psychosomatic symptoms, subjective well-being problems, and self-esteem issues).

The fact that the meta-analysis included 86 longitudinal studies allowed Paul and Moser to assess the causal links between unemployment and mental health. By examining the actual impact of unemployment on people over time, it would be possible to finally counter the downward drift hypothesis, which had contributed to the persistent notion that the victims of job loss were responsible to a significant extent for their employment struggles (due to personal deficits or mental health problems). The longitudinal studies were clear and compelling: Losing one's job is predictive of mental health problems, and locating a new job is associated with improvements in psychological functioning.

Further analyses of this rich data set revealed that long-term unemployment has a greater negative impact on men and blue-collar workers. This particular finding makes sense both logically and intuitively. Men tend to attribute more status and identity to their work role, which makes them more vulnerable to experiencing psychological distress during a long period of unemployment.[18] Blue-collar workers seem to struggle more because of their very real concerns about the viability of their skill set in a changing labor market as well as challenges in accessing viable support systems. One of the most striking findings by Paul and Moser was their observation that the best way to regain one's mental health after a period of unemployment is to locate a new job.

The large-scale perspective offered by Paul and Moser has been replicated in more recent integrative reviews and has had a profound impact on our thinking about the impact of long-term unemployment.[19] In fact, Paul and Moser thoughtfully countered a quietly emerging position that some degree of unemployment can lead to periods of personal growth. Their findings did not support that view; in fact, empirical research actually suggests that long-term unemployment is one of the most stressful and painful experiences in life.[20]

Next, I transition from the world of statistics and research findings to the lived experiences of the Boston College Working Project participants. This exploration of people's complex and heartfelt experiences dealing with access to work offers a needed vista into the emotionally evocative world of the contemporary workplace.

Unemployment: Lived Experiences

Interviewing the participants who were out of work and those who described their unemployment experiences in their past was one of the most painful aspects of this project for me. I came away shaken and moved, as I recounted at the outset of this book. In the sections that follow, I present the basic themes that emerged in our analysis of these narratives, primarily focusing on how the participants experienced and constructed meaning about unemployment and underemployment.

Psychological Experience of Unemployment

One of the questions that we asked of all the participants was to share their experiences of unemployment, either currently or in their past. This question evoked responses from nearly everyone. To provide some coherence to the narratives that follow, I first present a few illustrative quotations that capture the emotional aspects of being unemployed following by a few stark vignettes describing how they transitioned from working steadily to being unemployed.

The Feel of Unemployment. The raw experience of being unemployed was conveyed by numerous participants, who captured very striking emotional states in their descriptions of not being able to find work. In the next passage,

Joyce, a 31-year-old African American woman, described her experience of work in light of her extensive period of unemployment:

> Work is portrayed as a place that is not really helping anyone anymore—it's not doing it. . . . I can't go to a job today, and don't know if I'm going to be there tomorrow. I don't have the assurance there. I don't have the way of figuring out whether my check is going to come again, or whether I'm getting an unemployment check. I don't know whether I'm going to have food on my table or if I'm looking for a next bed in a shelter. You know, it's not guaranteed, and this is where it hurts people the most.

The feeling of unemployment for Joyce was one of pervasive insecurity; she was relating to the pressure of not having financial resources to support the basic necessities of life. In the next passage, Mitchell, a 58-year-old unemployed man who had worked in various trades but yearned to focus on his passionate calling of being an artist, described the experience of unemployment as follows:

> I think unemployment brings a heightened sense of engagement because you have a lot at stake. . . . I think that you have a different mindset when you aren't working. You tend to see people on the street or I notice people, who are destitute on the street more than I would normally. How has being unemployed affected me? I just think that it's the same feeling no matter when you're out of work; it's a feeling of the unknown. And you don't know when the next job is going to come around and the anxiety level, my anxiety level goes up substantially when I am unemployed.

Mitchell's description conveys his overriding uncertainty and a sense of hypervigilance that attuned him to notice those who are similarly on the margins, such as homeless people. He also attested to the anxiety that does not diminish even when he was working. The experience of being unemployed seems to have fundamentally reconfigured his perceptions and emotional reactivity, underscoring the psychological consequences of being on the margins of the labor market in a society that so clearly values marketplace work. A close examination of Mitchell's entire transcript revealed that he had many episodes of unemployment and underemployment, which have culminated in an inescapable sense of precariousness.

While most of the participants focused on the anguish of being unemployed, a small number experienced it as a respite from the grind of working in an unsatisfying job. In the next passage, Scott, a 29-year-old White teacher, described a period of unemployment that provided a hiatus that facilitated his continued career development:

I was on unemployment [benefits], so it wasn't the end of the world and again I had family resources to fall back on in terms of the financial part, which I didn't need to use. But it wasn't devastating economically and it also kind of gave me a kick in the butt to go back to school and that was when I first looked into getting my master's because I started taking classes. So I was able to get a job as a project assistant and I was able to get my tuition covered and I got a stipend every month so I was able to survive; but yeah it was a lot easier than maybe it would have been for others because I was prepared for it.

A critical factor for Scott was a safety net that existed for him, as reflected in his access to unemployment benefits and then the secondary resource of a supportive family. The financial support allowed him to reconfigure the unemployment phase as an opportunity for continued training. Scott, like a modest number of other participants, had financial resources to fall back on, which allowed them to use the break from work as an opportunity for growth.

As in other areas of life, ambivalence and shifts in our emotional reactions often become prominent features in how people experience a life-changing event such as unemployment. Joshua, a 45-year-old unemployed human resources professional, conveyed the complexity of reactions in the following quotation describing a period of unemployment early in his life:

Honestly, I was not pro-actively looking for work. For me, in my mind, I took it as like just a little recouping time, to just relax. . . . I was living with my mom and dad, so financially I really didn't have anything to worry about; they were paying for everything. But towards the end of being on unemployment, I just felt like a failure. I felt like a very unproductive member of society. And I just kept telling myself I never want to feel like that again.

Interestingly, Joshua's transition into feeling despair toward the end of this episode of unemployment foreshadowed his life during our interview, wherein he shared the powerful psychological and financial toll that being without work evoked in his life and in the lives of his family. In fact, he described his current situation as characterized by anger, which he recounted as follows:

We're very good at understanding purposefully where we want to go and what we want to do, but just because you identify that, it doesn't mean it exists in the world, readily and available. So that's been a bit of a challenge for us currently. And I think I have a bit of an anger problem about it sometimes. I find I've been more angry over the last 6 months than I think

I've ever been in my life, and . . . I've definitely noticed that as perhaps an offshoot from some of the frustrations that I've felt about my work world.

The Emotional Devastation of Becoming Unemployed . A striking observation in reading the narratives about unemployment has been the sheer terror that some of the participants experienced as they moved from being gainfully employed to losing their jobs. Elizabeth, a 51-year-old woman who lost her job when her supermarket job went out of business and then went on to work at the grocery chain that purchased the supermarket, shared the following, which describes how ordinary events in one's work life are suffused with intense feelings of marginalization and pain:

> The people that were in Organic Groceries—the people that were assisting in the store—resented us because we were taking their hours. All of a sudden, they had the people from the old store working with them; I mean we walked back to their break room and everybody'd shut up because there's people from the old store sitting there and I'm like hey, how you doing? You know, I'd be trying to be friendly and so finally somebody got a lady from the meat department to come over and she said that was awful brave of you. And I said, what do you mean brave of me? I work here now, why wouldn't I try to be nice to you people? I'm trying to do my job here. And then the last day, like I walked in, like, the only thing that was nasty about it, is they could have called me the day after they made the decision that they were going to let me go. They let the whole week, weekend go by. I called on Sunday for my hours and so you're working 2–10 tomorrow . . . to walk in there on that day and to be let go. And I said, you know, you could've called me and said look, we decided we're not going to keep you, we'll send your stuff in the mail. I wasted 6 dollars to get there.

In my interview with Elizabeth, she recounted in emotionally evocative tones how hard her transition to being unemployed has been. She was homeless, without financial resources, and overwhelmed with anxiety and despair. The telling of her unemployment story felt like unearthing a trauma, one that was profoundly painful, yet integrated into her being. In the next vignette, Rich, the teacher who also was struggling with cancer, described the day he learned that he was going to be fired:

> Well I knew it was going to happen on such and such a day: December 11th, 2002. I go into work that day, and I'm fearing that all these people I like will be fired. . . . At no point did I really think that I was going to be one of them. And what happened was, they brought in the

police—There were three police cars outside the building. . . . They [our managers] went around the building; your manager would come to your desk area, and say: So-and-so wants to see you . . . and they just did it in order. They didn't do it all at once; they just did it in order. And he did it with one of my friends, who I knew was on the list, and then he did the other guy, who I also knew was on the list. . . . It took maybe 5 minutes, and they come back, they give you a box: pack up your stuff, disable your computer, and show you out the door. And he's doing these desks that surround me. And next thing I knew, there he was at my desk, and I couldn't believe it. . . . When I saw him standing there I knew that I was next. And I guess I was in kind of a state of shock. You know, you get handed a little severance money. You get told your medical plan is good for the next 2 weeks. . . . You get a box, and the next thing you know you're out the door. And I had this huge house, my parents were aging, and . . . I get the box, and. . . . You know? I'm gone. I mean, I would have to say . . . without exception, it was the saddest, most depressing time of my life. Because I had this gigantic house, I had a family, I had a wife, I had two kids. . . . My oldest daughter was graduating high school that year. . . . And I've got to come home a tell them I'm . . . not working.

Rich's very striking description brings to mind the classic poem by Martin Niemöller, the German pastor who described the rapidly moving destruction of various groups during the Holocaust, which culminated in the final stanza wherein the author wrote, "Then they came for me—and there was no one left to speak for me."[21]

Rich continued to describe the impact that this had on his family and his life during the subsequent years:

I can honestly say that it was the most difficult time of my life. It was even more difficult than being diagnosed with cancer, because it affected so many people. It affected my wife. It affected my kids—an immediate effect on them. And it affected my parents. So, all of them were going to be affected by my loss of this job. And all of them were going to be requiring lifestyle changes.

A number of additional participants also spoke about the day of the firing or layoff in equally vivid and painful ways, describing a sense of a complete loss of security and psychological stability. Other participants depicted the process of becoming unemployed as a more subtle shift to a world where marketplace work became very elusive. Some of these participants struggled in the transition from high school to work or drifted into unemployment and underemployment in a more gradual manner, yet still producing very painful consequences.

An Inside Look at the Job Search

A common experience among the unemployed is the search for a job, which can be a very complex and emotionally challenging experience. Here again, our interviews offer important insights into a process that is often discussed in the popular media from the perspective of relatively privileged workers looking for their next new exciting venture.[22] The job search for the long-term unemployed is a very different process, one that is often described as entering a black hole. A particularly vivid illustration of the black hole is the experience of sending off applications and résumés and not hearing back, as if the submitted materials disappear into space. In the first passage, Lana, an unemployed 35-year-old college-educated White woman, described her job search process:

> My current situation is mostly making me look more for a job that will just pay me and sustain me to make sure I can live a decent life outside of work rather than me looking for a job that I feel is going to be something I want to do for the rest of my life. For the most part, my biggest issue is . . . just being out of the workforce for so long. Never when I was in the workforce did I really get a great feel for how well I was doing the job, so I don't really know where I stand, where my abilities are compared to others, where I will be able to perform at a high level. I believe I will basically be somewhere in the middle—good enough, but not great.

Lana's discussion of how she was looking for a survival job as opposed to something that would give her a sense of self-determination and meaningfulness was a common theme among many of the unemployed participants. Moreover, her lack of confidence was noteworthy and, again, reflected a theme that a number of other participants shared.

In the next passage, Stephen, a 51-year-old unemployed man, described his job search in his field of book publishing, which had been fruitless for over 2 years prior to the time of the interview:

> I am just trying to motivate myself to do anything. I have worked in book publishing and there is a lot of book publishing in Boston. And for 2 years, I've been applying to them [publishers] and I'm just reaching the point where, even though it's a new year and companies are hiring again, it's hard to motivate myself to apply for the same jobs that I didn't get

last year or the year before. I tried to look outside of publishing, but it's a buyer's market and people don't want to hire. They have a good pool to select from. And so, because I don't have enough of whatever experience in their industry, I don't get considered. The feedback I got was well he's a book publisher guy; we don't want to hire him so. It's hard to get the experience on my résumé; plus, I've got a big 2-year job gap. I really don't know what to do. I've got an interview tomorrow to work at the post office. So hopefully I won't break down like I did now and maybe I'll get some money there. I've used all the unemployment (insurance) that I'm entitled to.

Other participants shared equally grim narratives about their job search experiences. What seemed most compelling in the two quotations in this section and in other passages was the overwhelming sense of pessimism, particularly for people who had been out of the workforce for some time and for middle-aged and older workers. Younger job seekers were also struggling considerably, often without marketable skills, which exacerbated feelings of hopelessness.

Although the vast majority of the participants were out of work due to layoffs and lack of options, a few described the job search process from the vantage point of moving from one position to another, capturing the common narrative in the popular job search media of people seeking their next career challenge. In the next passage, David, the public administration worker who shifted his work life to follow his dream of being a massage therapist, described his one experience of being unemployed, which fits the notion of unemployment as a necessary gap between jobs that reflects a self-determined career path:

The only time I was unemployed was by choice. When I left Albany to come to D.C., I did not have a job. My intention was that I had just finished my political science degree and my intention was to get a job here in political science. As I had done my homework beforehand, I realize that these jobs pay a dime in this city. If you only have your bachelor's degree, you certainly aren't going very far. So, I got down here and started looking around in the political science sphere I was interested in and saw how little I was going to make that I realized, "Oh, that's not what I want to do." So it took me a while to find that job only because I had multiple offers, but there was nothing on the salary level that I wanted to accept. So it was 7 months before I got a job. I can't say I was too nervous except near the end because I said to myself that I had to have a job because I was going too far to not do something. I was burning through my savings, but I had saved up to do it, which is why I was comfortable with doing it. I was in a good position. I allowed myself longer to get that new job than I had intended.

David's experience exemplifies a different side of the unemployment world, one that reflects the natural movement that people engage in as they navigate their work lives. The difference in David's story in contrast to many of our other participants was that his comments did not reflect much anxiety and terror. These distinctive experiences represent two poles along a continuum, with working for survival at one end and seeking a self-determined and meaningful work life at the other end. Many of the participants described unemployment experiences that were located along this continuum. However, the prevalence of narratives that described the anguish and despair of unemployment was the most striking aspect of the full array of job search narratives.

Public Policy Impressions About Unemployment

Because the unemployment crisis has primarily been examined from the perspective of economists and policymakers, I felt that it was important to ask the participants about their thoughts on how society should manage the challenge of providing decent and stable work to all. Their responses varied extensively, covering solutions from both the political right and left. Their ideas also had the authentic touch of individuals who have lived through a horrific experience, one that affected many to the core of their being.

In the first passage, Dick, the 55-year-old artist and instructional aide, provides an illuminating perspective on how society should manage access to stable and decent work:

> Because both my parents worked in government, I saw the positive relationship it [i.e., the government] has, and that we need to start focusing on the bottom-up instead of the top-down. I think the top-down approach has been very destructive. . . . Having a philosophy that says one need to take more of what you don't have so that I can give more to you later is a false identity. I think we need to move towards loving our planet; we have to move towards loving all life on the planet; and we need to see everything on the planet as having importance. But as far as the crises that are facing the United States right now, I think intolerance is one of them, and I think that the solution is to give everybody a chance. Stop blaming people, stop blaming immigrants, stop blaming people who have to struggle to make a living, and stop blaming the victims, stop blaming people who don't have enough money to put food on the table, or don't have enough money for a

place to live, or education. So we need to go back to looking at, as much as possible, on the state level, like California providing education all the way through college. And I would start funding the schools and move towards a green economy. That would provide a lot of jobs. And the last thing I would say is any company, big company that does not provide health-care and does not provide for the payment of pensions—helping their employees get a lifelong pension so that they can retire—the tax structure should be in favor of those companies that do do that, and the ones that don't should be penalized because they are putting a strain on the system. . . . So I would be for more regulation, not less for protection for workers. That's it.

Dick's passionate appeal for more systemic and activist policies to protect workers certainly resonated with many of the participants. However, an alternative view was advanced by Jack, a president and chief operating officer of a software company, who offered the following recommendations:

We need to get the economy growing, which is really the fundamental thing. I don't think that the government can just create a whole lot of jobs. The government has to create an environment that leads to a little bit faster growth. The other aspect of it is education, because there are a lot of jobs out there that people just can't fit into. I mean there are plenty of software engineer jobs out there, a lot of them, and, we just don't have enough software engineers coming out of colleges in the U.S. So that's another aspect of it, is investing in programs that line up more with where the demand is for people.

Jack brought up an essential issue in the unemployment debate that relates to the question of how individuals can balance the marketplace and their career dreams in selecting career paths. The traditional view within the career development field has been to help people find their dreams and then provide them with the tools to map out their pathway so that they can make their dreams come alive. Within recent years, the view that Jack articulated has been debated by counselors and by people who are now faced with a rapidly changing labor market that does not consistently provide access to a broad array of jobs.

In the next passage, Mark, the educator turned successful entrepreneur, provided his advice for people trying to establish themselves in a more constricted labor market:

The point is that people are going to have to get comfortable with the fact that they're going to have to be more entrepreneurial—that the age of being a wage earner is slipping away, unless they want to be flipping hamburgers somewhere. They're going to have to reinvent themselves. They're going to have to be more in touch with their skills. They're also going to have to develop their skills and create niches for themselves. There's an expression that I believe in: there are riches in niches. If more people develop niches where they truly have little competition, they will thrive in the future. If they have generic skills that everybody has, they're going to find it a very tough go in the future.

One of the participants of the Boston College Working Project was Steve, a White 65-year old member of Congress who was in his last term of government service. His comments about the broader impressions of the challenges of unemployment certainly represent his policy-based focus, but also reflect his own life growing up in a rural part of his state that was not very wealthy or privileged. In the following passage, Steve shared the following recommendations about unemployment:

From my perspective, in the 60s and 70s, we walked away from teaching kids how to be plumbers and machine operators. We essentially gave them the message that this was lower-level work and that one should go college, when in fact that is an equally important part of the economy. And people need to be given the emotional freedom to pursue that because you can be very successful and very happy doing that. And we need it in the economy. I think that the American dream is much more difficult today that it was 60 years ago and 30 years ago. I think that it has become more difficult. I still think that it is achievable, but clearly we need to again allow people to see different pathways to that success, and also not to be quite as judgmental about what success is. Some of the most intelligent and interesting people I know are plumbers, and electricians, and laborers. And if they are happy, if they found contentment with their work and with the level of economic prosperity they have attained, then that is okay.

In the final passage in this section, we once again return to Stephen, who shared his thoughts about the job search process previously in this chapter. Here, he shares his thoughts about the impact of unemployment from a more global perspective:

I mean all this fighting over benefits and minimum wages and tax breaks. . . . . It's definitely class warfare that's going on now. I don't think people want to accept it, but it's greed. . . . I mean, I just assumed so long as I was working I would be rewarded for it. I'd always have a job and have a little salary and just like they used to do in the old days, which is not that long ago. I really don't want to raise a family on this planet because I just I don't think things are going to get any easier or better. And I wouldn't want my kids to suffer like I have. I feel like I'm suffering now. I failed to see what the work environment was going to become.

Stephen moved from the political to the personal and back in his very powerful comments about the impact that unemployment had been having on his inner experience and his impressions about the state of our nation. In effect, his passion, anger, and frustration spoke volumes and resonated powerfully with the voices of so many other participants who were eager to talk about the experience of unemployment and underemployment.

In putting this section together, I felt a bit like I was facilitating a grief group, with much anguish, anxiety, and despair evident in the extensive comments shared in the diverse vignettes. While the participants offered a wide range of ideas and reactions to their experience of the problems within the world of work, they all shared a sense that their stories needed to be told. In the next section, I return again to the psychological perspective, reviewing some important new insights that provide further illumination into the complex reactions that were gleaned in the interviews.

Being Without Work: A Psychological View

As in other social sciences, tension exists between qualitative and quantitative researchers, with each advocating the importance of their approach to a given set of problems. My position in this book and throughout my career has been to value both methods and to use both in generating inferences and ideas for people and communities. In the world of unemployment, quantitative research certainly has a major role in understanding the prevalence and impact of being without work. However, the essence of this chapter is to highlight the power of qualitative analyses (including narratives as well as direct observations) to develop deeper insights into the nature and impact of long-term unemployment. In the first part of this section, I provide a deeper dive into the brilliant book by Ofer Sharone, *Flawed System/Flawed Self: Job Searching and Unemployment Experiences* (discussed previously in this chapter), which offers very important insights about the "social games" that unemployed people are forced to play. I follow this summary with a psychologically informed analysis of the narratives that we have obtained in the Boston College Working Project, offering some new perspectives that I argue need to be considered as we move forward in thinking about the nature of work during this era.

Blaming the Self/Blaming the System

A striking observation about long-term unemployed in the United States is that people tend to blame themselves for their difficulty in obtaining work, often leading to mental health problems, which was noted previously, and, at times, to a gradual disengagement from the job search process. In Sharone's book, he examined this phenomenon and compared it to the situation in Israel, which also has had major problems with long-term unemployment, including among college-educated individuals. Sharone embarked on a very comprehensive study of long-term unemployment, conducting two interviews each with 162 unemployed Americans and Israelis. Most of the participants were white-collar workers; however, Sharone added a sample of American blue-collar workers from the same region as the white-collar workers to explore potential class distinctions. The conclusions that Sharone identified were striking: Whereas American unemployed workers tended to blame themselves for the difficulty in obtaining work, Israelis were more likely to blame the system. What is particularly compelling about this finding is that the differences between the U.S. and Israel cultures and economies, while clearly notable, were not overly dramatic. Both samples were drawn from college-educated workers from Tel Aviv, San Francisco, and Boston, where the technology industries were the driving force in their respective economies. A deeper analysis of these findings provided a more fine-tuned picture of the process of managing long-term unemployment.

Sharone's study is noteworthy for a number of reasons, including the very extensive sample and his use of a very rich theoretical perspective, which provided him with the intellectual tools to understand the depth of the participants' comments. Another advantage of this wonderfully insightful body of work is Sharone's extensive life experience in both the United States and Israel, which gave him the capacity to appreciate the cultural messages that people received about work, personal responsibility, and success. The conceptual framework that Sharone adopted was intriguing; using innovative ideas from sociology, he argued that the process of negotiating with the labor market was a sort of social game.[23] Sharone explored these new sociological theories because he felt that the perspectives offered by Marie Jahoda and other psychologists (regarding the loss of a sense of grounding that work provides) did not fully capture the subtleties of the differences that he noted in Israel and the United States among the long-term unemployed.

In Sharone's work, he proposed that fairly elaborate social expectations are conveyed to job seekers; these expectations were based on institutional practices as well as cultural norms. In the case of the labor market, Sharone observed that the American labor market conveyed the message that they should make a case that their personalities as well as background were a great fit with the organization that was hiring; in effect, the job seekers in the United States were selling themselves—their values and, indeed, their essence as human beings. In contrast, Israeli job seekers were used to a labor market that used specific skills and training to make hiring decisions, which is often a function of staffing agencies. Through a complex set of shifts in the Israeli economy over the past few decades, staffing agencies had become the modal human resources function for most employers. In contrast to interviewing with a hiring manager at an American firm, Israeli candidates were evaluated by a less experienced staffing employee, who looked for specific skills that an employer might be interested in. As a result, Israeli job candidates did not view themselves as having to market their personalities and their unique life histories to employers; rather, they were simply presenting their credentials.

The overarching story of Sharone's book was that the American job search system was based on chemistry (between the employer and the employee—like a first date), while the Israeli job search process was more like a match based on the specific needs of an employer and the skills of a potential employee (which Sharone called "specs"). The implications of this distinct social game are profound and were obvious to Sharone in his interviews and in his observations of job support groups in each country.

Because American job seekers were putting themselves on the line in their job search, they were prone to becoming discouraged as they experienced rejection and a sense of invisibility in the highly competitive and often-brutal game of getting a job, especially after a long period of unemployment. The Israeli job seekers were less likely to blame themselves but were prone to hold the system responsible. The ways in which the Israeli job seekers made sense of the failure of the system to provide them with work was often based on their sense that the Israeli system had adopted neoliberal economic policies from the West without considering the impact on individuals. Others felt that they had given the country so much in terms of military service and an abiding sense of patriotism, which left them feeling that the state did not care about them as individuals. Still others held staffing agencies and employers responsible for their arbitrary decisions. One of the implications of these different ways of constructing meaning about unemployment was that the Israeli job seekers tended not to become as discouraged and depressed as their American counterparts. Moreover, they were less likely to disengage from the job search process, which allowed them to continue looking for work, often with positive results.

The unemployment experiences of the blue-collar workers in the United States actually were more like the Israeli white-collar workers, which was quite a surprising observation. Sharone found that American blue-collar workers enacted what he called the "diligence game," which emphasized a strong work ethic and personal responsibility. These attributes essentially paralleled the notion of specs that characterized the Israeli job search. Interestingly, the blue-collar workers were not as prone to blame themselves because they did not envision that they had tried to sell themselves as people in making the case for their prospective employers.

When considering Sharone's study from a broader perspective, the impact of social forces, social class, and culture were all at play in determining how people managed the life-changing circumstances of long-term unemployment. A core takeaway from this study is that understanding individual reactions to long-term unemployment cannot be separated from the context in which one lives. Moreover, the ways in which social and cultural norms are conveyed, as reflected in the games that job seekers and hiring managers play, is highly sophisticated, requiring careful thought, reflection, and the wisdom of the social sciences. The insightful findings of Sharone's work inform the deeper perspective on the Boston College Working Project narratives, discussed next.

The Psychological Consequences of Unemployment: A Closer Look

Moving from the broader social context to the psychological or inner experience of unemployment, the narratives that were culled from the Boston College Working Project, when considered collectively, offered important insights about the nature of the process of being without work, representing new and important findings. While scholars have noted that mental health problems are more likely to emerge as a result of unemployment, a number of the participants in our interviews revealed a more disturbing set of experiences. A key observation in the narratives was the deep sense of psychological disruption that people felt as they moved from being employed to unemployed. In addition to Rich and Elizabeth, previously mentioned in this chapter, other participants recounted the days when they lost their jobs as events that shaped them in painful ways; indeed, for many of these individuals, the job loss experience was profoundly traumatic. Moreover, other studies that have relied on in-depth interviews with unemployed people also described the process in a similar fashion.[24]

What emerged in many of the narratives was a feeling of abject terror in learning that one would be without work. This was most pronounced in those individuals who were told that they were losing their jobs in a dispassionate and bureaucratic manner, as was the case with both Rich and Elizabeth (and a number of others in the sample). One of the prominent images that occurred to my research team and me was the sense that the bottom was falling out of the lives of the people who were losing their jobs. The image was one in which the job was creating a source of support, structure, and stability, all of which became instantly inaccessible in a decision made by people who, for the most part, did not care at all about the employees that they were firing.

Another important trend in our interviews was the experience of being in a black hole, particularly in long-term unemployment. As I noted previously, some of the long-term unemployed have described sending their résumés into what felt like a black hole, which seemingly evaporated their application materials. Closer examinations of the narratives, taken together, revealed that the participants themselves reported that they felt invisible, almost as if they disappeared. The outlines of this experience were in fact discernible from the quantitative research findings that were reported in the first part of this chapter; however, the vast darkness of the psychological and social lives of the long-term unemployed was palpable throughout their interviews. Many of the long-term unemployed participants felt invisible and sought to avoid social contact so that they would not have to disclose their status. Consistent with the insightful study by Sharone, some of the participants in our interviews were masters at blaming themselves for their struggles, recounting, in often very harsh terms, how they could have handled things better.

In a sense, the findings from the interviews seemed to provide needed depth about the psychological consequences of unemployment, especially long-term unemployment. Yet, something felt different about the depth of despair that was recounted in the narratives. The changes in the external occupational land-scape, as reflected in the growth of long-term unemployment and the parallel increase in precarious work (i.e., short-term, unstable contract jobs), seem to have created a parallel change in the internal landscape of how people are relating to work and to not working. Once people lose their jobs or search for new work unsuccessfully, they become submerged in a world that offers no mercy. Being without work for many of the participants was like being without access to the core necessities of life, akin to a feeling of walking in a dessert without water or food.

Two interrelated elements seemed to be contributing to the experience of being without resources and support. One of these factors is best described by the survival needs that I have outlined as a core need that working can fulfill. And, indeed for many of the participants, the loss of work often meant that they lost access to food, shelter, and other fundamental resources. A second factor was the self-determination needs also presented previously, which refer to the aspiration of having work be a meaningful and purposeful experience. For those who had their survival needs met (via financial support from loved ones or other resources), the desire to do something important and useful in their lives was essential, and the loss of that option felt devastating for many.

In sum, the narratives that we obtained about unemployment and under-employment represent a new and stark set of findings about the psychological consequences of being without work. While the qualitative research that we conducted builds on the seminal work of Jahoda and the remarkable meta-analysis by Paul and Moser, the overarching conclusion of the interviews that we analyzed raised the stakes of these findings markedly. The major theme in these personal narratives is more about the emotional tone than the actual content. People were in considerable psychological pain about their lack of access to decent and stable work, an experience that was profound and expressed with considerable intensity and thoughtfulness. The vast majority of the participants spoke about unemployment as one of the most traumatic events in their lives, one that had a long reach into their families and their future.

Conclusion

This chapter started off by describing the touching stories that were told in the boot camp for long-term unemployed adults, followed by an equally evocative discussion of the devastating impact of unemployment in Marienthal, Austria, the town that was put on the map in Marie Jahoda's insightful analysis of unemployment during the Great Depression. So, what has changed during these many decades of unemployment research? Certainly, our nation is not facing anything like the Depression, with soup lines dotting our cities and mass migration from dust bowl rural areas to the West Coast. However, I believe that the very moving stories that were shared by the Boston College Working Project participants as well as the compelling research findings that I have reviewed have foreshadowed the psychological landscape of a growing proportion of Americans.

As I summarized in the first chapter, technology and automation are game changers in the world of work. And, although there is considerable debate about the overall impact of these changes on employment, it does seem clear that some considerable degree of marketplace disruption will become the norm for many adults in America. What may emerge are two different trajectories of unemployment that may have distinct psychological features. Long-term unemployment will likely continue as it has during the past decade, casting aside people who want and need to work in the marketplace. The consequences of this experience are clear, although not necessarily predetermined for all those who must go through long periods of unemployment. Increasing risk for mental health problems, disengagement, and, for some, a sense of the bottom falling out will be ever more present as the labor market makes harsh choices about who is in and who is out of the marketplace at any given point in time.

A second group, known as precarious workers, also is likely to expand as short-term work contracts become more popular.[25] For those whose lot in life is to transition in and out of the marketplace work depending on the whims of the economy, equally compelling psychological challenges are likely. As reflected in considerable research, precarious workers are also more likely to experience mental health problems and other social and physical problems, much like their long-term unemployed peers.[26] The growth of precarious work may result in creating islands of work and nonwork experience, which will involve far more psychological stress as people navigate seemingly endless transitions and losses.

Perhaps one of the primordial fears in our individual and collective psyches is the fear of annihilation and starvation.[27] Indeed, this theme was prominently represented in some of the interviews conducted for this book, particularly for those participants who were struggling with unemployment, underemployment, and homelessness. This highly internalized fear is not an irrational belief, to quote a common cognitive therapy reframe intervention. As we have seen, some of the participants were indeed on the verge of collapse, both financially and psychologically. In some nations, not being able to find work, while stressful, does not necessarily evoke intense anxiety because of accessible safety nets (e.g., long-term unemployment benefits; coverage for food costs and housing).[28] Indeed, at various points during the Great Recession, the U.S. government was able to provide extensive unemployment benefits, at times encompassing 99 weeks; however, the work culture in the United States remains one where the safety net is limited, an issue that reflects a hotly contested aspect of the political landscape.

The problems of unemployment and precarious work are really central to this entire book. In fact, each of the chapters of this book attests to the extensive functions that work optimally can provide and that are central to being alive. However, as we enter a period where many will face a jobless future or one where joblessness will be a recurring part of their lives, we may need to revisit this idea. As discussed further in Chapter 9, a viable option for a jobless life may be the guaranteed basic income. While financial support will clearly help to ward off the intense fear of annihilation, it may not suffice to provide access to meaning and purpose, which also emerged as important aspects of this chapter and other chapters in this book. In the closing chapter of this book, I revisit the notion of a jobless future and integrate observations culled from the qualitative analyses of the narratives by the Boston College Working Project participants and the insights from my colleagues around the world who have studied unemployment throughout their own careers. However, some central themes from this chapter reveal important implications for systemic changes that function as an apt closing for this chapter.

My work here and the work of others reveals that we need to provide a clear and strong safety net for people that includes financial resources, emotional support, and a clear message that functions to reframe the experience so that it is not characterized by self-blame. Indeed, the self-blame theme that was evident in Sharone's work was replicated here and is integral to the causal connection between unemployment and mental health problems. In addition, we need to provide thoughtful opportunities for people during periods of unemployment that include retraining, enhancing supports for caregiving, which does not stop in the face of marketplace unemployment, and meaningful projects.

In closing, this chapter has provided an in-depth view of the pain and anguish of unemployment. The solutions to this problem clearly involve public policy, economics, and other social sciences; however, the empathic connection that we achieved in reading these narratives and examining some of the prominent research findings underscores that people who are struggling in their work lives need to be an integral part of the solutions. I have felt humbled in my interviews of these brave people, and I hope that their voices are heard clearly as our society seeks solutions to the precariousness and pain that define the lives of so many who are simply seeking their place in the world of work.

9

Being Able to Work With Dignity and Opportunity

I begin this final chapter in a lovely hotel room in Turin, Italy, after completing a 2-day workshop sponsored by the Future of Work initiative of the International Labor Organization (ILO). The meeting included 31 experts on work and society from across the globe; the charge was to develop informed solutions in response to the radical changes in the labor market. As the lone psychologist at the meeting (which was primarily attended by economists and leaders from labor, the private sector, and various government and nonprofit agencies), I was struck by some of the same impressions that I have been considering throughout this book project.

Many people at work and who are seeking work are struggling and in pain across the globe—the image of the upwardly mobile professional that occupies so many conversations about work in the public forum and media is clearly not the norm in most locations in the world (and, indeed, in many sectors of the United States).[1] The helicopter view of many of the economists at this meeting was important and, in many ways, quite alarming, touching on the growth of precarious work and the palpable anxiety about the impact of automation on the availability and quality of jobs currently and in the future. However, missing from the dialogue and debates at this workshop were the voices from people on the ground. This book, and the collective efforts of my many colleagues in psychology and related fields (as well as the brave souls who share their life stories via memoirs, art, music, poetry, theatre, and other forms of personal expression), has given voice to the diverse inner experiences of work. As I have argued throughout this book, we cannot move forward as a society toward a just and dignified approach to working unless we include those who are most affected: those who work and who are seeking work, particularly those who have been squeezed out of the American dream.

In my comments about this book project at the ILO meeting, I highlighted some of the same thoughts that I hope to clarify and deepen in this final chapter. Work is indeed central to our sense of aliveness in the world. The participants at this ILO meeting each conveyed compassion for people and concern about how we, as a society, will fare with growing instability in the workplace. Indeed, the overriding sense that I have taken away from writing this book was shared by the labor leaders, policy analysts, and economists from various sectors of the world at this ILO meeting. The experience of working across the globe is very diverse. The contrasts that my research team and I witnessed in the interviews obtained for this project captures the essence of a major conclusion of this book. We are living in a world where, for some, work is a source of pride, accomplishment, connection, and creativity. For many others, regrettably, work is a source of enduring anguish and anxiety, particularly given the sad reality that there does not seem to be enough decent work within the United States, and across the globe, for all of those who need to work to sustain themselves.

In this concluding chapter, I flesh out my firsthand experience of living with the moving stories from the Boston College Working Project participants in the context of the scholarly and policy literature as well as my own immersion in this field for over three decades. When considering the full scope of the narratives in light of the changes that the participants so clearly articulated at this ILO meeting, the conclusions about the state of work in America are clearly complex, but do cohere into some meaningful themes and implications for individuals and society.[2] In this chapter, I provide a road map of these ideas, with the goal of infusing an empathic, psychological perspective into current debates about how to support efforts toward fair and dignified means of earning a living and finding meaning in the world.

Emerging Themes

Throughout this book, we have moved back and forth from individual psychological experiences to the broader social and economic world, often seamlessly, which is often how our lives organically take shape. In this section, I consider themes that emerged from an individual perspective at the outset, followed by a more macro-level analysis. As we shall see, the division is arbitrary but provides a means of linking some of the more important and unique observations culled in this project.

Psychological Experiences of Working

Much of the impetus for this book was to put the individual in the foreground of our considerations of the impact of work in an age of such uncertainty and anxiety. The cohering links among these chapters clearly affirm some fundamental conclusions that, while obvious to many academics and working people, merit our attention and can connect us to other, more subtle, points. Working is a fundamentally psychological act.[3] The psychological aspects of working are evident throughout this book. Of course, working is a social and economic act as well, but the actual process of initiating, sustaining, and making meaning from working is deeply personal and unique for each of us.[4] Collapsing people's reactions to their experience of working by quantifying their employment status, satisfaction at work, and their diverse attitudes about work, while clearly necessary, is limited. The participants in this book and my very honest and engaged therapy clients tell this part of the story clearly and with conviction. Working matters to each of us and provides a profoundly important context for our well-being.

Working is also fundamentally a relational act, as my colleague Hanoch Flum, a gifted Israeli psychologist, has proposed.[5] The narratives that were shared in this project have underscored that work serves as a means of connecting to others and to the broader social good. In addition, working provides a means of informing our engagement in the social and economic world with roles, responsibilities, and relationships, generating a core sense of our identities.[6] In effect, our work role furnishes a link to the ground that nourishes us—as a source of sustenance, people, and projects. In my view, the way that people described their work often paralleled how they conveyed their most intimate relationships. When work let people down, either via unemployment or feeling marginalized or hurt, the impact was often like that of a rupture of a romantic relationship. In addition, people have the potential to feel deeply connected to their projects and tasks, which we observed in some of the narratives that have been included in previous chapters. However, the stark reality is that many people do not have an opportunity to engage in work that is meaningful and compelling; indeed, significant numbers of people in the United States (and indeed, globally) cannot even locate work to sustain themselves and their families.[7]

Another important current running through the narratives was the complex ways that marketplace work and care work function in our lives. While the overt content of comments about care work was seemingly quite disparate, a number of themes were identified in Chapter 6. Care work is often outsourced by more privileged working people who can afford to hire others to care for their children and other family members.[8] Yet, my impression is that the marginalization of care work in our society has made it hard for those who feel called to care for others to fully inhabit this integral part of life.

Sustainable Livelihoods and Working

One of the most common refrains that I have heard both in these interviews and in conversations with therapy clients is that they are struggling to survive;

many people actually use this phrase, which underscores a central truth about work, both historically and currently. What emerged in the interviews with the participants, which is also evident in the academic literature as well as in many literary and artistic contributions, is that work functions as a means of survival for most people.[9] Indeed, one of the important attributes of work is its relationship to our need for a sustainable life: the capacity to earn money to pay for the necessities in life. While this connection is part of our evolutionary heritage, it is not clear that it needs to be carried forward exclusively within the marketplace because many jobs, particularly within less skilled occupations, are potentially replaceable by technology.[10]

Before I venture into this quagmire of a debate, I first want to reflect on the psychological experience of struggling for survival. In short, not having access to work and not having the resources needed to survive is a painful psychological as well as economic burden for people. As we have seen in the previous chapters, some of the participants felt forced to do almost anything to have a roof over their heads and a source of nutrition. It is hoped the inner experience of this struggle was palpable for readers; by exposing ourselves to these powerful stories, I believe that we have been transformed in our understanding of the gravity of this problem.

An aspect of struggling for survival certainly has played a role in helping us, as human beings, in being challenged and enhancing our capacity to learn, connect, and solve problems. However, as growing inequality becomes entrenched within the United States, and indeed, in many parts of the world, one needs to question the moral purpose of not providing for people who need to survive. Those who are not able to obtain work that can pay their bills (including the largest number of the poor people in the United States: the working poor) have created an enormous challenge for us all. Their stories and their experiences are part of the fabric of American society, yet we have continued to link sustainable livelihoods to work, which is often very elusive, particularly for those without marketable skills or other barriers (such as marginalized identities, disabling conditions, or prior prison record). As discussed further in this chapter, the question of maintaining the connection between work and sustainability is being seriously debated and may become a major hot button issue in years to come.

The Broad Landscape of Contemporary Work

In contrast to the popular narrative of the intentional, upwardly mobile career that reflects one's values and interests, the reality of work lives in the United States is far more complex and not very linear for most people. While some

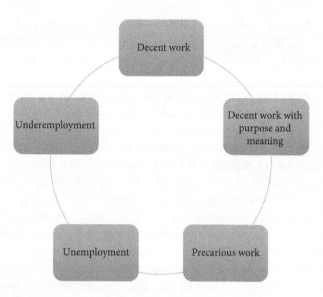

Figure 9.1 Contemporary work contexts.

of the participants in the Boston College Working Project certainly were able to develop purposeful and meaningful work lives, the hard reality of work is that people are exposed to very diverse opportunities and experiences. As reflected in Figure 9.1, the landscape of work for many includes some periods of unemployment, underemployment, precarious work, decent work that is not necessarily meaningful, and decent work that provides a sense of purpose and meaning. For some, the movement from less stable working contexts to more stable decent working conditions is linear, while for others, the movement is far less predictable.[11] As reflected in some of the passages and in research on precarious work, the labor market is increasingly not offering people the sort of stability and upward mobility that has been so prized in many Western cultures.[12]

The impact of this highly unstable work context for people is a notable elevation in anxiety and stress. The search for a stable environment that reduces our risk has been a driving force in human evolution, one that has inspired human beings to settle most of the planet's inhabitable regions.[13] In a similar vein, people have sought security in their work lives, hoping that they can find some meaning and value in their efforts to create a firm foundation for their lives. The growth of precariousness, in particular, which is reflected in short-term work, gig economy jobs, and temporary work assignments, underscores that people are faced with a sense that the world of work feels like standing on quicksand.[14]

One of the more problematic consequences of the growth of unstable work options is that people may not have an opportunity to find joy and a sense of accomplishment in their work. A sizable minority of the Boston College Working Project participants described their enthusiasm for their career lives and work-related projects; indeed, an integral aspect of the work lives for some people is the opportunity to engage in intrinsically interesting activities that promote self-determination and contributions to the broader social good. When people are consumed with the need to work for survival, their capacity to experience flow or, perhaps, a less lofty goal of being able to engage in meaningful projects and tasks is compromised. For some, however, significant life projects may not be connected to marketplace work; some people find considerable meaning in caregiving, hobbies, leisure activities, relationships, and other life roles. However, one's capacity to engage in projects that are highly compelling or interesting outside the marketplace is frequently a function of privilege. Individuals who have adequate financial resources are often able to carve out wonderful life projects that are disconnected from their marketplace work needs.[15] As reflected throughout this book, the very essence of working is multifaceted, with some individuals experiencing sheer delight in meeting the challenges of marketplace work, while many others experience work as their sole means of survival and not much more.

Social and Psychological Erosion of the Workplace

Another very powerful and disconcerting trend in the narratives and in the psychological literature is the reality of the growing social and psychological erosion within the workplace, which has been evident throughout this book. (When I refer to the workplace, I am also considering the struggle to enter the labor market: the daunting process of searching for work.) In many of the narratives, we learned about very damaging experiences directly related to work, including being exposed to long-term unemployment, interpersonal abuse, sexual harassment, racism, marginalization, and unsafe working conditions. The participants eloquently described this growing sharp edge in their lives, which was manifested in so many insidious ways. From a psychological perspective, I have witnessed in my therapy clients as well as research participants over the past decade or so the devastating impact of an erosion of decency in many aspects of the workplace. As indicated in previous chapters, some of the participants described situations that evoked trauma for them, such as living in shelters because of long-term unemployment and being abused by those with more power in the workplace. The deteriorating nature of the workplace is also evident in many social scientific studies on work, which have

documented the association between harsh working conditions and various indices of well-being and ill-being.[16]

The consequences of this erosion of social support and economic sustenance
are profound. Although some readers will no doubt counter this observation
by arguing that the workplace never really promised us security or kindness,
the picture that emerged in the narratives surprised my research team and me.
Some of the participants described horrific experiences that were magnified because of lack of support both at work and in their lives more broadly. Relational
support can certainly help to reduce the impact of the erosion of the workplace; however, the convergence of the narratives from this project, research
data from many recent studies about working, and reports from major policy
institutions points to a more troubling state of affairs. Many of our workplaces
and, indeed, the systems in place that ostensibly support people in preparing for
work are losing their capacity to nourish people.[17] The result is that people are
suffering and are struggling to find a way of holding themselves up in the face
of headwinds of change and uncertainty. As I discuss further in the chapter, this
state of affairs requires a radical reconsideration of the way in which we construct working in our society.

Assessing Causality in the Workplace Crises

The complex pull of individual initiative and external barriers and resources has
been and continues to be a highly contentious debate in psychology and many
other scholarly and policy-based considerations of work. In the political debates
of our time, some leaders and policy experts argue that individuals can use their
inner resources to pull themselves up by their bootstraps. Psychologists like myself often work with clients who have internalized this narrative, which, as Ofer
Sharone, the talented occupational sociologist noted in Chapter 8, can become
the prevailing way that people explain their struggles at work and in life. At the
same time, developmental economists, such as Amartya Sen, have gone to great
lengths to introduce the notion of human agency in their considerations of how
to alleviate global poverty.[18] However, Sen clearly infused a deeply contextual
view of agency, observing that people need to feel secure and free in order to
develop the internal capacity to initiate and sustain effective actions in their
lives. So, how does this book provide any meaningful insight into this debate?

The short answer is that the material presented in previous chapters confirms
the view that both macro-level and internal psychological factors interact in
highly complex and often-unpredictable ways to shape our work lives.[19] As Sen
noted in his Nobel Prize–winning book, *Development as Freedom*, people are
most likely to develop the capacity to implement their goals in their lives (which

he calls agency) when they experience political freedom, access to economic resources, social opportunities, transparency guarantees, and protection security.[20] Similar insights have emerged in various aspects of psychology: Human agency is indeed very important, but it is not a given.[21] People clearly need access to the goodies of life, such as stable families, nutrition, healthcare, safe neighborhoods, excellent education, and ongoing social support.[22] In addition, the labor market is one of the major limiting factors for people, even if they have worked incredibly hard and if they have had access to the antecedents of a good life.[23]

In my view, the typical messages conveyed in the United States (and many other Western nations) about success are infused with an overreliance on personal causality in considerations of how people fare in their work lives. The narratives that we obtained for this project underscored how readily people assumed blame for their troubles in making a living and in finding meaning at work. The empirical research in economics, psychology, and related fields does not support this tendency within the United States for people to hold themselves responsible for their struggles.[24] Access to opportunity is a powerful force in American society and is perhaps even more potent as the crisis about growing inequality continues to be played out. In the next section of this chapter, I explore some of the most compelling implications for individuals and public policies that emerge in my synthesis of the collective insights that have been shared in this book.

A Way Forward: Individual and Community Perspectives

Taken together, the themes that I have explored thus far underscore that work in an age of uncertainty is creating a highly stressful and anxiety-laden existence for people and communities. As I worked on this book, I also read extensively about the changing nature of the workplace and the diverse array of recommendations that have been posited about how our society should move forward in creating a more just and sustainable future for people at work. I will also chime in with my thoughts about a way forward, rooting my recommendations in a careful analysis of existing macro-level trends and equally precise attention to the psychological experiences, values, and insights that emerged from the participants who we interviewed for this project. Clearly, I do not have access to a magic wand of solutions for the crises affecting people and communities with respect to their working lives. However, at the very minimum, I hope to infuse a psychological perspective, informed by the values that were conveyed by the participants in the Boston College Working Project and related research literature, into current debates as our nation moves into an era of work that is evoking anxiety in so many sectors of our society.

Coping With Uncertainty: An Individual Perspective

Prior to exploring systemic ideas about how to enhance the quality and availability of decent work, I identify the most disconcerting stressors that impact people as they cope with eroding work conditions. In my view, people often cope with multiple stressors at once as they seek sustainable livelihoods, as summarized next.

Unpredictability. A core theme in the narratives obtained for this project was the pervasive sense of unpredictability that people felt as the working context increasingly became less stable and secure. Many of the participants spoke eloquently about the need to cope with the feeling that they did not know what the future would bring; indeed, some of the participants (particularly those who were unemployed for some time) were uncertain about where they would live and how they would find food to eat. The reactions to unpredictability ranged from resignation and apathy to anger and rage, with many gradations in between. Managing uncertainty is clearly a challenge for people; indeed, the reactions that we observed in the narratives were completely understandable and expected. While living in states of uncertainty is part of the human condition, by and large, people do not generally like to experience these feelings continuously as they tend to evoke deep anxiety.

Inequality. The emergence of growing inequality is rapidly changing the nature of working. Increasingly, the United States is becoming a divided nation, with a smaller cohort of our population living a life of privilege, self-determination, and accomplishment while a growing proportion is living in poverty or in a state of precariousness because of lack of work or the availability of only short-term work, often not in the field for which one has prepared.[25] Coping with inequality is a challenge psychologically because it can evoke envy, frustration, self-blame, and despair.[26] For those who are living in the America that is economically constricting, seeing wealth and status in their lives and in the media provides a benchmark that may serve to underscore the difficult conditions that exist in one's own life. How do people deal with inequality when they are the ones in the down position? Some strive harder and set their goals at a higher bar, hoping that effort and perseverance will yield upward mobility. However, as we know from recent trends in the United States, others become disillusioned and may turn to drugs, maladaptive lifestyles, and, alarmingly, political ideologies that provide a prescribed (but ultimately self-defeating and ineffective) outlet for anger and envy.[27]

The responses to inequality, like many aspects of life, vary enormously, depending on a host of individual and contextual factors. However, the narratives from the Boston College Working Project coupled with my clinical experience and reading of relevant literature revealed that many people are not comfortable living in such an unequal society. Moreover, those who live in more affluent communities also suffer from inequality as they may feel guilty about their status in life as well as anxiety that what they have attained can be easily taken away.

Dreams Deferred or Dashed. For some in our society, work has resulted in an ongoing sense of disappointment as one's dreams for a meaningful life and capacity to earn a living are either deferred or completely unattainable. There are interview passages in this book that convey this deep sense of despair, which often culminated in depression and other forms of psychic pain. For some, internal psychological resources, such as being very proactive, resilient, or optimistic, may get them through and allow for some adaptations that result in a decent work life. For others, the collective sense of marginalization that exists in inhabiting a highly precarious work life becomes overwhelming, crushing one's capacity to fight back.

Managing the Stress and Despair. Entire books and counseling strategies have been developed to help people deal with unpredictability, disappointments, anxiety, and depression. (I refer readers to some of the best self-help resources in the Notes at the end of the book.[28]) At this point, I identify some of the core issues that emerged as we examined these individual responses to a world of work that is increasingly evoking distress rather than serving as a source of engagement and connection.

The first step in managing unpredictability in life is to accurately label the experience and link it to some likely causes that may be evoking the feelings. In the United States, the contract between employers and employees has changed dramatically since World War II, leaving many feeling alone and frightened, without any source of stability or security. Many psychologists might suggest the use of various coping strategies, such as mindfulness and cognitive behavioral strategies to minimize internal reactivity to these experiences.[29] Most certainly, people should be able to access tools that will help to reduce anxiety in the face of uncertainty. However, seeking solely to adapt to conditions that are increasingly harsh and unfair is not always in the best interest of people. Being aware of the inequity of American society with respect to access to decent work can actually help to mobilize individuals and communities, thereby providing people with adaptive coping strategies and engagement in the sort of critical thinking that will demand more humane policies about work.

In a highly individualistic culture like ours, the tendency is to view oneself as the architect of one's own life. In many ways, this approach has some upsides in that it encourages action and persistence and can be motivating for many people. However, the downside of an individualistic ethos is holding oneself overly responsible for both positive events and negative outcomes. Many positive experiences in our lives not only are linked to hard work, but also may reflect the input of others in our lives and the broader social and economic contexts, which provide access to schools, good healthcare, and other modern amenities. The overly individualistic approach may result in some people taking more credit for their successes and not acknowledging the support of others or of social capital that may be a function of the family or community into which one is born.

In a similar vein, a common observation that I had in reading the interviews in depth was that the participants tended to view themselves as responsible for their work-related problems, which often resulted in depressive moods and stagnation.[30] Optimally, the material presented in this book will help to reframe the issue of causality to a more nuanced and sophisticated view that identifies the role of the individual in a complex web of factors that are at play in our work lives.

Another important individual strategy is the adoption of critical consciousness, which was discussed in Chapter 7. As I noted, individuals who are able to read the world and critically assess the nature of systemic influences in life are often better able to manage hardship and cope with distress.[31] In effect, critical consciousness not only provides us with a perspective that helps to reduce self-blame and can empower social advocacy, but also furnishes an important source of psychological protection that many people will find essential as we move into a more unstable period of work in the coming years and decades. In the next section, we move out from the individual perspective to the community level, which also has an important role to play in creating a more sustainable work life.

Coping With Uncertainty: A Community Perspective. One of the takeaways from this book project has been the sense of isolation that many people are experiencing as they cope with unemployment, underemployment, and growing precariousness in their lives. As I noted in many of the chapters, particularly Chapter 3, people have an inherent need for connection and relationships. These needs can be met in a multitude of ways, but one of the most consistent vehicles for social and community engagement in adulthood is in our work lives. The loss of these connections has left many of the participants from our sample feeling disengaged and alone, which clearly echoes the state of many community connections throughout the United States.[32] As such, I believe that our local communities, including faith-based institutions; community-based programs; vocational support services (such as government-sponsored and nonprofit employment and career counseling offices); mental health services;

education and training; and friends and family need to be mobilized to provide support and connection for those who are struggling in their work lives.

One particularly important strategy for the United States moving forward is to invest in our career counseling, education, and training services for young adults and adults who are facing increasingly challenging transitions between work and nonwork roles. Although we have an existing set of support services in the One-Stop Career Centers in the United States, I propose that this network of resources is insufficient to manage the depth and breadth of the need that exists now and will no doubt grow in the coming years.[33] Considerable research evidence supports the use of career counseling as a tool for people who are navigating changes in their work lives.[34] High-quality career counseling can help people identify new directions that may fit well with their interests, values, and abilities.[35] Also, the counseling aspect of this resource can be very important in helping people work through the psychological consequences of losing the solid foundation that work provides for many people in cohering their identities, providing a source of sustenance, and in connecting them to the broader social world. I also believe that an invigorated career services resource needs to provide people access to training and education, which clearly is a lifelong endeavor for people as we enter the challenging depths of the information age.[36]

In relation to the need for ongoing education and training, I propose that accessible, affordable, and responsive postsecondary training will be increasingly needed by people across the full spectrum of the occupational landscape. Thomas Friedman, the noted *New York Times* columnist and author, has argued compellingly in his book, *Thank You for Being Late: An Optimist's Guide to Thriving in the Age of Accelerations,* for the need for lifelong learning, which he proposes will be increasingly necessary as skills required for new jobs become more complex and sophisticated.[37] I also believe that community colleges, which are so entrenched in our society (but often underfunded), can become nimble resources that can provide both vocational training and relational support for people negotiating planned or unplanned changes in their lives. Furthermore, colleges and universities will increasingly need to expand their offerings for adults who may be squeezed out of the labor market. Here again, an infusion of career and mental health counseling, provided as resources for all students and learners, will be essential if we are to create the pathway for decent and dignified work.

The support mechanisms that I have outlined in this section will clearly require revamping of our current institutions, particularly those that provide education, counseling, and training. More important, these sorts of changes will also require a different sort of social contract with each other and with the broader social world. The new social contract that will be needed is based on several important values that have emerged in this book. First, people need to be supported, both emotionally and instrumentally, as they seek to manage the growing complexity of work in America. The emergence of a rigid adoption of neoliberal economic policies (discussed in further depth in material that follows) has resulted in a glorification of individualism and self-absorption, which has left people feeling untethered to their communities and to each other. Second, we need to rebuild our infrastructure, both tangibly (better schools, roads, and medical care) and psychologically. The tangible infrastructure would be characterized by a comprehensive investment in the resources that are needed to create the conditions for meaningful and decent work, such as job creation efforts, evidence-based counseling and training for all who want to enter the workforce, and the creation of systems to support people and communities as they seek to create and sustain decent working conditions. (Further details on this vision are forthcoming further in the chapter.)

The psychological infrastructure that I am referring to is the sense that we are responsible for each other. By clearly stating that our society values connection and caring, we will be better able to design the sort of community-based resources and macro-level policies that will support access to decent and meaningful work.[38] I realize that I am asking a lot here; also, I am aware that not all readers will concur with this value system. I acknowledge that my appeals in this chapter (and, indeed, throughout this book) may not change the norms that so overtly endorse liberalizing our regulations so that free markets can thrive; however, I do hope that this book will become part of the debate that is needed as our nation sorts out its policies about work moving forward. In the section that follows, I infuse these values for care, compassion, and connection into existing and future deliberations about how to manage a society where stable and secure work is available to a decreasing proportion of our nation's workforce.

Changing the Context of Work: A Psychological Perspective of Macro-Level Solutions

In the concluding section of this chapter, I enter the highly contentious fray about how our society ought to deal with the many problems that exist in the world of work. My vantage point in this section is based on an explicit infusion of a psychological perspective that affirms the fundamental human needs that working can optimally fulfill.

Human Rights and Working: A Second Look

In the first chapter, I summarized some notable efforts to infuse a human rights agenda into our considerations of work. After considering the various ways in which work serves to sustain people and provide a sense of aliveness in the world, I would like to revisit this perspective, with the added wisdom of the collective voices of the participants from the Boston College Working Project and the scholars who have been so informative in documenting the impact of work in people's lives. In short, I propose that access to decent work is integral to a decent life and is an inherent part of our human rights.[39]

One of the major themes that emerged in the narratives was a sense of outrage about the difficulty that people had in locating decent work and being able to sustain themselves in jobs that offer security, stability, and dignity. While there were some in the sample who were quite satisfied with their lives and with their experiences at work, a surprising number of participants, even those with fairly extensive educational backgrounds, recounted a sense of being deprived of their natural striving to work. In short, people wanted to work and wanted to be able to earn their livelihood, contribute to the greater social good, and do something meaningful with their lives. For many, the sense of constraints was palpable, underscoring the struggles that exist in moving into the world of work with both dignity and purpose.

While most would concur that access to work and access to the building blocks of a decent life are critical for all, the sad reality is that the efforts of the United Nations, ILO, and other multinational and government-based groups to achieve the goal of infusing human rights into our working lives has not been fully successful. The notion of guaranteeing a capacity to earn a fair income with decent work conditions, which was articulated in the UN Declaration of Human Rights after World War II, remains fundamentally elusive. That said, some of the related UN initiatives, such as the Millennium Development Goals, advanced in 2000, have resulted in a notable decrease in global poverty, particularly the sort of poverty that has resulted in starvation, malnutrition, and even death.[40] The promise of the efforts to eliminate poverty does give some hope to similar objectives by the ILO and other groups to establish human rights–based initiatives to guarantee access to decent work for all who want and who need to work. I unequivocally affirm this view: People need to sustain themselves and find sources of meaning and purpose in their lives. In the sections that follow, I expand my position with further details about how individuals and societies can manage to sustain the fundamental right of people to work in decent and fair conditions.

Neoliberal Policies and the Psychological Experience of Working

At this point, I enter a debate about work that includes a rather large meta-phorical elephant in our discussion that casts a deep shadow across many conversations about work, encompassing personal, psychological, and political contexts. The elephant in this particular room is the economic system—neoliberalism—that has dominated the United States (and many other regions of the globe) for the past four decades. Americans do indeed love freedom and liberty; these concepts are integral to our nation's fundamental political values and to our beliefs about our individual rights and, increasingly, our views about our economic systems. The emergence of neoliberal policies, which may sound reasonable to some people who have libertarian leanings, is actually quite a complex stew of ideas and policies that, in many ways, shifts the risks about work from employers to employees.[41]

The fundamental assumption that underlies neoliberal policies about economics is that too much regulation constrains the freedom of business enterprises to innovate and expand and therefore slows the quasi-mystical properties of capitalist markets. The outcomes of neoliberal policies include the reduction of regulations supporting unions, the diminishment of legal protections for workers, easy access to outsourcing human resources, reduced corporate taxes, and the overall reduction of supports for vulnerable people and institutions within the labor market and economy, writ large.[42]

The advent of neoliberal policies in the United States took shape during the Reagan years and has affected all political and economic perspectives, many of which have shifted toward neoliberal policies, even while some political movements do try to shore up the safety net for people. According to many neoliberal advocates, it is impossible to turn the clock back to a system where social welfare benefits were more robust and where markets were constrained by regulation and norms that affirmed the rights of workers. The rationale for continuing to advance neoliberal agendas is that globalization has changed the nature of competition, elevating the need for highly responsive and lean organizations that can adapt to changes swiftly while also being creative and innovative.

The hard reality of neoliberal policies is that sustaining free markets has indeed become the dominant discourse in many political and economic circles within the United States (although clearly not all perspectives endorse neoliberal policies), leaving many workers to fend for themselves as they seek stability and dignity in the labor market. I realize that some readers may feel that I am moving into an arena that may be beyond my calling as a psychologist who thinks about and writes about work primarily from the perspective of

individuals and communities. However, I have chosen to write about this because the debate requires a psychological perspective and because I want to
encourage all citizens to join complex debates about work and equality in our
society. Rather than examining economic systems via the lens of aggregate data
that focus on market growth, unemployment statistics, interest rates, and global
competitiveness, I argue that we need to infuse an explicit focus on how neoliberal policies affect people and communities.

What are the consequences of neoliberal policies for people, particularly for
those who are not profiting from increasingly unrestrained markets? One of the
overriding themes in the narratives has been the erosion of safety, decency, and
security in the workplace. In addition to the observations of the participants,
I have detailed research in this book that underscores the psychological and
social consequences of diminishing work opportunities coupled with a lack of
protections for workers across the occupational spectrum. When considered
collectively, the picture that emerges is indeed affected by the shadows of neoliberal policies. The brazen focus on ensuring freedom for employers has
resulted in a significant reduction in opportunities for employees and their
families to enjoy the stability and security of decent work.

Clearly, this book alone will not change the neoliberal policies that have
taken hold in the United States and across many other regions of the world.
However, it is time that those of us who are concerned about the welfare of
people and communities speak up about the economic systems that consider
corporations as needing protections while individuals are often left to fend for
themselves. What may change the neoliberal sway is for authors and scholars
like myself and others to name the problem and to advocate for more humane
policies, using arguments and data that will compel our society to insist on
change.[43] In the sections that follow, I outline some other features of the macro-
level structures that I believe need to be actively considered as we strive for
more humane policies about work in the United States.

Sustainable Livelihoods: Is It Time to Unpack Work From Making a Living?

Throughout this book, I have written about how work serves to fulfill our needs
for survival, social connection, self-determination, contributions to the social
good, and capacity to care for others. As policy analysts have assessed the impact of automation and artificial intelligence on the workforce of the future
(even the very near future), considerable concern exists about the capacity for
our society to create enough jobs for all who need to work. A heated debate is
under way about the potential impact of automation and artificial intelligence

on the workforce, with some experts predicting massive job losses and others offering more restrained projections.[44] Perhaps the most common theme among the various predictions is that automation will indeed reduce opportunities for many working people, particularly for individuals whose skills are not consistent with the needs of the workplace.[45] For example, workers who are not able to function in highly automated workplaces may be squeezed out by information technology and by the continued outsourcing of jobs to places with lower labor wages. In addition, various pockets of higher skilled occupations will suffer from job losses as artificial intelligence replaces the need for such positions as attorneys, legal assistants, middle-level managers, programmers, and others.

One option that has been debated is to separate the need for earning a living from having to work. These discussions often center on such ideas as the guaranteed basic income (GBI). In short, the GBI would provide people with an allocation of funds from the government that would provide for one's survival needs.[46] These funds would be provided to all, regardless of their status in the workforce, thereby releasing people from the stress of having to find work to sustain themselves. (There are debates within the GBI community about the pros and cons of providing resources to people who are well supported by their work or their own financial capital. The notion of means testing these payments is also being considered, although some are concerned that doing so will involve a more intrusive level of government control of this process.) In some European nations, the extensive level of social welfare support simulates many aspects of basic income.[47] In the United States, the closest parallel to basic income guarantees exist only for those who are significantly underresourced, perhaps best reflected in welfare benefits, which require careful means testing and which also necessitate work, except for those with very young children or disabling conditions.

A contentious debate is under way about nearly every aspect of the GBI. One of the most complex questions is whether the GBI best serves people, many of whom, for various reasons, want a stake in the labor market. As I have described in this book, work, at its best, serves a number of psychological functions, such as providing a means of engaging in meaningful tasks that allow one to contribute and create as well as connect to society and to others. However, it is possible for many to find meaning and purpose in nonmarketplace activities, such as hobbies, caregiving work, creative pursuits, and leisure. Indeed, in my conversations with students in my classes on this topic, typically a few state that they would be happy not to work if their financial needs were taken care of and if they had opportunities to do what they really love. Other students chime in that they would prefer to engage in tasks within the traditional workforce: a regular job that reflects their interests, values, and dreams. Clearly, psychologists and other social scientists need to conduct research on the impact of basic income guarantees on such issues as individuals' well-being, meaning about life, physical and psychological health, and quality of relationships. In addition, we may need to develop resources for people to choose purposeful activities outside the marketplace.

A second issue is the question of how the GBI should be constructed and distributed. One line of thought is that everyone should receive the same amount of money, while another perspective advocates that the amount of GBI should be adjusted based on a family's resources and needs, similar to means testing, which is the case with many social welfare benefits in North America and Europe. The interest in basic income has actually emerged from both the political left and right, with predictable sort of gradations depending on one's ideological orientation. Policy advocates from the right propose that income guarantees should replace all other social welfare supports, such as unemployment insurance and disability payments. Those on the left view income guarantees as a means of ensuring that people can survive, especially during periods when work is not available or decent; another feature of the left-leaning view of income guarantees is that it provides redistributive economic justice, a clear counter to growing social and economic inequality.

The underlying theme in this debate is actually quite profound: unpacking survival needs from the marketplace. If projections about massive job losses are accurate, the GBI will likely be needed to sustain the social and economic cohesion of our society. As we have observed in history and currently in other regions of the world, large-scale unemployment is associated with disturbing levels of social disintegration, which can manifest in a host of unpleasant ways (increases in crime, violent political movements, substance abuse, and alienation from one's community).[48]

Based on the observations from this book and from the voluminous literature on work and well-being, I believe that people do need to engage in tasks that are meaningful and that provide them with the psychological and social resources to feel fully alive in the world.[49] Whether these tasks need to be linked to the marketplace is not entirely clear and merits careful consideration and research. My take on this issue is that if work does disappear for some, we will need more than income guarantees to help people have a meaningful life. We will need to develop ways to help people find outlets for their interests and for their natural striving to engage in projects that provide meaning and purpose in their lives.

The precise shape that this future society may take is unclear with respect to how work and nonwork roles will be manifested and distributed. However, the psychological literature strongly supports the notion that people function best when they are engaged in activities and tasks that have some meaning to them.

Education and Work in the Age of Uncertainty

Education serves many roles in American society, including a means of socializing young people, providing them with cognitive and interpersonal skills, and preparing students for their adult lives, optimally with a sense of purpose and decency. One of the major strands in education is helping young people transition to the world of work. While this is not the only purpose, it is clearly important, and this issue drives many reform efforts in education.[50] As we enter a world where work may no longer be as necessary for sustainability, what will happen to education? How will educators motivate students to work hard if they no longer can link education to success in their future careers? These are complex questions that have actually not been examined in much depth in the educational world or, for that matter, in other public discourses and the future of work.

At the outset of education in the United States, the goals for schools were quite rudimentary: teach students to read, write, and use basic math skills while also socializing them into the most basic norms of our society. Around the time of the Industrial Revolution, education expanded to encompass broader goals, such as enhancing the sense of citizenship for students and helping youth to prepare for a world of work that increasingly required more elaborate training and skills. This set of objectives has sustained the educational enterprise for over a century and still, for the most part, defines the landscape of education.

However, the prospect of a world without sufficient work will likely change the game for education and for schooling in general. It is not quite clear how education will adapt to this shifting context, but I do believe that it is timely for educators and policy leaders to debate the purpose of education with respect to preparing students for adulthood. One viable set of ideas that emerged for me in this book project is the need to help students understand the nature of the changes in the workforce, underscoring the importance of lifelong learning and engaged effort in school. In addition, I believe that educators should double down on such psychological factors as purpose and meaning, which students will need to consider carefully as they mull over their options. Finally, educating people not only to read but also to read the world, via critical consciousness training, will help to prepare a citizenry that can discern the nature of the social and economic forces that are constricting opportunity and to become advocates for more just solutions.

Developing Humane Public Policies About Work

While the previous sections have certainly examined some prominent policy issues that are shaping the nature of working in America, I believe that we need a broader commitment to developing a psychologically informed and value-based set of policies that will inform how we approach work in the years to come. From my vantage point, the risks that many individuals are facing with respect to their work lives are overwhelming. The growth of precarious work and underemployment and the very real fears of a jobless future are creating heightened levels of anxiety for some and for others a sense of despair and apathy. Like climate change, which experts identified as a potential calamity many decades ago, scholars and experts on work (including me) are raising a cautionary warning that we are facing major crises in people's experiences of work. As reflected in Chapter 1, the recovery from the Great Recession has been characterized by further transformations of the labor market, which is reflected in so many of the passages that have been shared in this book by the participants from the Boston College Working Project.

My recommendation is that public leaders in our country need to establish policies about the rights and privileges of people with respect to work. As I indicated previously, the full endorsement of the UN Declaration of Human Rights would necessitate radical changes in our society, similar to the sort of policies that Franklin Roosevelt implemented in the Great Depression. Prior to providing some examples of a more humane approach to developing policies about work, I would like to underscore the basic tenets of contemporary public policy about work:

- People should have access to decent conditions at the workplace as detailed in the ILO's Decent Work Agenda (reviewed in Chapter 1).
- Human rights, in all forms and manifestations, need to be defined and regulated by legislation and legal protections. This would include rights for individuals from diverse racial and ethnic backgrounds as well as for individuals who express varied sexual orientations and gender identities.
- Access to work and the development of sustainable conditions for survival and self-determination need to be considered shared responsibilities that people in our society value as part of our citizenship in a modern democratic state. Achieving humane policies about work will require sacrifices from many. Optimally, an educational system that is constructed around the notion that we share responsibility for each other may yield a citizenry that affirms this caring view of society's responsibilities for establishing decent work for all.
- During periods of unemployment, people should have access to generous unemployment benefits that will also include career counseling, job training, and lifelong learning.

- New work forms, such as the gig economy and short-term contract work, should be viewed as opportunities for people to gain new skills and should not be construed as viable long-term options for people who are seeking more stability in their work lives, except in cases where these short-term work projects are consistent with an individual's needs and aspirations.
- Alternative means of ensuring that people can sustain themselves with a decent income that does not involve humiliating means testing or forced work assignments need to be developed and evaluated.
- Education and training need to be affordable and fair; the era of crushing student debt needs to be reformed as a major means of reducing inequality.

It is clear that many of these recommendations will be viewed as far too idealistic, costly, and perhaps politically risky in an era where individualistic policies have a strong presence in our discourse. I concur that many of these ideas may be a challenge to even introduce into policy debates. However, the alternatives are far more radical and disruptive, as well as morally questionable. As the Organization for Economic Cooperation and Development (OECD) report on sustainable futures articulated, information technology and growing inequality could lead to major political and economic changes that can completely transform our societies into chaotic and dangerous places.[51] Consider the impact of such radical changes in the availability of work in Europe during the Great Depression, which resulted in many being attracted to the simplistic and nationalistic ideologies of fascism.

I am not necessarily predicting anarchy in the United States if we do not introduce more humane work policies, but I believe many experts would concur that the shifts in the political climate to more radical solutions may be a result of a population that feels deeply anxious about its capacity to sustain itself in a world with declining opportunities in the labor market. In the next section, I outline some of the ways of introducing a humane public policy about work, optimally providing some fuel for thought as we mull over the future of work in the United States.

Implementing Humane Policies About Work

The framework for humane and humanistic policies about work is evident by examining existing practices in our own history as well as in some other countries in the Western world. In the material that follows, I summarize a few means of implementing humane policies about work; of course, many more ideas exist and it is hoped will be generated by readers of this book.

- *Creating Work.* For much of the neoliberal period within the past few decades, we have viewed the free market as the primary and, for some, the only way to create work. If we go back to the Great Depression, with unemployment rates of 30% and more, there was a great need for more jobs immediately. Franklin Roosevelt introduced an expansive array of government-funded jobs that helped to create the infrastructure that is still supporting many institutions in the United States. Other efforts at introducing government-sponsored "make work" programs ensued during different periods of American history (and, indeed, in many other nations). I am not suggesting that the state become the sole employer, such as in the Communist states of the second half of the twentieth century; this clearly did not work and did result in both stagnation and totalitarian societies. Rather, the middle ground between harsh neoliberal policies and harsh communist policies is needed, where societies are sufficiently flexible to create work when needed. Using best practices based on psychological and social scientific research, I am confident that government-sponsored employment opportunities can be crafted so that they result in innovation, excellent training, and important contributions to society.

- *New Contexts for Work.* Much of the labor force in the United States (and many other countries) is focused on business: making products to sell or creating services that people will buy. In this environment, jobs that are focused on creative endeavors (generally artistic or intellectual) and caregiving have become somewhat marginalized. Interestingly, a number of scholars and policy analysts predict that caring and creating tasks will be the most robust occupations in the face of automation and artificial intelligence.[52] In this context, I envision that a humane public policy toward work would include efforts to fund and sustain work that does not necessarily add to the gross national product or business profits. Rather, the development of meaningful and decent work for people that is fair, sustainable, and decent ought to be a viable end in and of itself. If we adopt a view by which work can be created by institutions, paid for by more egalitarian tax policies, and sustained by policies that value creating and connecting, it is possible to envision a future where work is not solely linked to production. Once we unpack work from the neoliberal policies that have reified productivity, consumption, and profits, we may be able to conceptualize work as contributing to people's well-being and the welfare of communities. One particularly compelling exemplar of needed work projects is in teaching, counseling, social work, and other helping professions. For example, why do we need to continue to staff only one teacher for every 30 students when there are many people in our society who would be happy to teach and are working part-time or in precarious gig jobs? Paying for increased social services, naturally, will be contentious. However, if we are approaching a period of needing to support people via GBI allocations, it seems reasonable to assume that we can obtain public funds to ramp up education, healthcare, and other helping and nurturing roles.

• *Caregiving Work and Sustainability.* In various sections of this book, I have discussed caregiving as an inherent part of being alive in the world and an integral part of our work lives (and of our relational lives). A number of scholars have described the very complex issues nested in caregiving in American society, ranging from the ongoing sexist nature of policies about care work to the low-paid aspects of contemporary care work.[53] One idea that may have some merit in a context where stable jobs are diminishing is to link personal care work to guaranteed income payments. While the concept of basic income has traction well beyond considerations of economically rewarding care work, the legitimization of personal care work via stable pay and benefits may have some merit. The income for personal care work would be far more substantial than welfare payments and can be linked to ongoing training and support for caregivers, who would likely benefit considerably from the financial and social support.

• *Paying for Humane Policies About Work.* It is relatively easy to create a wish list of supports and services that will infuse more humanity into our work policies. However, it is much more daunting to think about the reality that many of my proposals are out of sync with the current political winds in the United States that are under the sway of neoliberal forces. As such, it might seem naïve for me simply to suggest increasing taxes on the wealthy and introducing greater equity throughout American society, which I do believe are viable and needed options. Political winds do shift, and I am hopeful that the American people will realize that a crisis exists in the workplace that is significantly responsible for the overriding sense of anxiety that was so evident in our interviews. Perhaps the most important contribution that I can make to the question of how we pay for all of these ideas about work is to articulate the need and rationale for more activism and humaneness in our approach to work. Entering a period of diminished work opportunities will evoke a major debate about inequality and the distribution of resources, as evident in the GBI debates. In my view, the preoccupation currently with lowering taxes on corporations and the wealthy will soon give way to more realistic approaches about reducing inequality in a fair and morally responsible way. The harshness of this neoliberal era does not need to endure indefinitely.

When considered collectively, the proposals that I have outlined seek to respond to the calls for more support and empathy throughout the interviews that we conducted and, indeed, throughout much of the recent research on work from psychology and related fields. I close this chapter with a synthesis of the unique and important observations that emerged in this project, which serve to inspire a clarion call for more kindness, caring, and shared responsibility as our nation (and indeed the world) enters a period of great uncertainty.

Conclusion

The psychological aspects of working are complex, especially during this very unsettling period of instability and precariousness in the workplace. Amidst this complexity, a number of prominent themes have emerged in this book; these themes provide a coherent way to summarize this journey into the inner life of people as they interact with work. Despite all of the changes in the external world of work, the psychological experience of this fundamental aspect of life is consistent with many of the attributes of work earlier in our evolutionary history. Work is inextricably intertwined with survival and with the capacity to furnish a deeper sense of meaning and purpose in our lives. At the same time, work puts people into contact with the social world in ways that can be both affirming and, at times, painful. While work offers the capacity for deep rootedness in our social and economic lives, it also can provide the sharpest edge of our capacity to marginalize people by excluding them from the workplace or degrading and harassing those who do find work.

The diverse mix of psychological experiences can indeed feel like an amorphous part of life that defies logic or control. The material that I have presented here, emerging both from the analyses of the interviews and the very insightful contributions from my peers in the social sciences, do offer some ways of understanding the psychological nature of work. One of the most common themes in this book is the intersection of our need to sustain ourselves economically with work. Changes in the nature of work have the potential to unpack this connection, especially if the added wealth from automation is used wisely and fairly to support people across the United States and the world.

However, our track record in creating an equal playing field and in supporting those who are struggling to gain a foothold in the world of work in recent decades does not engender confidence. My view is that we will need to advocate strongly for the humane and caring policies that I have outlined in this final chapter. I do not believe that this advocacy struggle will be easy or without conflict. Much like climate change, some may respond to the recommendations that I have offered in this book with claims that counter the strong evidence from the social sciences about the impact of inequality, unpredictability, and dashed dreams in the lives of people and communities.

Another major theme that we identified is the role of work in providing a means to feel fully alive. What does it mean to feel fully alive? Clearly, the experience of feeling fully alive is not isolated to our work lives; many relationships and experiences in life provide us with a deep sense of joy, meaning, purpose, and engagement. We witnessed the sense of feeling fully alive at work in many of the interviews that were gathered for this project; indeed, these narratives echoed observations from the arts and literature on the role of work in creating a rich and full life for those who are fortunate to have access to decent and meaningful work. In addition, people can feel fully alive by being able to support themselves and their families, even in work that is not necessarily meaningful or interesting.

For those who do not find a way to feel fully alive in the marketplace due to a lack of decent jobs, diminished opportunities, or unsatisfying jobs, I propose that our society is responsible for providing the framework for a life of meaning and purpose in other ways. If we assume that some form of basic income guarantees will be used when work opportunities are severely compromised by automation, then we will also need to think about ways of creating opportunities for people to engage in projects that provide a connection to one's sense of inner purpose. What this may look like is not entirely clear, but the outlines are evident in the observations generated in this book. People strive to be engaged and challenged while also enjoying their time and tasks. The intense purpose that children exhibit when they are playing, in my view, integral to our natural state; we will need to create the contexts for these sorts of experiences throughout the life span.

As a counterpoint to the eroding nature of stability and security that was so evident in this book, I would like to close with a call for more caring and shared responsibility in our considerations of the current state and the future of work. It is clear that we are at a crossroads, with considerable evidence suggesting that work will likely be less available and stable in the years to come. Given the observations gleaned in this book, I believe that we can make a case for thoughtful responses to shifts in the labor market by clearly advocating for people over profits. While the struggle will not be so easy, the alternatives are not viable. Maintaining the investment in neoliberal policies that treat people as commodities or costs that can be offloaded without consequences is the complete opposite of the findings that have prevailed in the Boston College Working Project and in psychology more broadly. To feel fully alive and engaged in decent work should not be confined to the privileged; rather, it is a core human right, one that I believe all of us need to share. Rather than passively observing the eroding work experience in America, I advocate that we all commit to creating the conditions in which our natural human striving to create, contribute, and collaborate is nurtured and affirmed: To engage in work that is decent and dignified is in our DNA, and it is central to our well-being and the welfare of our communities.

Notes

Preface

1. Didion, J. (2005). *The year of magical thinking.* New York: Knopf.
2. Hyman, L. (2018). *TEMP: How American work, American business, and the American dream became temporary.* New York: Penguin-Random House; Kalleberg, A. L., & Vallas, S. P. (2017). Probing precarious work: Theory, research, and politics. In A. L. Kalleberg & S. P. Vallas (Eds.), *Precarious work* (pp. 1–30). Bingley, England: Emerald; Katz, L. F., & Krueger, A. B. (2016). *The rise and nature of alternative work arrangements in the United States, 1995–2015.* Retrieved from https://krueger.princeton.edu/sites/default/files/akrueger/files/katz_krueger_cws_-_march_29_20165.pdf; International Labor Organization. (2018). *World employment social outlook: Trends 2018.* Geneva: International Labor Office; Organization for Economic Cooperation and Development. (2015). *Securing livelihoods for all: Foresight for action.* Development Centre Studies. Paris: Author. doi:10.1787/9789264231894-en
3. Blustein, D. L. (Ed.). (2013). *The Oxford handbook of the psychology of working.* New York: Oxford University Press. ;Organization for Economic Cooperation and Development. (2015). *Securing livelihoods for all: Foresight for action.* Development Centre Studies. Paris: Author. doi:10.1787/9789264231894-en, Sharone, O. (2013). *Flawed system/flawed self: Job searching and unemployment experience.* Chicago: University of Chicago Press; Vallas, S. P. (2011). Work: A critique. Malden, MA: Policy Press.
4. Blustein, D. L. (2006). *The psychology of working: A new perspective for career development, counseling, and public policy.* New York: Routledge; Guichard, J. (2009). Self-constructing. *Journal of Vocational Behavior, 75,* 251–258; Jahoda, M. (1982). *Employment and unemployment: A social–psychological analysis.* Cambridge, England: Cambridge University Press; Lent, R. W., & Brown, S. D. (2013). Social cognitive model of career self-management: Toward a unifying view of adaptive career behavior across the life span. *Journal of Counseling Psychology, 60,* 557–568; Leong, F. T. L., & Flores, L. Y. (2015). Career interventions with racial and ethnic minority clients. In P. J. Hartung, M. L. Savickas, & W. B. Walsh (Eds.), *APA handbook of career intervention, Volume 1: Foundations* (pp. 225–242). Washington, DC: American Psychological Association. doi:10.1037/14438-013; Richardson, M. S. (2012). Counseling for work and relationship. *The Counseling Psychologist, 40,* 190–242. doi:10.1177/0011000011406452; Savickas, M. L., Nota, L., Rossier, J., Sauwalder, J., Duarte, J. E., Guichard, J., & van Vianen, A. E. M. (2009). Life designing: A paradigm

for career construction in the 21st century. *Journal of Vocational Behavior, 75,* 139–250;Super, D. E. (1980). A life-span, life-space approach to career development. *Journal of Vocational Behavior, 16,* 282–298; Vondracek, F. W., Ford, D. H., & Porfeli, E. (2014). *A living systems theory of vocational behavior and development.* Boston: Sense.

5. Clandinin, D. J. (Ed.). (2007). *Handbook of narrative inquiry: Mapping a methodology.* Thousand Oaks, CA: Sage; Hsieh, H. F., & Shannon, S. E. (2005). Three approaches to qualitative content analysis. *Qualitative Health Research, 15,* 1277–1288. doi:10.1177/1049732305276687, Lieblich, A., Tuval-Mashiach, R., & Zilber, T. (1998). *Narrative research: Reading, analysis, and interpretation.* Thousand Oaks, CA: Sage.

6. Hsieh, H. F., & Shannon, S. E. (2005). Three approaches to qualitative content analysis. *Qualitative Health Research, 15,* 1277–1288. doi:10.1177/1049732305276687

7. Bowen, G. A. (2008). Naturalistic inquiry and the saturation concept: A research note. *Qualitative Research, 8,* 137–152. doi:10.1177/1468794107085301; Hill, C. E., Knox, S., Thompson, B. J., Williams, E. N., Hess, S. A., & Ladany, N. (2005). Consensual qualitative research: An update. *Journal of Counseling Psychology, 52,* 196–205. http://dx.doi.org/10.1037/0022-0167.52.2.196.

8. Arulmani, G., Bakshi, A. J., Leong, F. T. L., & Watts, A. G. (Eds.). (2014). *Handbook of career development: International perspectives.* New York: Springer. doi:10.1007/978-1-4614-9460-7; Blustein, D. L. (Ed.). (2013). *The Oxford handbook of the psychology of working.* New York: Oxford University Press; Hartung, P. J., Savickas, M. L., & Walsh, W. B. (Eds.). (2015). *APA handbook of career intervention, Volumes 1 and 2.* Washington, DC: American Psychological Association; Nota, L., & Rossier, J. (Eds.). (2015). *Handbook of life design: From practice to theory and from theory to practice.* Boston: Hogrefe; Walsh, W. B., Savickas, M. L., &. Hartung, P. J. (Eds.). (2013). *Handbook of vocational psychology* (4th ed.). New York: Routledge; Zedeck, S. (Ed.). (2011). *APA handbook of industrial and organizational psychology.* Washington, DC: American Psychological Association.

Chapter 1

1. Blustein, D. L. (2006). *The psychology of working: A new perspective for counseling, career development, and public policy.* New York: Routledge; Fouad, N. A. (2007). Work and vocational psychology: Theory, research, and applications. *Annual Review of Psychology, 58,* 543–564; Kalleberg, A. (2009). Precarious work, insecure workers: Employment relations in transition. *American Sociological Review, 71*(1), 1–22. doi:10.1177/000312240907400101; Sharone, O. (2013). *Flawed system/flawed self: Job searching and unemployment experience.* Chicago: University of Chicago Press; Vallas, S. P. (2011). *Work: A critique.* Malden, MA: Policy Press; Weil, D. (2014). *The fissured workplace: Why work became so bad for so many and what can be done to improve it.* Cambridge, MA: Harvard University Press.

2. Bowe, J., Bowe, M., & Streeter, S. (2000). *Gig: Americans talk about their jobs.* New York: Three Rivers Press; Terkel, S. (1974). *Working: People talk about what they do all day and how they feel about what they do.* New York: Pantheon Books.

3. Blustein, D. L. (2006). *The psychology of working: A new perspective for counseling, career development, and public policy.* New York: Routledge; Donkin, R. (2010). *The history of work.* London: Palgrave.

4. Budd, J. W. (2011). *The thought of work.* Ithaca, NY: ILR-Cornell Paperbacks; Richardson, M. S. (2012). Counseling for work and relationship. *The Counseling Psychologist, 40,* 190–242. doi:10.1177/0011000011406452; Standing, G. (2014). *A precariat charter: From denizens to citizens.* New York: Bloomsbury.

5. Brynjolfsson, E., & McAfee, A. (2014). *The second machine age: Work, progress, and prosperity in a time of brilliant technologies.* New York: Norton; Kalleberg, A. L., & Vallas, S. P. (2017). Probing precarious work: Theory, research, and politics. In A. L. Kalleberg & S. P. Vallas (Eds.), *Precarious work* (pp. 1–30). Bingley, England: Emerald. doi:10.1108/S0277-283320170000031017; Organization for Economic Cooperation and Development. (2015). *Securing livelihoods for all: Foresight for action* (Development Centre Studies). Paris: Author. doi:10.1787/9789264231894-en

6. Savickas, M. L. (2013). Career construction theory and practice. In S. D. Brown & R. W. Lent (Eds.), *Career development and counseling: Putting theory and research to work* (2nd ed., pp. 42–70). Hoboken, NJ: Wiley; Super, D. E. (1980). A life-span, life-space approach to career development. *Journal of Vocational Behavior, 16,* 282–298. doi:10.1016/0001-8791(80)90056-1

7. Blustein, D. L. (2001). Extending the reach of vocational psychology: Toward an inclusive and integrative psychology of working. *Journal of Vocational Behavior, 59,* 171–182. doi:10.1006/jvbe.2001.1823; Brown, S. D., & Lent, R. W. (2013). *Career development and counseling: Putting theory and research to work* (2nd ed.). Hoboken, NJ: Wiley.

8. Brynjolfsson, E., & McAfee, A. (2014). *The second machine age: Work, progress, and prosperity in a time of brilliant technologies.* New York: Norton.

9. Ford, M. (2015). *Rise of the robots: Technology and the threat of a jobless future.* New York: Basic Books; National Academies of Sciences. (2017). *Information technology and the US workforce: Where are we and where do we go from here?* Washington, DC: National Academies Press. doi:10.17226/24649

10. Organization for Economic Cooperation and Development. (2015). *Securing livelihoods for all: Foresight for action* (Development Centre Studies). Paris: Author. doi:10.1787/9789264231894-en

11. Mishel, L., & Bivens, J. (2017). *The zombie robot argument lurches on: There is no evidence that automation leads to joblessness or inequality.* Washington, DC: Economic Policy Institute. Retrieved from https://www.epi.org/files/pdf/126750.pdf

12. National Academy of Sciences. (2017). *Information technology and the US workforce: Where are we and where do we go from here?* Washington, DC: National Academies Press. doi:10.17226/24649

13. US Department of Labor, Bureau of Labor Statistics. (2018). *Economic news release: Table A-12. Unemployed persons by duration of employment.* Retrieved from https://www.bls.gov/news.release/empsit.t12.htm

14. Blustein, D. L., Kozan, S., & Connors-Kellgren, A. (2013). Unemployment and underemployment: A narrative analysis about loss. *Journal of Vocational Behavior, 82,* 256–265. doi:10.1016/j.jvb.2013.02.005; Blustein, D. L., Connors-Kellgren, A., Olle, C., & Diamonti, A. (2017). Promising career and workforce development practices in supporting the needs of unemployed populations. In V. S. Solberg & S. Ali (Eds.), *Handbook of career and workforce development: Practice and policy* (pp. 97–123). New York: Routledge; Herbert, B. (2014). *Losing our way: An intimate portrait of a troubled America.* New York: Penguin-Random House.

15. Stiglitz, J. (2015). *The great divide: Unequal societies and what we can do about them.* New York: Norton.

16. Stiglitz, J. E. (2012). *The price of inequality: How today's divided society endangers our future.* New York: Norton.

17. Blustein, D. L., Connors-Kellgren, A., Olle, C., & Diamonti, A. (2017). Promising career and workforce development practices in supporting the needs of unemployed populations. In V. S. Solberg & S. Ali (Eds.), *Handbook of career and workforce development: Practice and policy* (pp. 97–123). New York: Routledge; Hyman, L. (2018). *TEMP: How American work, American business, and the American dream became temporary.* New York: Penguin-Random House; Kalleberg, A. L., & Vallas, S. P. (2017). Probing precarious work: Theory, research, and politics. In A. L. Kalleberg & S. P. Vallas (Eds.), *Precarious work* (pp. 1–30). Bingley, England: Emerald. doi:10.1108/S0277-283320170000031017

18. Standing, G. (2011). *The precariat: The new dangerous class.* New York: Bloomsbury; Standing, G. (2014). *A precariat charter: From denizens to citizens.* New York: Bloomsbury.

19. UN General Assembly. (1948, December 10). *Universal declaration of human rights* [217 A (III)]. Retrieved from http://www.refworld.org/docid/3ae6b3712c.html

20. Blustein, D. L., Masdonati, J., & Rossier, J. (2017). *Psychology and the International Labor Organization: The role of psychology in the Decent Work Agenda.* Retrieved from https://www.ilo.org/global/research/publications/WCMS_561013/lang--en/index.htm; International Labor Organization. (2018). *World employment social outlook: Trends 2018.* Geneva: Author.

21. International Labor Organization. (2008). *ILO declaration on social justice for a fair globalization.* Retrieved from http://www.ilo.org/wcmsp5/groups/public/---dgreports/---cabinet/documents/genericdocument/wcms_371208.pdf

22. International Labor Organization. (2008). *ILO declaration on social justice for a fair globalization.* Retrieved from http://www.ilo.org/wcmsp5/groups/public/---dgreports/---cabinet/documents/genericdocument/wcms_371208.pdf

23. Applebaum, H. (1984). *Work in non-market and transitional societies.* Albany: State University of New York Press; Applebaum, H. (1992). *The concept of work: Ancient, medieval, and modern.* Albany: State University of New York Press.

24. Donkin, R. (2010). *The history of work.* London: Palgrave.

25. Budd, J. W. (2011). *The thought of work*. Ithaca, NY: ILR-Cornell Paperbacks.

26. Donkin, R. (2010). *The history of work*. London: Palgrave; Budd, J. W. (2011). *The thought of work*. Ithaca, NY: ILR-Cornell Paperbacks.

27. Budd, J. W. (2011). *The thought of work*. Ithaca, NY: ILR-Cornell Paperbacks; Olle, C. (2018). Exploring politics at the intersection of critical psychology and career guidance: A Freudo-Marxist case for radical refusal. In T. Hooley & R. Sultana (Eds.), *Career guidance for social justice: Contesting neoliberalism* (pp. 159–176). New York: Routledge; Parker, I. (2009). Critical psychology and revolutionary Marxism. *Theory & Psychology*, *19*, 71–92. doi:10.1177/0959354308101420

28. Jahoda, M. (1981). Work, employment, and unemployment: Values, theories, and approaches in social research. *American Psychologist*, *36*, 184–191. doi:10.1037/0003-066x.36.2.184; Wanberg, C. R. (2012). The individual experience of unemployment. *Annual Review of Psychology*, *63*, 369–396. doi:10.1146/annurev-psych-120710-100500

29. Erikson, E. H. (1994). *Identity and the life cycle*. New York: Norton.

30. Brown, A., & Bimrose, J. (2015). Identity development. In P. Hartung, M. Savickas, & W. B. Walsh (Eds.), *APA handbook of career intervention, Volume 2: Applications* (pp. 241–254). Washington, DC: American Psychological Association; Blustein, D. L. (1994). The question of "Who am I?": A cross-theoretical analysis. In M. L. Savickas & R. W. Lent (Eds.), *Convergence in career development theories: Implications for science and practice* (pp. 139–154). Palo Alto, CA: Consulting Psychologist Press; Savickas, M. L., Nota, L., Rossier, J., Dauwalder, J., Duarte, M. E., Guichard, J., Van Vianen, A. E. (2009). Life designing: A paradigm for career construction in the 21st century. *Journal of Vocational Behavior*, *75*, 239–250. doi:10.1016/j.jvb.2009.04.004; Leary, M. R., & Tangney, J. P. (Eds.). (2011). *Handbook of self and identity*. New York: Guilford Press.

31. Creed, P., & Hood, M. (2015). Process variables: Maturity, identity, decision making, and adjustment. In P. J. Hartung, M. L. Savickas, & W. B. Walsh (Eds.), *APA handbook of career intervention* (Vol. 1, pp. 351–372). Washington, DC: American Psychological Association; Skorikov, V. B., & Vondracek, F. W. (2011). Occupational identity. In S. J. Schwartz, K. Luyckx, & V. L. Vignoles (Eds.), *Handbook of identity theory and research* (pp. 693–714). New York: Springer.

32. Leary, M. R., & Tangney, J. P. (Eds.). (2011). *Handbook of self and identity*. New York: Guilford Press.

33. Savickas, M. (2019). *Career counseling* (2nd ed.). Washington, DC: American Psychological Association; McAdams, D. P., Josselson, R. E., & Lieblich, A. E. (2001). *Turns in the road: Narrative studies of lives in transition*. Washington, DC: American Psychological Association; McAdams, D. P. (2008). Personal narratives and the life story. In O. P. John, R. W. Robins, & L. A. Pervin (Eds.), *Handbook of personality: Theory and research* (pp. 242–262). New York: Guilford Press.

34. Savickas, M. (2019). *Career counseling* (2nd ed.). Washington, DC: American Psychological Association.

35. Blustein, D. L., Masdonati, J., & Rossier, J. (2017). *Psychology and the International Labor Organization: The role of psychology in the Decent Work Agenda*. Retrieved from https://www.ilo.org/global/research/publications/WCMS_561013/lang--en/index.htm

Chapter 2

1. Maslow, A. H. (1943). A theory of human motivation, *Psychological Review, 50*, 370–96. doi:10.1037/h0054346; Maslow, A. (1968). *Toward a psychology of being* (2nd ed.). New York: Van Nostrand Reinhold.

2. Latham, G. P. (2012). *Work motivation: History, theory, research, and practice.* Thousand Oaks, CA: Sage; Tay, L., & Diener, E. (2011). Needs and subjective well-being around the world. *Journal of Personality and Social Psychology, 101*, 354–365. doi:10.1037/a0023779

3. Maslow, A. (1968). *Toward a psychology of being* (2nd ed.). New York: Van Nostrand Reinhold.

4. Ali, S. R. (2013). Poverty, social class, and working. In D. L. Blustein (Ed.), *The Oxford handbook of the psychology of working* (pp. 127–140). New York: Oxford University Press. doi:10.1093/oxfordhb/9780199758791.001.0001; Flores, L. (2013). Race and working. In D. L. Blustein (Ed.), *The Oxford handbook of the psychology of working* (pp. 71–84). New York: Oxford University Press. doi:10.1093/oxfordhb/9780199758791.013.0001; Duffy, R. D., Blustein, D. L., Diemer, M. A., & Autin, K. L. (2016). The psychology of working theory. *Journal of Counseling Psychology, 63*, 127–148. doi:10.1037/cou0000140; Kenny, M. E., Blustein, D. L., Liang, B., Klein, T., & Etchie, Q. (2019). Applying the psychology of working theory for transformative career education. *Journal of Career Development.* https://doi.org/10.1177/0894845319827655; Juntunen, C. L. (2006). The psychology of working: The clinical context. *Professional Psychology: Research and Practice, 37*, 342–350.

5. Blustein, D. L. (2001). Extending the reach of vocational psychology: Toward an inclusive and integrative psychology of working. *Journal of Vocational Behavior, 59*, 171–182; Blustein, D. L. (2006). *The psychology of working: A new perspective for counseling, career development, and public policy.* New York: Routledge.

6. O'Brien, K. M. (2001). The legacy of Parsons: Career counselors and vocational psychologists as agents of social change. *The Career Development Quarterly, 50*, 66–76. doi:10.1002/j.2161-0045.2001.tb00891

7. Blustein, D. L. (2017). Integrating theory, research, and practice: Lessons learned from the evolution of vocational psychology. In J. P. Sampson, E. Bullock-Yowell, V. C. Dozier, D. S. Osborn, & J. G. Lenz (Eds.), *Integrating theory, research, and practice in vocational psychology: Current status and future directions* (pp. 179–187). Tallahassee: Florida State University.

8. Blustein, D. L. (2011). A relational theory of working. *Journal of Vocational Behavior, 79*, 1–17. doi:10.1016/j.jvb.2010.10.004; Kenny, M. E., Blustein, D. L., & Meerkins, T. M. (2018). Integrating relational perspectives in career counseling practice. *The Career Development Quarterly, 66*, 135–48. doi:10.1002/cdq.12128; Reich, T. C., & Hershcovis, M. S. (2011). Interpersonal relationships at work. In S. Zedeck (Ed.), *APA handbook of industrial and organizational psychology, Vol 3: Maintaining, expanding, and contracting the organization* (pp. 223–248). Washington, DC: American Psychological Association. doi:10.1037/12171-006; Richardson, M. S. (2012). Counseling for work and relationship. *The Counseling Psychologist, 40*, 190–242. doi:10.1177/0011000011406452

9. Savickas, M., Silling, S., & Schwartz, S. (1984). Time perspective in vocational maturity and career decision making. *Journal of Vocational Behavior, 25*, 258–269. doi:10.1016/0001-8791(84)90049-6

10. Ferrari, L., Nota, L., & Soresi, S. (2010). Time perspective and indecision in young and older adolescents. *British Journal of Guidance & Counselling, 38*, 61–82. doi:10.1080/03069880903408612

11. Taber, B. (2015). Enhancing future time perspective and exploring occupational possible selves. In P. Hartung, M. L. Savickas, & W. B. Walsh (Eds.), *The APA handbook of career intervention* (Vol. 2, pp. 101–111). Washington, DC: American Psychological Association.

12. Fieulane, N., & Apostolidis, T. (2015). Precariousness as a time horizon: How poverty and social insecurity shape individuals' time perspective. In M. Stolarski, N. Fieulane, & W. van Beek (Eds.), *Time perspective theory review, research and application* (pp. 213–228). New York: Springer.

13. Blustein, D. L. (2006). *The psychology of working: A new perspective for counseling, career development, and public policy.* New York: Routledge.

14. Duffy, R. D., Diemer, M. A., Perry, J. C., Laurenzi, C., & Torrey, C. L. (2012). The construction and initial validation of the Work Volition Scale. *Journal of Vocational Behavior, 80*, 400–11. doi:10.1016/j.jvb.2011.04.002

15. Blustein, D. L., Chaves, A. P. Diemer, M. A., Gallagher, L. A. Marshall, K. G., Sirin, S., & Bhati, K. S. (2002).Voices of the "forgotten half": The role of social class in the school-to-work transition. *Journal of Counseling Psychology, 49*, 311–323. doi:10.1037/0022-0167.49.3.311

16. Vuolo, M., Staff, J., & Mortimer, J. T. (2012). Weathering the Great Recession: Psychological and behavioral trajectories in the transition from school to work. *Developmental Psychology, 48*, 1759–1773. doi:10.1037/a0026047

17. Allan, B. A., Autin, K. L., & Duffy, R. D. (2016). Self-determination and meaningful work: Exploring socioeconomic constraints. *Frontiers in Psychology, 7*, 71. doi:10.3389/fpsyg.2016.00071; Blustein, D. L. (Ed.). (2013). *The Oxford handbook of the psychology of working.* New York: Oxford University Press. doi:/10.1093/oxfordhb/9780199758791.001.0001; Duffy, R. D., Blustein, D. L., Diemer, M. A., & Autin, K. L. (2016). The psychology of working theory. *Journal of Counseling Psychology, 63*, 127–148. doi:10.1037/cou0000140; Lyons, H. Z. (2011). Responding to hard times in the "Big Easy": Meeting the vocational needs of low-income African-American New Orleans residents. *The Career Development Quarterly, 59*, 290–301. doi:10.1002/j.2161-0045.2011.tb00070

18. Lewis, M., & Rudolph, K. D. (Eds.). (2014). *Handbook of developmental psychopathology* (3rd ed.). New York: Springer; Lipina, S. J., & Colombo, J. A. (2009). *Poverty and brain development during childhood: An approach from cognitive psychology and neuroscience.* Washington, DC: American Psychological Association; Yoshikawa, H., Aber, J. L., & Beardslee, W. R. (2012). The effects of poverty on the mental, emotional, and behavioral health of children and youth: Implications for prevention. *American Psychologist, 67*, 272–284.

19. Heckman, J. (2012). *Giving kids a fair chance.* Cambridge, MA: MIT Press.

Chapter 3

1. Marcus, P. (2017). *The psychoanalysis of career choice, job performance, and satisfaction: How to flourish in the workplace*. New York: Routledge.
2. Freud, S. (2002). *Civilization and its discontents* (D. McLintock, Trans.) [DX Kindle Edition]. Retrieved from https://www.amazon.com/Civilization-Discontents-Penguin-Modern-Classics-ebook/dp/B002RI9K8Q/ref=sr_1_2?s=digital-text&ie=UTF8&qid=1540129706&sr=1-2&keywords=Freud+civilization+and+its+discontents
3. Marcus, P. (2017). *The psychoanalysis of career choice, job performance, and satisfaction: How to flourish in the workplace*. New York: Routledge.
4. Mitchell, S. A. (1988). *Relational concepts in psychoanalysis*. Cambridge, MA: Harvard University Press; Wachtel, P. (2007). *Relational theory and the practice of psychotherapy*. New York: Guilford Press.
5. Donkin, R. (2010). *The history of work*. London: Palgrave.
6. Blustein, D. L. (2006). *The psychology of working: A new perspective for counseling, career development, and public policy*. New York: Routledge; Blustein, D. L. (2011). A relational theory of working. *Journal of Vocational Behavior, 79*, 1–17.
7. Blustein, D. L., Kozan, S., & Connors-Kellgren, A. (2013). Unemployment and underemployment: A narrative analysis about loss. *Journal of Vocational Behavior, 82*, 256–265; Paul, K. I., & Moser, K. (2009). Unemployment impairs mental health: Meta-analyses. *Journal of Vocational Behavior, 74*, 264–282.
8. Freud, S. (1995). *The Freud reader* (P. Gay, Ed.). New York: Norton.
9. Freud, S. (1995). *The Freud reader* (P. Gay, Ed.). New York: Norton; Kohlberg, L. (1981). *The philosophy of moral development: Moral stages and the idea of justice* (Essays on moral development, Vol. 1). San Francisco: Harper & Row.
10. Bowlby, J. (1973). *Attachment and loss, Vol. 2: Separation*. New York: Basic Books; Bowlby, J. (1988). *A secure base: Parent-child attachment and healthy human development*. New York: Basic Books; Gergen, K. J. (2009). *Relational being: Beyond self and community*. New York: Oxford University Press; Gilligan, C. (1982). *In a different voice*. Cambridge, MA: Harvard University Press; Jordan, J. M. (2009). *Relational-cultural therapy*. Washington, DC: American Psychological Association; Josselson, R. (1992). *The space between us: Exploring the dimensions of human relationships*. San Francisco: Jossey-Bass; Mitchell, S. A. (1988). *Relational concepts in psychoanalysis*. Cambridge, MA: Harvard University Press.
11. Bowlby, J. (1988). *A secure base: Parent-child attachment and healthy human development*. New York: Basic Books; Siegel, D. J. (2015). *The developing mind: How relationships and the brain interact to shape who we are* (2nd ed.). New York: Guilford Press.
12. Bowlby, J. (1988). *A secure base: Parent-child attachment and healthy human development*. New York: Basic Books; Cassidy, J., & Shaver, P. R. (Eds.). (2018). *Handbook of attachment: Theory, research, and clinical applications* (3rd ed.). New York: Guilford Press.

13. Bowlby, J. (1988). *A secure base: Parent-child attachment and healthy human development*. New York: Basic Books; Mayseless, O. (2016). *The caring motivation: An integrated theory*. New York: Oxford University Press.
14. Cassidy, J., & Shaver, P. R. (Eds.). (2018). *Handbook of attachment: Theory, research, and clinical applications* (3rd ed.). New York: Guilford Press.
15. Gilligan, C. (1982). *In a different voice*. Cambridge, MA: Harvard University Press.
16. Blustein, D. L. (2011). A relational theory of working. *Journal of Vocational Behavior, 79*, 1–17; Flum, H. (2001). Relational dimensions in career development. *Journal of Vocational Behavior, 59*, 1–16; Flum, H. (2015). Relationships and career development: An integrative approach. In P. J. Hartung, M. L. Savickas, & W. B. Walsh (Eds.), *APA handbook of career intervention* (Vol. 1, pp. 145–158). Washington, DC: American Psychological Association; Kenny, M. E., & Medvide, M. B. (2013). Relational influences. In S. D. Brown & R. W. Lent (Eds.), *Career development and counseling: Putting theory and research to work* (2nd ed., pp. 329–356). Hoboken, NJ: Wiley; Reich, T. C., & Hershcovis, M. S. (2011). Interpersonal relationships at work. In S. Zedeck (Ed.), *APA handbook of industrial and organizational psychology: Vol. 3. Maintaining, expanding, and contracting the organization* (pp. 233–248). Washington, DC: American Psychological Association; Richardson, M. S. (2012). Counseling for work and relationship. *Counseling Psychologist, 40*, 190–242; Schultheiss, D. E. P. (2003). A relational approach to career counseling: Theoretical integration and practical application. *Journal of Counseling & Development, 81*, 301–310. doi:10.1002/j.1556-6678.2003.tb00257.x; Schultheiss, D. E. P. (2007). The emergence of a relational cultural paradigm for vocational psychology. *International Journal of Educational and Vocational Guidance, 7*, 191–201.
17. Greenberg, J., & Mitchell, S. (1983). *Object relations in psychoanalytic theory*. Cambridge, MA: Harvard University Press; Mitchell, S. A. (1988). *Relational concepts in psychoanalysis*. Cambridge, MA: Harvard University Press; Wachtel, P. (2007). *Relational theory and the practice of psychotherapy*. New York: Guilford Press.
18. Kohut, H. (2009). *The analysis of the self: A systematic approach to the psychoanalytic treatment of narcissistic personality disorders*. Chicago: University of Chicago Press. (Original work published 1971).
19. Krieshok, T. S., Black, M. D., & McKay, R. A. (2009). Career decision making: The limits of rationality and the abundance of non-conscious processes. *Journal of Vocational Behavior, 75*, 275–290. dOi:l0.l016/j.jvb.2009.04.006; Phillips, S. D., Christopher-Sisk, E., & Gravino, K. (2001). Making career decisions in a relational context. *The Counseling Psychologist, 29*, 193–213.
20. Betz, N., & Fitzgerald, L. (1987). *The career psychology of women*. Orlando, FL: Academic Press; Gordon, E. W. (1974). Vocational guidance: Disadvantaged and minority populations. In E. L. Herr (Ed.), *Vocational guidance and human development* (pp. 452–477). Boston: Houghton Mifflin; Hackett, G., & Betz, N. (1981). A self-efficacy approach to the career development of women. *Journal of Vocational Behavior, 18*, pp. 326–339;, Helms, J. E., & Cook, D. A. (1999). *Using race and culture in counseling and psychotherapy: Theory and process*. Needham Heights, MA: Allyn & Bacon.

21. Blustein, D. L. (2011). A relational theory of working. *Journal of Vocational Behavior,79*, 1–17; Flum, H. (2001). Relational dimensions in career development. *Journal of Vocational Behavior, 59*, 1–16; Flum, H. (2015). Relationships and career development: An integrative approach. In P. J. Hartung, M. L. Savickas, & W. B. Walsh (Eds.), *APA handbook of career intervention* (Vol. 1, pp. 145–158). Washington, DC: American Psychological Association; Kenny, M. E., & Medvide, M. B. (2013). Relational influences. In S. D. Brown & R. W. Lent (Eds.), *Career development and counseling: Putting theory and research to work* (2nd ed., pp. 329–356). Hoboken, NJ: Wiley; Richardson, M. S. (2012). Counseling for work and relationship. *Counseling Psychologist, 40*, 190–242; Reich, T. C., & Hershcovis, M. S. (2011). Interpersonal relationships at work. In S. Zedeck (Ed.), *APA handbook of industrial and organizational psychology: Vol. 3. Maintaining, expanding, and contracting the organization* (pp. 233–248). Washington, DC: American Psychological Association; Schultheiss, D. E. P. (2003). A relational approach to career counseling: Theoretical integration and practical application. *Journal of Counseling & Development, 81*, 301–310. doi:10.1002/j.1556-6678.2003.tb00257; Schultheiss, D. E. P. (2007). The emergence of a relational cultural paradigm for vocational psychology. *International Journal of Educational and Vocational Guidance, 7*, 191–201.

22. Arthur, M. B., & Rousseau, D. M. (Eds.). (1996). *The boundaryless career.* New York: Oxford University Press; Hall, D. T. (1996). *The career is dead—Long live the career: A relational approach to careers.* San Francisco: Jossey-Bass; Arthur, M. B., & Rousseau, D. M. (Eds.). (1996). *The boundaryless career.* New York: Oxford University Press; Sennett, R. (1998). *The corrosion of character: The personal consequences of work in the new capitalism.* New York: Norton; Vallas, S. (2011). *Work: A critique.* Cambridge, MA: Polity.

23. Blustein, D. L., Fama, L. D., White, S. F., Ketterson, T. U., Schaefer, B. M., Schwam, M. F., . . . Skau, M. (2001). A qualitative analysis of counseling case material: Listening to our clients. *The Counseling Psychologist, 29*, 240–258; Bowe, J., Bowe, M., & Streeter, S. (2000). *Gig: Americans talk about their jobs.* New York: Three Rivers Press; Terkel, S. (1974). *Working: People talk about what they do all day and how they feel about what they do.* New York: Pantheon Books.

24. Blustein, D. L. (2011). A relational theory of working. *Journal of Vocational Behavior, 79*, 1–17; Flum, H. (2015). Relationships and career development: An integrative approach. In P. J. Hartung, M. L. Savickas, & W. B. Walsh (Eds.), *APA handbook of career intervention* (Vol. 1, pp. 145–158). Washington, DC: American Psychological Association; Kenny, M. E., Blustein, D. L., & Meerkins, T. (2018). Integrating relational perspectives in counseling. *Career Development Quarterly, 66*, 135–148.

25. Flum, H. (2015). Relationships and career development: An integrative approach. In P. J. Hartung, M. L. Savickas, & W. B. Walsh (Eds.), *APA handbook of career intervention* (Vol. 1, pp. 145–158). Washington, DC: American Psychological Association.

26. Blustein, D. L. (2011). A relational theory of working. *Journal of Vocational Behavior, 79*, 1–17; Kenny, M. E., Blustein, D. L., & Meerkins, T. (2018). Integrating relational perspectives in counseling. *Career Development Quarterly, 66*, 135–48; Phillips, S. D.,

Christopher-Sisk, E., & Gravino, K. (2001). Making career decisions in a relational context. *The Counseling Psychologist, 29*, 193–213.

27. Baillien, E., Neyens, I., DeWitte, H., & DeCuyper, N. (2009). A qualitative study on the development of workplace bullying: Towards a three-way model. *Journal of Community and Applied Social Psychology, 19*, 1–16; Flum, H. (2015). Relationships and career development: An integrative approach. In P. J. Hartung, M. L. Savickas, & W. B. Walsh (Eds.), *APA handbook of career intervention* (Vol. 1, pp. 145–158). Washington, DC: American Psychological Association.

28. Kossek, E. E., Pichler, S., Bodner, T., & Hammer, L. B. (2011). Workplace social support and work–family conflict: A meta-analysis clarifying the influence of general and work–family-specific supervisor and organizational support. *Personnel Psychology, 64*, 289–313. doi:10.1111/j.1744-6570.2011.01211.x; Viswesvaran, C., Sanchez, J. I., & Fisher, J. (1999). The role of social support in the process of work stress: A meta-analysis. *Journal of Vocational Behavior, 54*, 314–334.

29. Blustein, D. L. (2011). A relational theory of working. *Journal of Vocational Behavior, 79*, 1–17.

30. Liu, S., Huang, J. L., & Wang, M. (2014). Effectiveness of job search interventions: A meta-analytic review. *Psychological Bulletin, 140*, 1009–1041; Phillips, S. D., Christopher-Sisk, E., & Gravino, K. (2001). Making career decisions in a relational context. *The Counseling Psychologist, 29*, 193–213.

31. Blustein, D. L. (2011). A relational theory of working. *Journal of Vocational Behavior, 79*, 1–17.

32. Piketty, T. (2017). *Capital in the twenty-first century.* Cambridge, MA: Belknap Press of Harvard University Press. (Original work published 2014)

33. Aquino, K., & Lamertz, K. (2004). A relational model of workplace victimization: Social roles and patterns of victimization in dyadic relationships. *Journal of Applied Psychology, 89*, 1023–1034. doi:10.1037/0021-9010.89.6.1023; Einarsen, S., Hoel, H., Zapf, D., & Cooper, C. (2010). *Bullying and harassment in the workplace: Developments in theory, research, and practice.* Boca Raton, FL: CRC Press; Samnani, A., & Singh, P. (2012). 20 years of workplace bullying research: A review of the antecedents and consequences of bullying in the workplace. *Aggression and Violent Behavior, 17*, 581–589. doi:10.1016/j.avb.2012.08.004

34. Blustein, D. L. (2011). A relational theory of working. *Journal of Vocational Behavior, 79*, 1–17; Greenberg, J., & Mitchell, S. (1983). *Object relations in psychoanalytic theory.* Cambridge, MA: Harvard University Press; Mitchell, S. A. (1988). *Relational concepts in psychoanalysis.* Cambridge, MA: Harvard University Press;, Wachtel, P. (2007). *Relational theory and the practice of psychotherapy.* New York: Guilford Press.

35. Kohut, H. (2009). *The analysis of the self: A systematic approach to the psychoanalytic treatment of narcissistic personality disorders.* Chicago: University of Chicago Press. (Original work published 1971)

36. Brown, S. D., Ryan Krane, N. E., Brecheisen, J., Castelino, P., Budisin, I., Miller, M., & Edens, L. (2003). Critical ingredients of career choice interventions: More analyses and new hypotheses. *Journal of Vocational Behavior, 62*, 411–428; Whiston, S. C., Li, Y., Mitts, N. G., & Wright, L. (2017). Effectiveness of career choice interventions: A

meta-analytic replication and extension. *Journal of Vocational Behavior, 100,* 175–184.

37. Bolles, R. (2018). *What color is your parachute? A practical manual for job-hunters and career-changers* (Rev. ed.). Emeryville, CA: Ten Speed Press;, Liu, S., Huang, J. L., & Wang, M. (2014). Effectiveness of job search interventions: A meta-analytic review. *Psychological Bulletin, 140,* 1009–1041.

38. Blustein, D. L., Prezioso, M., & Schultheiss, D. E. (1995). Attachment theory and career development: Current status and future direction. *The Counseling Psychologist, 23,* 416–432; Cassidy, J., & Shaver, P. R. (Eds.). (2018). *Handbook of attachment: Theory, research, and clinical applications* (3rd ed.). New York: Guilford Press.

39. Blustein, D. L. (2011). A relational theory of working. *Journal of Vocational Behavior, 79,* 1–17; Dahling, J. J., & Librizzi, U. A. (2015). Integrating the theory of work adjustment and attachment theory to predict job turnover intentions. *Journal of Career Development, 42,* 215–28. doi:10.1177/0894845314545169; Kvitkovičová, L., Umemura, T., & Macek, P. (2017). Roles of attachment relationships in emerging adults' career decision-making process: A two-year longitudinal research design. *Journal of Vocational Behavior, 101,* 119–132. doi:10.1016/j.jvb.2017.05.006;, Flum, H. (2015). Relationships and career development: An integrative approach. In P. J. Hartung, M. L. Savickas, & W. B. Walsh (Eds.), *APA handbook of career intervention* (Vol. 1, pp. 145–158). Washington, DC: American Psychological Association.

40. Blustein, D. L., Walbridge, M., Friedlander, M. L., & Palladino, D. E. (1991). Contributions of psychological separation and parental attachment to the career development process. *Journal of Counseling Psychology,38,* 39–50.

41. Braunstein-Bercovitz, H. (2014). Self-criticism, anxious attachment, and avoidant attachment as predictors of career decision making. *Journal of Career Assessment, 22,* 176–87. doi:10.1177/1069072713492938; Keller, B. K., & Whiston, S. C. (2008). The role of parental influences on young adolescents' career development. *Journal of Career Assessment, 16,* 198–217; Wright, S. L., & Perrone, K. M. (2008). The impact of attachment on career-related variables: A review of the literature and proposed theoretical framework to guide future research. *Journal of Career Development, 35,* 87–106. Retrieved from https://doi.org/10.1177/0894845308325643.

42. Kenny, M. E., Blustein, D. L., Chaves, A., Grossman, J. M., & Gallagher, L. A. (2003). The role of perceived barriers and relational support in the educational and vocational lives of urban high school students. *Journal of Counseling Psychology, 50,* 142–155.

43. Diemer, M. A. (2007). Parental and school influences upon the career development of poor youth of color. *Journal of Vocational Behavior, 70,* 502–524.

44. Haasler, S. R. (2015). Voices of older women in Germany. In J. Bimrose, M. McMahon, & M. Watson (Eds.), *Women's career development throughout the lifespan: An international perspective* (pp. 152–163). New York: Routledge.

45. Ragins, B., & Kram, K. E. (2007). *The handbook of mentoring at work theory, research, and practice.* Thousand Oaks, CA: Sage; Passmore, J., Peterson, D. B., & Freire, T. (Eds.). (2013). *The Wiley-Blackwell handbook of the psychology of coaching and mentoring.* Chichester, England: Wiley Blackwell.

46. Tong, C., & Kram, K. E. (2013). The efficacy of mentoring—The benefits for mentees, mentors, and organizations. In J. Passmore, D. Peterson, & T. Freire (Eds.), *The Wiley-Blackwell handbook of the psychology of coaching and mentoring* (pp. 217–242). Chichester, England: Wiley Blackwell.

47. Dobrow, S., Chandler, D., Murphy, W., & Kram, K. (2012). A review of developmental networks: Incorporating a mutuality perspective. *Journal of Management, 38*, 210–242.

48. Liu, S., Huang, J. L., & Wang, M. (2014). Effectiveness of job search interventions: A meta-analytic review. *Psychological Bulletin, 140*, 1009–1041; Sharone, O. (2013). *Flawed system, flawed self: Job searching and unemployment.* Chicago: University of Chicago Press.

49. Vallas, S. (2011). *Work: A critique.* Cambridge, MA: Polity.

50. Liu, S., Huang, J. L., & Wang, M. (2014). Effectiveness of job search interventions: A meta-analytic review. *Psychological Bulletin, 140*, 1009–1041; Sharone, O. (2013). *Flawed system, flawed self: Job searching and unemployment.* Chicago: University of Chicago Press; Vallas, S. (2011). *Work: A critique.* Cambridge, MA: Polity.

51. Whiston, S. C., & Cinamon, R. G. (2015). The work–family interface: Integrating research and career counseling practice. *Career Development Quarterly, 63*, 44–56.

52. Blustein, D. L. (2006). *The psychology of working: A new perspective for counseling, career development, and public policy.* New York: Routledge; Blustein, D. L., & Spengler, P. M. (1995). Personal adjustment: Career counseling and psychotherapy. In W. B. Walsh & S. H. Osipow (Eds.), *Handbook of vocational psychology* (2nd ed., pp. 295–329). Mahwah, NJ: Erlbaum.

53. Gergen, K. J. (2009). *Relational being: Beyond self and community.* New York: Oxford University Press; Gilligan, C. (1982). *In a different voice.* Cambridge, MA: Harvard University Press; Jordan, J. M. (2009). *Relational-cultural therapy.* Washington, DC: American Psychological Association; Josselson, R. (1992). *The space between us: Exploring the dimensions of human relationships.* San Francisco: Jossey-Bass; Mitchell, S. A. (1988). *Relational concepts in psychoanalysis.* Cambridge, MA: Harvard University Press.

54. Blustein, D. L., Kozan, S., & Connors-Kellgren, A. (2013). Unemployment and underemployment: A narrative analysis about loss. *Journal of Vocational Behavior, 82*, 256–265; Paul, K. I., & Moser, K. (2009). Unemployment impairs mental health: Meta-analyses. *Journal of Vocational Behavior, 74*, 264–282; Sharone, O. (2013). *Flawed system, flawed self: Job searching and unemployment experiences.* Chicago: University of Chicago Press; Wanberg, C. R. (2012). The individual experience of unemployment. *Annual Review of Psychology, 63*, 369–396.

Chapter 4

1. Gardner, H. E., Csikszentmihalyi, M., & Damon, W. (2008). *Good work: When excellence and ethics meet.* New York: Basic Books.

2. Allison, W. T. (2012). *My Lai: An American atrocity in the Vietnam War.* Baltimore, MD: John Hopkins Univeristy Press.
3. Manning, R., Levine, M., & Collins, A. (2007). The Kitty Genovese murder and the social psychology of helping: The parable of the 38 witnesses. *American Psychologist, 62*(6), 555–562.
4. Batson, C. D., & Powell, A. A. (2003). Altruism and prosocial behavior. In T. Millon & M. J. Lerner (Eds.), *Handbook of psychology, Volume 5: Personality and social psychology* (pp. 463–484). Hoboken, NJ: Wiley.
5. Penner, L. A., Dovidio, J. F., Pilavin, J. A., Schroeder, D. A. (2005). Prosocial behavior: Multilevel perspective. *Annual Review of Psychology, 56,* 365–392; Blustein, D. L. (2006). *The psychology of working: A new perspective for counseling, career development, and public policy.* New York: Routledge; Duffy, R. D., Blustein, D. L., Diemer, M. A., & Autin, K. L. (2016). The psychology of working theory. *Journal of Counseling Psychology, 63,* 127–148; Gardner, H. E., Csikszentmihalyi, M., & Damon, W. (2008). *Good work: When excellence and ethics meet.* New York: Basic Books.
6. Gardner, H. E., Csikszentmihalyi, M., & Damon, W. (2008). *Good work: When excellence and ethics meet.* New York: Basic Books.
7. Budd, J. W. (2011). *The thought of work.* Ithaca, NY: ILR-Cornell Paperbacks.
8. Zweig, D. (2014). *Invisibles: Celebrating the unsung heroes of the workplace.* New York: Portfolio/Penguin.
9. Rose, M. (2004). *The mind at work: Valuing the intelligence of the American worker.* New York: Viking/Penguin.
10. Dik, B. J., Byrne, Z. S., & Steger, M. F. (Eds.). (2011). *Purpose and meaning in the workplace.* Washington, DC: American Psychological Association.
11. Savickas, M. L. (2013). Career construction theory and practice. In S. D. Brown & R. W. Lent (Eds.), *Career development and counselling: Putting theory and research to work* (2nd ed., pp. 42–70). Hoboken, NJ: Wiley. doi:/10.4135/9781412952675. n34; Schultheiss, D. (2009). To mother or to matter: Can women do both? *Journal of Career Development, 36,* 25–48.
12. Blustein, D. L. (2006). *The psychology of working: A new perspective for counseling, career development, and public policy.* New York: Routledge; Savickas, M. L. (2013). Career construction theory and practice. In S. D. Brown & R. W. Lent (Eds.), *Career development and counselling: Putting theory and research to work* (2nd ed., pp. 42–70). Hoboken, NJ: Wiley. doi:/10.4135/9781412952675.n34
13. Dik, B. J., & Duffy, R. D. (2015). Strategies for discerning and living a calling. In P. Hartung, M. Savickas, & B. Walsh (Eds.), *APA handbook of career intervention* (pp. 305–317).Washington, DC: American Psychological Association; Duffy, R. D., & Dik, B. J. (2013). Research on calling: What have we learned and where are we going? *Journal of Vocational Behavior, 83,* 428–436.
14. Duffy, R. D., & Dik, B. J. (2013). Research on calling: What have we learned and where are we going? *Journal of Vocational Behavior, 83,* 428–436.
15. Dik, B. J., & Duffy, R. D. (2015). Strategies for discerning and living a calling. In P. Hartung, M. Savickas, & B. Walsh (Eds.), *APA handbook of career intervention* (pp.

305–317).Washington, DC: American Psychological Association; Duffy, R. D., & Dik, B. J. (2013). Research on calling: What have we learned and where are we going? *Journal of Vocational Behavior, 83*, 428–436.

16. Duffy, R. D., Douglass, R. P., Autin, K. A., England, J. W., & Dik, B. J. (2016). Does the dark side of a calling exist? Examining potential negative effects. *Journal of Positive Psychology, 11*, 634–646.

17. Dik, B. J., & Duffy, R. D. (20145 B. Walsh (Eds.), *APA handbook of career intervention* (pp. 305–317).Washington, DC: American Psychological Association; Duffy, R. D., Douglass, R. P., Autin, K. A., England, J. W., & Dik, B. J. (2016). Does the dark side of a calling exist? Examining potential negative effects. *Journal of Positive Psychology, 11*, 634–646.

18. Dik, B. J., & Duffy, R. D. (2015). Strategies for discerning and living a calling. In P. Hartung, M. Savickas, & B. Walsh (Eds.), *APA handbook of career intervention* (pp. 305–317).Washington, DC: American Psychological Association.

19. Schwartz, B. (2015). *Why we work*. New York: Simon & Schuster.

20. Parker, S. K. (2014). Beyond motivation: Job and work design for development, health, ambidexterity, and more. *Annual Review of Psychology, 65*, 661–691. doi:10.1146/annurev-psych-010213-115208; Wrzesniewski, A., & Dutton, J. E. (2001). Crafting a job: Revisioning employees as active crafters of their work. *Academy of Management Review, 26*, 179–201.

21. Dik, B. J., Byrne, Z. S., & Steger, M. F. (Eds.). (2011). *Purpose and meaning in the workplace*. Washington, DC: American Psychological Association.

22. Dik, B. J., & Duffy, R. D. (2015). Strategies for discerning and living a calling. In P. Hartung, M. Savickas, & B. Walsh (Eds.), *APA handbook of career intervention* (pp. 305–317).Washington, DC: American Psychological Association.

23. Dik, B. J., & Duffy, R. D. (2012). *Make your job a calling: How the psychology of vocation can change your life at work*. Philadelphia: Templeton Press.

24. Frankl, V. E. (1959/2006). *Man's search for meaning*. Boston: Beacon Press.

25. Dik, B. J., & Duffy, R. D. (2012). *Make your job a calling: How the psychology of vocation can change your life at work*. Philadelphia: Templeton Press; Schwartz, B. (2015). *Why we work?* New York: Simon & Schuster; Grant, A. (2014). *Give and take: Why helping others drives our success*. New York: Penguin Group.

26. UN General Assembly. (1948, December 10). *Universal declaration of human rights* [217 A (III)]. Retrieved from http://www.refworld.org/docid/3ae6b3712c.html

27. Blustein, D. L. (Ed.). (2013). *The Oxford handbook of the psychology of working*. New York: Oxford University Press; Duffy, R. D., Blustein, D. L., Diemer, M. A., & Autin, K. L. (2016). The psychology of working theory. *Journal of Counseling Psychology, 63*, 127–148; Herbert, B. (2014). *Losing our way: An intimate portrait of a troubled America*. New York: Penguin-Random; Ryan, W. (1976). *Blaming the victim*. New York: Vintage.

28. Herbert, B. (2014). Losing our way: An intimate portrait of a troubled America. New York: Penguin-Random; Putnam, R. (2016). *Our kids: The American dream in crisis*. New York: Simon & Schuster.

Chapter 5

1. Kanfer, R., & Chen, G. (2016). Motivation in organizational behavior: History, advances and prospects. *Organizational Behavior and Human Decision Processes*, *136*, 6–19; Kanfer, R., Frese, M., & Johnson, R. E. (2017). Motivation related to work: A century of progress. *Journal of Applied Psychology*, *102*, 338–355; Latham, G. P. (2012). *Work motivation: History, theory, research, and practice*. Thousand Oaks, CA: Sage.

2. Blustein, D. L. (2006). *The psychology of working: A new perspective for counseling, career development, and public policy*. New York: Routledge.

3. Blustein, D. L. (2017). Integrating theory, research, and practice: Lessons learned from the evolution of vocational psychology. In J. P. Sampson, E. Bullock-Yowell, V. C. Dozier, D. S. Osborn, & J. G. Lenz (Eds.), *Integrating theory, research, and practice in vocational psychology: Current status and future directions* (pp. 179–187). Tallahassee: Florida State University.

4. Latham, G. P. (2012). *Work motivation: History, theory, research, and practice*. Thousand Oaks, CA: Sage.

5. Kanfer, R., & Chen, G. (2016). Motivation in organizational behavior: History, advances and prospects. *Organizational Behavior and Human Decision Processes*, *136*, 6–19; Kanfer, R., Frese, M., & Johnson, R. E. (2017). Motivation related to work: A century of progress. *Journal of Applied Psychology*, *102*, 338–355; Latham, G. P. (2012). *Work motivation: History, theory, research, and practice*. Thousand Oaks, CA: Sage.

6. Highhouse, S. (2007). Applications of organizational psychology: Learning through failure or failure to learn. In L. L. Koppes (Ed.), *Historical perspectives in industrial and organizational psychology* (pp. 331–352). Mahwah, NJ: Erlbaum; Latham, G. P. (2012). *Work motivation: History, theory, research, and practice*. Thousand Oaks, CA: Sage.

7. Highhouse, S. (2007). Applications of organizational psychology: Learning through failure or failure to learn. In L. L. Koppes (Ed.), *Historical perspectives in industrial and organizational psychology* (pp. 331–352). Mahwah, NJ: Erlbaum; Latham, G. P. (2012). *Work motivation: History, theory, research, and practice*. Thousand Oaks, CA: Sage.

8. Blustein, D. L. (2017). Integrating theory, research, and practice: Lessons learned from the evolution of vocational psychology. In J. P. Sampson, E. Bullock-Yowell, V. C. Dozier, D. S. Osborn, & J. G. Lenz (Eds.), *Integrating theory, research, and practice in vocational psychology: Current status and future directions* (pp. 179–187). Tallahassee: Florida State University.

9. Csikszentmihalyi, M. (2009). *Flow: The psychology of optimal experience*. New York: Harper Row.

10. Kowal, J., & Fortier, M. (1999). Motivational determinants of flow: Contributions from self- determination theory. *Journal of Social Psychology*, *139*, 355–368. https://doi.org/10.1080/00224549909598391; Nielsen, K., & Cleal, B. (2010). Predicting flow at work: Investigating the activities and job characteristics that predict flow

states at work. *Journal of Occupational Health Psychology, 15,* 180–190. https://doi.org/10.1037/a0018893.

11. Csikszentmihalyi, M. (2014). *Applications of flow in human development and education: The collected works of Mihaly Csikszentmihalyi.* Dordrecht, Netherlands: Spring erdoi:10.1007/978-94-017-9094-9; Linley, P. A., Harrington, S., & Garcea, N. (Eds.). (2013). *The Oxford handbook of positive psychology and work.* New York: Oxford University Press;, Pink, D. H. (2011). *Drive: The surprising truth about what motivates us.* New York: Riverhead Books.

12. Deci, E. L., & Ryan, R. M. (2000). The "what" and "why" of goal pursuits: Human needs and the self-determination of behavior. *Psychological Inquiry, 11,* 227–268. https://doi.org/10.1207/S15327965PLI1104_01; Latham, G. P. (2012). *Work motivation: History, theory, research, and practice.* Thousand Oaks, CA: Sage; Lent, R. W., Brown, S. D., & Hackett, G. (1994). Toward a unifying social cognitive theory of career and academic interest, choice, and performance. *Journal of Vocational Behavior, 45,* 79–122.

13. Deci, E. L., & Ryan, R. M. (2000). The "what" and "why" of goal pursuits: Human needs and the self-determination of behavior. *Psychological Inquiry, 11,* 227–268. https://doi.org/10.1207/S15327965PLI1104_01; Ryan, R. M., & Deci, E. L. (2000). Self-determination theory and the facilitation of intrinsic motivation, social development, and well-being. *American Psychologist, 55,* 68–78https://doi.org/10.1037/0003-066X.55.1.68; Ryan, R. M., & Deci, E. L. (2000). Intrinsic and extrinsic motivations: Classic definitions and new directions. *Contemporary Educational Psychology, 25,* 54–67. https://doi:10.1006/ceps.1999.1020.

14. Pine, F. (1990). *Drive, ego, object, and self: A synthesis for clinical work.* New York: Basic Books; Safran, J. D. (2012). *Psychoanalysis and psychoanalytic therapies.* Washington, DC: American Psychological Association.

15. Schneider, K. J., Bugental, J. F. T., & Pierson, J. F. (2014). *Handbook of humanistic psychology: Leading edges in theory, research, and practice.* Thousand Oaks, CA: Sage; Rogers, C. R. (1995). *On becoming a person: A therapist's view of psychotherapy.* New York: Houghton Mifflin.

16. Gagné, M. (2014). *The Oxford handbook of work engagement, motivation, and self-determination theory.* New York: Oxford University Press.

17. Gagné, M. (2014). *The Oxford handbook of work engagement, motivation, and self-determination theory.* New York: Oxford University Press; Ryan, R. M., & Deci, E. L. (2000). Self-determination theory and the facilitation of intrinsic motivation, social development, and well-being. *American Psychologist, 55,* 68–78.

18. Gagné, M. (2014). *The Oxford handbook of work engagement, motivation, and self-determination theory.* New York: Oxford University Press; Ryan, R. M., & Deci, E. L. (2000). Intrinsic and extrinsic motivations: Classic definitions and new directions. *Contemporary Educational Psychology, 25,* 54–67. https://doi:10.1006/ceps.1999.1020.

19. Gagné, M. (2014). *The Oxford handbook of work engagement, motivation, and self-determination theory.* New York: Oxford University Press; Ryan, R. M., & Deci, E. L. (2000). Self-determination theory and the facilitation of intrinsic motivation, social development, and well-being. *American Psychologist, 55,* 68–78.

20. Blustein, D. L. (Ed.). (2013). *The Oxford handbook of the psychology of working.* New York: Oxford University Press; Blustein, D. L., Kenny, M. E., Di Fabio, A., & Guichard, J. (2019). Expanding the impact of the psychology of working: Engaging psychology in the struggle for decent work and human rights. *Journal of Career Assessment, 27,* 3–28. https://doi.org/10.1177/1069072718774002; Blustein, D. L., Olle, C., Connors-Kellgren, A., & Diamonti, A. J. (2016). Decent work: A psychological perspective. *Frontiers in Psychology, 7,* 407. https://doi:10.3389/fpsyg.2016.00407; Duffy, R. D., Blustein, D. L., Diemer, M. A., & Autin, K. L. (2016). The psychology of working theory. *Journal of Counseling Psychology, 63,* 127-148. doi:https://doi.org/10.1037/cou0000140

21. Colquitt, J., Conlon, D., Wesson, M., Porter, C., Yee Ng, K., & Murphy, Kevin R. (2001). Justice at the millennium: A meta-analytic review of 25 years of organizational justice research. *Journal of Applied Psychology, 86,* 425–445; Cropanzano, R., Bowen, D., & Gilliland, S. (2007). The management of organizational justice. *The Academy of Management Perspectives, 21,* 34–48.

22. Greenberg, J., & Colquitt, J. A. (Eds.). (2005). *Handbook of organizational justice.* Mahwah, NJ: Erlbaum.

23. Cropanzano, R., Bowen, D., & Gilliland, S. (2007). The management of organizational justice. *The Academy of Management Perspectives, 21,* 34–48.

24. Walsh, W. B., Savickas, M. L., & Hartung, P. J. (Eds.). (2013). *Handbook of vocational psychology.* New York: Routledge; Zedeck, S. (Ed.). (2011). *APA handbook of industrial and organizational psychology.* Washington, DC: American Psychological Association.

25. Walsh, W. B., Savickas, M. L., & Hartung, P. J. (Eds.). (2013). *Handbook of vocational psychology.* New York: Routledge; Zedeck, S. (Ed.). (2011). *APA handbook of industrial and organizational psychology.* Washington, DC: American Psychological Association.

26. Hooley, T., Sultana, R. G., & Thomsen, R. (Eds.). (2018). *Career guidance for social justice: Contesting neoliberalism.* New York: Routledge.

Chapter 6

1. Budd, J. W. (2011). *The thought of work.* Ithaca, NY: ILR-Cornell Paperbacks; Mayseless, O. (2016). *The caring motivation: An integrated theory.* New York: Oxford University Press.

2. Folbre, N. (Ed.). (2012). *For love and money: Care provision in the United States.* New York: Russell Sage Foundation; Richardson, M. S. (2012). Counseling for work and relationship. *The Counseling Psychologist, 40,* 190–242. https://doi.org/10.1177/0011000011406452

3. Budd, J. W. (2011). *The thought of work.* Ithaca, NY: ILR-Cornell Paperbacks; Tronto, J. C. (1993). *Moral boundaries: A political argument for an ethic of care.* New York: Routledge; Tronto, J. C. (2006). Vicious circles of unequal care. In M.

Hamington (Ed.), *Socializing care* (pp. 3–26). Lanham, MD: Rowman and Littlefield; Noonan, M. C. (2001). The impact of domestic work on men's and women's wages. *Journal of Marriage and Family, 63,* 1134–1145. https://doi.org/10.1111/j.1741-3737.2001.01134.x; Schultheiss, D. E. P. (2006). The interface of work and family life. *Professional Psychology: Research and Practice, 37,* 334–341. http://dx.doi.org/10.1037/0735-7028.37.4.334

4. Hochschild, A. R. (2000). Global care chains and emotional surplus value. In W. Hutton & A. Giddens (Eds.), *On the edge: Living with global capitalism* (pp. 130–146). London: Cape; Hochschild, A. R. (2003). *The commercialization of intimate life: Notes from home and work.* Berkeley: University of California Press; Whiston, S. C., & Cinamon, R. G. (2015). The work–family interface: Integrating research and career counseling practice. *Career Development Quarterly, 63,* 44–56. https://doi.org/10.1002/j.2161-0045.2015.00094.x

5. Fassinger, R. E. (2008). Workplace diversity and public policy: Challenges and opportunities for psychology. *American Psychologist, 63,* 252–268. doi:10.1037/0003-006X.63.4.252; Kantamneni, N. (2013). Gender and the psychology of working. In D. L. Blustein (Ed.), *The Oxford handbook of the psychology of working* (pp. 85–102). New York: Oxford University Press.

6. Mayseless, O. (2016). *The caring motivation: An integrated theory.* New York: Oxford University Press; Richardson, M. S. (2012). Counseling for work and relationship. *The Counseling Psychologist, 40,* 190–242. https://doi.org/10.1177/0011000011406452; Richardson, M. S., & Schaefer, C. (2013). From work and family to a dual model of working. In D. L. Blustein (Ed.), *The Oxford handbook of the psychology of working* (pp. 141–159). New York: Oxford University Press.

7. Folbre, N. (Ed.). (2012). *For love and money: Care provision in the United States.* New York: Russell Sage Foundation; Budd, J. W. (2011). *The thought of work.* Ithaca, NY: ILR-Cornell Paperbacks; Tronto, J. C. (1993). *Moral boundaries: A political argument for an ethic of care.* New York: Routledge.

8. Folbre, N. (Ed.). (2012). *For love and money: Care provision in the United States.* New York: Russell Sage Foundation.

9. Mayseless, O. (2016). *The caring motivation: An integrated theory.* New York: Oxford University Press.

10. Folbre, N. (Ed.). (2012). *For love and money: Care provision in the United States.* New York: Russell Sage Foundation; Mayseless, O. (2016). *The caring motivation: An integrated theory.* New York: Oxford University Press.

11. Mayseless, O. (2016). *The caring motivation: An integrated theory.* New York: Oxford University Press.

12. Bowbly, J. (1988). *A secure base: Clinical applications of attachment theory.* London: Routledge; Mayseless, O. (2016). *The caring motivation: An integrated theory.* New York: Oxford University Press.

13. Ainsworth, M. S. (1989). Attachments beyond infancy. *American Psychologist, 44,* 709–716. http://dx.doi.org/10.1037/0003-066X.44.4.709; Cassidy, J., & Shaver, P. R. (Eds.). (2010). *Handbook of attachment: Theory, research, and clinical applications.* New York: Guilford Press.

14. Ainsworth, M. S. (1989). Attachments beyond infancy. *American Psychologist, 44*(4), 709–716. http://dx.doi.org/10.1037/0003-066X.44.4.709; Cassidy, J., & Shaver, P. R. (Eds.). (2010). *Handbook of attachment: Theory, research, and clinical applications.* New York: Guilford Press.

15. Richardson, M. S. (2012). Counseling for work and relationship. *The Counseling Psychologist, 40,* 190–242. https://doi.org/10.1177/0011000011406452; Richardson, M. S., & Schaefer, C. (2013). From work and family to a dual model of working. In D. L. Blustein (Ed.), *The Oxford handbook of the psychology of working* (pp. 141–159). New York: Oxford University Press.

16. Richardson, M. S. (2012). Counseling for work and relationship. *The Counseling Psychologist, 40,* 190–242. https://doi.org/10.1177/0011000011406452; Richardson, M. S., & Schaefer, C. (2013). From work and family to a dual model of working. In D. L. Blustein (Ed.), *The Oxford handbook of the psychology of working* (pp. 141–159). New York: Oxford University Press.

17. Richardson, M. S. (2012). Counseling for work and relationship. *The Counseling Psychologist, 40,* 190–242. https://doi.org/10.1177/0011000011406452; Richardson, M. S., & Schaefer, C. (2013). From work and family to a dual model of working. In D. L. Blustein (Ed.), *The Oxford handbook of the psychology of working* (pp. 141–159). New York: Oxford University Press.

18. Betz, N., & Fitzgerald, L. (1987). *The career psychology of women.* Orlando, FL: Academic Press; Fassinger, R. E. (2008). Workplace diversity and public policy: Challenges and opportunities for psychology. *American Psychologist, 63,* 252–268. doi:10.1037/0003-006X.63.4.252; Friedan, B. (2001). *The feminine mystique.* New York: Norton.

19. Budd, J. W. (2011). *The thought of work.* Ithaca, NY: ILR-Cornell Paperbacks.

20. Budd, J. W. (2011). *The thought of work.* Ithaca, NY: ILR-Cornell Paperbacks; Folbre, N. (Ed.). (2012). *For love and money: Care provision in the United States.* New York: Russell Sage Foundation; Mayseless, O. (2016). *The caring motivation: An integrated theory.* New York: Oxford University Press.

21. Murdock, G. P., & Provost, C. (1973). Measurement of cultural competency. *Ethnology, 12,* 379–392. doi:10.2307/3773367

22. Betz, N., & Fitzgerald, L. (1987). *The career psychology of women.* Orlando, FL: Academic Press; Fassinger, R. E. (2008). Workplace diversity and public policy: Challenges and opportunities for psychology. *American Psychologist, 63,* 252–268. doi:10.1037/0003-006X.63.4.252

23. Betz, N. E. (2005). Women's career development. In S. D. Brown & R. W. Lent (Eds.), *Career development and counseling: Putting theory and research to work* (pp. 253–277). Hoboken, NJ: Wiley; Kantamneni, N. (2013). Gender and the psychology of working. In D. L. Blustein (Ed.), *The Oxford handbook of the psychology of working* (pp. 85–102). New York: Oxford University Press.

24. Bianchi, S., Folbre, N., & Wolf, D. (2012). Unpaid care work. In N. Folbre (Ed.), *For love and money: Care provision in the United States* (pp. 40–64). New York: Russell Sage Foundation.

25. Richardson, M. S., & Schaefer, C. (2013). From work and family to a dual model of working. In D. L. Blustein (Ed.), *The Oxford handbook of the psychology of working* (pp. 141–159). New York: Oxford University Press.

26. Folbre, N. (Ed.). (2012). *For love and money: Care provision in the United States.* New York: Russell Sage Foundation.

27. Bianchi, S., Folbre, N., & Wolf, D. (2012). Unpaid care work. In N. Folbre (Ed.), *For love and money: Care provision in the United States* (pp. 40–64). New York: Russell Sage Foundation; Osterman, P. (2017). *Who will care for us: Long-term care and the long-term workforce.* New York: Russell Sage Foundation; Richardson, M. S., & Schaefer, C. (2013). From work and family to a dual model of working. In D. L. Blustein (Ed.), *The Oxford handbook of the psychology of working* (pp. 141–159). New York: Oxford University Press.

28. Budd, J. W. (2011). *The thought of work.* Ithaca, NY: ILR-Cornell Paperbacks.

29. Folbre, N. (Ed.). (2012). *For love and money: Care provision in the United States.* New York: Russell Sage Foundation.

30. O'Brien, K. M., Ganginis Del Pino, H. V., Yoo, S. K., Cinamon, R. G., & Han, Y. J. (2014). Work, family, support, and depression: Employed mothers in Israel, Korea, and the United States. *Journal of Counseling Psychology, 61,* 461–472. doi:10.1037/a0036339

31. Mayseless, O. (2016). *The caring motivation: An integrated theory.* New York: Oxford University Press.

32. Mayseless, O. (2016). *The caring motivation: An integrated theory.* New York: Oxford University Press.

33. Mayseless, O. (2016). *The caring motivation: An integrated theory.* New York: Oxford University Press; Tronto, J. C. (2006). Vicious circles of unequal care. In M. Hamington (Ed.), *Socializing care* (pp. 3–26). Lanham, MD: Rowman and Littlefield.

34. Mayseless, O. (2016). *The caring motivation: An integrated theory.* New York: Oxford University Press.

35. Osterman, P. (2017). *Who will care for us: Long-term care and the long-term workforce.* New York: Russell Sage Foundation.

36. Gergen, K. J. (2009). *Relational being: Beyond self and community.* New York: Oxford University Press; Gilligan, C. (1982). *In a different voice: Psychological theory and women's development.* Cambridge, MA: Harvard University Press; Jordan, J. M. (2009). *Relational-cultural therapy.* Washington, DC: American Psychological Association; Jordan, J., Kaplan, A., Miller, J. B., Stiver, I., & Surrey, J. (1991). *Women's growth in connection: Writings from the Stone Center.* New York: Guilford Press; Josselson, R. (1992). *The space between us: Exploring the dimensions of human relationships.* San Francisco: Jossey-Bass.

37. Cinamon, R. G. (2015). The synergy project: A group career counseling intervention to enhance work-family management. In P. J. Hartung, M. L. Savickas, & W. B. Walsh (Eds.), *Handbook of career interventions, Volume 2: Applications* (pp. 413–425). Washington, DC: American Psychological Association; Hochschild, A. R. (2003). *The commercialization of intimate life: Notes from home and work.* Berkeley: University of California Press; Richardson, M. S. (2012). Counseling for work and relationship. *The Counseling Psychologist, 40,* 190–242. https://doi.org/10.1177/0011000011406452; Schultheiss, D. E. P. (2009). To mother or matter: Can women do both? *Journal of Career Development, 36,* 25–47. https://doi.org/10.1177/0894845309340795; Whiston, S. C., & Cinamon, R. G. (2015). The work–family

interface: Integrating research and career counseling practice. *Career Development Quarterly*, *63*, 44–56. https://doi.org/10.1002/j.2161-0045.2015.00094.x

38. Richardson, M. S., & Schaefer, C. (2013). From work and family to a dual model of working. In D. L. Blustein (Ed.), *The Oxford handbook of the psychology of working* (pp. 141–159). New York: Oxford University Press.

39. <<<REFO:BK>>>Folbre, N. (Ed.). (2012). *For love and money: Care provision in the United States*. New York: Russell Sage Foundation<<<REFC>>>.

40. Stiglitz, J. E. (2012). *The price of inequality: How today's divided society endangers our future*. New York: Norton.; Stiglitz, J. E. (2015). *The great divide: Unequal societies and what we can do about them*. New York: Norton.

41. Budd, J. W. (2011). *The thought of work*. Ithaca, NY: ILR-Cornell Paperbacks; Gilligan, C. (1982). *In a different voice: Psychological theory and women's development*. Cambridge, MA: Harvard University Press; Mayseless, O. (2016). *The caring motivation: An integrated theory*. New York: Oxford University Press.

42. Standing, G. (2011). *The precariat: The new dangerous class*. London: Bloomsbury Academic.

43. Standing, G. (2011). *The precariat: The new dangerous class*. London: Bloomsbury Academic.

Chapter 7

1. Boston Latin School. (2018, October 31). *Wikipedia, The Free Encyclopedia*. Retrieved November 16, 2018, from https://en.wikipedia.org/w/index.php?title=Boston_Latin_School&oldid=866582065

2. Ferguson, A. D., & Miville, M. L. (Eds.). (2014). *Handbook of race, ethnicity, and gender in psychology*. New York: Springer; Neville, H. A., Tynes, B. M., & Utsey, S. O. (Eds.). (2009). *Handbook of African American psychology*. Thousand Oaks, CA: Sage; Valsiner, J. (Ed.). (2012). *The Oxford handbook of culture and psychology*. New York: Oxford University Press; Roberson, Q. (2013). *The Oxford handbook of diversity and work*. New York: Oxford University Press; Broadbridge, A. M., & Fielden, S. L. (2018). *Research handbook of diversity and careers*. Northampton, MA: Elgar.

3. Flores, L. (2013). Race and working. In D. L. Blustein (Ed.), *The Oxford handbook of the psychology of working* (pp. 71–84). New York: Oxford University Press.

4. Helms, J. E., & Cook, D. A. (1999). *Using race and culture in counseling and psychotherapy: Theory and process*. Boston: Allyn & Bacon; Helms, J. E., Jernigan, M., & Mascher, J. (2005). The meaning of race in psychology and how to change it: A methodological perspective. *American Psychologist*, *60*, 27–36.

5. Helms, J. E. (2012). A legacy of eugenics underlies racial-group comparisons in intelligence testing. *Industrial and Organizational Psychology: Perspectives on Science and Practice*, *5*, 176–179. doi:10.1111/j.1754-9434.2012.01426.x; Helms, J. E., Jernigan, M., & Mascher, J. (2005). The meaning of race in psychology and how to change

it: A methodological perspective. *American Psychologist, 60,* 27–36. doi:10.1037/0003-066X.60.1.27.

6. *Microaggressions and marginality: Manifestation, dynamics, and impact.* NY: Wiley.

7. Blustein, D. L. (Ed.). (2013). *The Oxford handbook of the psychology of working.* New York: Oxford University Press. doi:/10.1093/oxfordhb/9780199758791.001.0001; Karsten, M. F. (Ed.). (2016). *Gender, race, and ethnicity in the workplace: Emerging issues and enduring challenges.* Santa Barbara, CA: Praeger.

8. Institute for Women Policy Research. (2018). *Pay equity & discrimination.* Retrieved from https://iwpr.org/issue/employment-education-economic-change/pay-equity-discrimination/

9. Kantamneni, N. (2013). Gender and the psychology of working. In D. L. Blustein (Ed.), *The Oxford handbook of the psychology of working* (pp. 85–102). New York: Oxford University Press. doi:/10.1093/oxfordhb/9780199758791.013.0006

10. Betz, N., & Fitzgerald, L. (1987). *The career psychology of women.* Orlando, FL: Academic Press; Harmon, L. W. (1972). Variables related to women's persistence in educational plans. *Journal of Vocational Behavior, 2,* 143–153.

11. Betz, N., & Fitzgerald, L. (1987). *The career psychology of women.* Orlando, FL: Academic Press; Heppner, M. J. (2013). Women, men, and work: The long journey to gender equity. In S. D. Brown & R. W. Lent (Eds.), *Career development and counseling: Putting theory and research to work* (2nd ed., pp. 187–214). Hoboken, NJ: Wiley.

12. Fassinger, R. E. (2008). Workplace diversity and public policy: Challenges and opportunities for psychology. *American Psychologist, 63,* 252–268. doi:10.1037/0003-066x.63.4.252; Fouad, N. A., Singh, R., Cappaert, K., Chang, W. H., & Wan, M. (2016). Comparison of women engineers who persist in or depart from engineering. *Journal of Vocational Behavior, 92,* 79–93. doi:10.1016/j.jvb.2015.11.002; Karsten, M. F. (Ed.). (2016). *Gender, race, and ethnicity in the workplace: Emerging issues and enduring challenges.* Santa Barbara, CA.

13. Chronister, K. M., & McWhirter, E. H. (2006). An experimental examination of two career intervention programs for battered women. *Journal of Counseling Psychology, 53,* 151–164; Cinamon, R. G. (2015). The synergy project: A group career counseling intervention to enhance work-family management. In P. J. Hartung, M. L. Savickas, & W. B. Walsh (Eds.), *Handbook of career interventions, Volume 2: Applications* (pp. 413–425). Washington, DC: American Psychological Association; Kossek, E. E., Su, R., & Wu, L. (2017). "Opting Out" or "Pushed Out"? Integrating perspectives on women's career equality for gender inclusion and interventions. *Journal of Management, 43,* 228–254. https://doi.org/10.1177/0149206316671582; Walsh, W. B., & Heppner, M. (Eds.). (2006). *Handbook of career counseling for women* (2nd ed). Mahwah, NJ: Erlbaum.

14. Fielden, S., & Hunt, C. (2014). Sexual harassment in the workplace. In S. Kumra, R. Simpson, & R. J. Burke (Eds.), *The Oxford handbook of gender in organizations* (pp. 353–370). New York: Oxford University Press; Fitzgerald, L. (2017). Still the last great open secret: Sexual harassment as systemic trauma. *Journal of Trauma & Dissociation, 18,* 483–489; Fitzgerald, L. F., Drasgow, F., Hulin, C. L., Gelfand,

M. J., & Magley, V. J. (1997). Antecedents and consequences of sexual harassment in organizations: A test of an integrated model. *Journal of Applied Psychology, 82,* 578–589; Mueller, C., De Coster, S., & Estes, S. (2001). Sexual harassment in the workplace: Unanticipated consequences of modern social control in organizations. *Work and Occupations, 28,* 411–446. https://doi.org/10.1177/0730888401028004003

15. Anderson, M. Z., & Croteau, J. M. (2013). Toward an inclusive LGBT psychology of working. In D. L. Blustein (Ed.), *The Oxford handbook of the psychology of working* (pp. 103–126). New York: Oxford University Press.

16. Anderson, M. Z., & Croteau, J. M. (2013). Toward an inclusive LGBT psychology of working. In D. L. Blustein (Ed.), *The Oxford handbook of the psychology of working* (pp. 103–126). New York: Oxford University Press.

17. Fabian, E. (2013). Disability and work. In D. L. Blustein (Ed.), *The Oxford handbook of the psychology of working* (pp. 185–200). New York: Oxford University Press.

18. *Americans With Disabilities Act of 1990,* Pub. L. No. 101-336, 104 Stat. 328 (1990). Retrieved from https://www.ada.gov/; Fabian, E. (2013). Disability and work. In D. L. Blustein (Ed.), *The Oxford handbook of the psychology of working* (pp. 185–200). New York: Oxford University Press.

19. Bureau of Labor Statistics. (2018). *Persons with a disability: Labor force characteristics summary.* Retrieved from https://www.bls.gov/news.release/disabl.nr0.htm

20. Dunn, E. C., Wewiorski, N. J., & Rogers, E. S. (2008). The meaning and importance of employment to people in recovery from serious mental illness: Results of a qualitative study. *Psychiatric Rehabilitation Journal, 32,* 59–62; Fabian, E., & Liesener, J. (2005). Promoting the career potential of youth and young adults with disabilities. In S. D. Brown & R. W. Lent (Eds.), *Career development and counseling: Putting theory and research to work* (pp. 551–573). Hoboken, NJ: Wiley; Millner, U. C., Rogers, E. S., Bloch, P., Costa, W., Pritchett, S., & Woods, T. (2015). Exploring the work lives of adults with serious mental illness from a vocational psychology perspective. *Journal of Counseling Psychology, 62,* 642–654. http://dx.doi.org/10.1037/cou0000109; Szymanski, E. M., Enright, M. S., Hershenson, D. B., & Ettinger, J. M. (2010). Career development theories and constructs: Implications for people with disabilities. In E. M. Szymanski & R. M. Parker (Eds.), *Work and disability: Contexts, issues and strategies for enhancing employment outcomes for people with disabilities* (pp. 87–131). Austin, TX: Pro-Ed.

21. Desmond, M. (2017). *Evicted: Poverty and profit in the American city.* New York: Broadway Books (Original work published in 2016); Herbert, B. (2014). *Losing our way: An intimate portrait of a troubled America.* New York: Penguin-Random House; Smith, L. (2010). *Psychology, poverty, and the end of social exclusion: Putting our practice to work.* New York: Teachers College Press, Columbia University; Stiglitz, J. E. (2015). *The great divide: Unequal societies and what we can do about them.* New York: Norton.

22. Ali, S. R. (2013). Poverty, social class, and working. In D. L. Blustein (Ed.), *The Oxford handbook of the psychology of working* (pp. 127–140). New York: Oxford University Press, 2013. doi:10.1093/oxfordhb/9780199758791.001.0001; Heckman, J. J. (2006). Skill formation and the economics of investing in disadvantaged children. *Science, 312*(5782),

1900–1902. doi:10.1126/science.1128898; Heberle, A. E., & Carter, A. S. (2015). Cognitive aspects of young children's experience of economic disadvantage. *Psychological Bulletin, 141,* 723–746. http://dx.doi.org/10.1037/bul0000010; Schilbach, F., Schofield, H., & Mullainathan, S. (2016). The psychological lives of the poor. *American Economic Review, 106,* 435–440 https://www.aeaweb.org/articles?id=10.1257/aer.p20161101

23. Liu, W. (2013). *The Oxford handbook of social class in counseling.* New York: Oxford University Press.

24. Shultz, K. S., & Adams, G. A. (2018). *Aging and work in the 21st century* (2nd ed.). New York: Routledge.

25. Nelson, T. (2016). The age of ageism. *Journal of Social Issues, 72,* 191–198. https://doi.org/10.1111/josi.12162;, Marcus, J., & Fritzsche, B. A. (2015). One size doesn't fit all: Toward a theory on the intersectional salience of ageism at work. *Organizational Psychology Review, 5,* 168–188. https://doi.org/10.1177/2041386614556015

26. Colella, A., & King, E. B. (Eds.). (2018). *The Oxford handbook of workplace discrimination.* New York: Oxford University Press. Retrieved November 29, 2018, from http://www.oxfordhandbooks.com/view/10.1093/oxfordhb/9780199363643.001.0001/oxfordhb-9780199363643; Jean, Y., & Feagin, J. (1998). *Double burden: Black women and everyday racism.* New York: Routledge.

27. Blustein, D. L. (2011). A relational theory of working. *Journal of Vocational Behavior, 79,* 1–17; Bowlby, J. (1988). *A secure base: Parent-child attachment and healthy human development.* New York: Basic Books; Jordan, J. M. (2009). *Relational-cultural therapy.* Washington, DC: American Psychological Association.

28. Helms, J. E. (Ed.). (1990). *Black and White racial identity: Theory, research, and practice.* New York: Greenwood Press; Helms, J. E., & Cook, D. A. (1999). *Using race and culture in counseling and psychotherapy: Theory and process.* Needham Heights, MA: Allyn & Bacon.

29. Carter, R. T., & Constantine, M. G. (2000). Career maturity, life role salience, and racial/ethnic identity in black and Asian American college students. *Journal of Career Assessment, 8,* 173–187. https://doi.org/10.1177/106907270000800206; Helms, J. E., & Piper, R. E. (1994). Implications of racial identity theory for vocational psychology. *Journal of Vocational Behavior. 44,* 124–138; Chavous, T., Bernat, D., Schmeelk-Cone, K., Caldwell, C., Kohn-Wood, L., & Zimmerman, M. (2003). Racial identity and academic attainment among African American adolescents. *Child Development, 74,* 1076–1090; Seaton, E., Scottham, K., & Sellers, R. (2006). The status model of racial identity development in African American adolescents: Evidence of structure, trajectories, and well-being. *Child Development, 77,* 1416–1426.

30. Liu, W. M., Soleck, G., Hopps, J., Dunston, K., & Pickett, T. (2004). A new framework to understand social class in counseling: The social class worldview and modern classism theory. *Journal of Multicultural Counseling and Development, 32,* 95–122; Liu, W. M., Ali, S. R., Soleck, G., Hopps, J., Dunston, K., & Pickett, T. (2004). Using social class in counseling psychology research. *Journal of Counseling Psychology, 51,* 3–18.

31. Liu, W. (2011). *Social class and classism in the helping professions research, theory, and practice.* Thousand Oaks, CA: Sage; Liu, W. (Ed.). (2013). *The Oxford handbook of social class in counseling.* New York: Oxford University Press.

32. Carter, R. T., & Pieterse, A. L. (2005). Race: A social and psychological analysis of the term and its meaning. In R. T. Carter (Ed.), *Handbook of racial-cultural psychology and counseling: Theory and research* (Vol. 1, pp. 41–63). Hoboken, NJ: Wiley; Helms, J. E., & Cook, D. A. (1999). *Using race and culture in counseling and psychotherapy: Theory and process*. Boston: Allyn & Bacon.

33. Carter, R. T. (2007). Racism and psychological and emotional injury: Recognizing and assessing race-based traumatic stress. *The Counseling Psychologist, 35*, 13–105. https://doi.org/10.1177/0011000006292033; Coates, T. (2015). *Between the world and me*. New York: Spiegel & Grau; Kendi, I. (2017). *Stamped from the beginning: The definitive history of racist ideas in America*. New York: Nation Books. (Original work published in 2016).

34. Carter, R. T., Forsyth, J., Mazzula, S., & Williams, B. (2005). Racial discrimination and race-based traumatic stress. In R. T. Carter (Ed.), *Handbook of racial-cultural psychology and counseling: Training and practice* (Vol. 2, pp. 447–476). New York: Wiley; Dovidio, J. F., & Gaertner, S. L. (1998). On the nature of contemporary prejudice: The causes, consequences and challenges of aversive racism. In S. T. Fiske & J. L. Eberhardt (Eds.), *Racism: The problem and the response* (pp. 123–134). Newbury Park, CA: Sage.

35. Betz, N., & Fitzgerald, L. (1987). *The career psychology of women*. Orlando, FL: Academic Press; Gordon, E. W. (1974). Vocational guidance: Disadvantaged and minority populations. In E. L. Herr (Ed.), *Vocational guidance and human development* (pp. 452–477). Boston: Houghton Mifflin; Helms, J. E., & Cook, D. A. (1999). *Using race and culture in counseling and psychotherapy: Theory and process*. Needham Heights, MA: Allyn & Bacon; Smith, E. J. (1983). Issues in racial minorities' career behavior. In W. B. Walsh & S. H. Osipow (Eds.), *Handbook of vocational psychology: Vol. 1, Foundations* (pp. 161–222). Hillsdale, NJ: Erlbaum.

36. Ali, S. R. (2013). Poverty, social class, and working. In D. L. Blustein (Ed.), *The Oxford handbook of the psychology of working* (pp. 127–140). New York: Oxford University Press; Roberson, Q. (Ed.). (2013). *The Oxford handbook of diversity and work*. New York: Oxford University Press; Walsh, W. B., & Heppner, M. (Eds.). (2006). *Handbook of career counseling for women* (2nd ed). Mahwah, NJ: Erlbaum; Byrd, M. Y., & Scott, C. L. (Eds.). (2014). *Diversity in the workforce: Current issues and emerging trends*. New York: Routledge.

37. Farmer, H. (1985). Model of career and achievement motivation for women and men. *Journal of Counseling Psychology 32*, 363–390; Harmon, L. W. (1981). The life and career plans of young adult college women: A follow-up study. *Journal of Counseling Psychology, 28*, 416–27. http://dx.doi.org/10.1037/0022-0167.28.5.416

38. Fabian, E. (2013). Disability and work. In D. L. Blustein (Ed.), *The Oxford handbook of the psychology of working* (pp. 185–200). New York: Oxford University Press.

39. Cole, E. (2009). Intersectionality and research in psychology. *American Psychologist, 64*(3), 170–180; Moradi, B., & Grzanka, P. R. (2017). Using intersectionality responsibly: Toward critical epistemology, structural analysis, and social justice activism. *Journal of Counseling Psychology, 64*, 500–513.

40. Ali, S. R. (2013). Poverty, social class, and working. In D. L. Blustein (Ed.), *The Oxford handbook of the psychology of working* (pp. 127–140). New York: Oxford University

Press; Smith, L. (2010). *Psychology, poverty, and the end of social exclusion: Putting our practice to work* (Vol. 7). New York: Teachers College Press; Stiglitz, J. (2015). *The great divide: Unequal societies and what we can do about them.* New York: Norton.

41. Flores, L. (2013). Race and working. In D. L. Blustein (Ed.), *The Oxford handbook of the psychology of working* (pp. 71–84). New York: Oxford University Press. doi:10.1093/oxfordhb/9780199758791.013.0001; Neville, H. A., Gallardo, M. E., & Sue, D. W. E. (Eds.). (2016). *The myth of racial color blindness: Manifestations, dynamics, and impact.* Washington, DC: American Psychological Association.

42. Helms, J. E. (2012). A legacy of eugenics underlies racial-group comparisons in intelligence testing. *Industrial and Organizational Psychology: Perspectives on Science and Practice, 5,* 176–179. doi:10.1111/j.1754-9434.2012.01426.x; Helms, J. E., Jernigan, M., & Mascher, J. (2005). The meaning of race in psychology and how to change it: A methodological perspective. *American Psychologist, 60,* 27–36. doi:10.1037/0003-066X.60.1.27; Suzuki, L. A., & Valencia, R. R. (1997). Race–ethnicity and measured intelligence: Educational implications. *American Psychologist, 52,* 1103–1114. http://dx.doi.org/10.1037/0003-066X.52.10.1103; Zuckerman, M. (1990). Some dubious premises in research and theory on racial differences: Scientific, social, and ethical issues. *American Psychologist, 45,* 1297–1303. http://dx.doi.org/10.1037/0003-066X.45.12.1297

43. Neville, H., Awad, G., Brooks, J., Flores, M., & Bluemel, J. (2013). Color-blind racial ideology: Theory, training, and measurement implications in psychology. *American Psychologist, 68,* 455–466; Neville, H. A., Gallardo, M. E., & Sue, D. W. E. (Eds.). (2016). *The myth of racial color blindness: Manifestations, dynamics, and impact.* Washington, DC: American Psychological Association.

44. Bureau of Labor Statistics. (2017). *Unemployment rate and employment-population ratio vary by race and ethnicity.* Retrieved from https://www.bls.gov/opub/ted/2017/unemployment-rate-and-employment-population-ratio-vary-by-race-and-ethnicity.htm; Flores, L. (2013). Race and working. In D. L. Blustein (Ed.), *The Oxford handbook of the psychology of working* (pp. 71–84). New York: Oxford University Press. doi:10.1093/oxfordhb/9780199758791.013.0001

45. Neville, H., Awad, G., Brooks, J., Flores, M., & Bluemel, J. (2013). Color-blind racial ideology: Theory, training, and measurement implications in psychology. *American Psychologist, 68,* 455–466.

46. Block, C. J. (2016). The impact of color-blind racial ideology on maintaining racial disparities in organizations. In H. A. Neville, M. E. Gallardo, & D. W. Sue (Eds.), *The myth of racial color blindness: Manifestations, dynamics, and impact* (pp. 243–259). Washington, DC: American Psychological Association.

47. Steele, C. M. (2011). *Whistling Vivaldi: And other clues to how stereotypes affect us (issues of our time).* New York: Norton.

48. Diemer, M. A. (2009). Pathways to occupational attainment among poor youth of color the role of sociopolitical development. *The Counseling Psychologist, 37,* 6–35. doi:10.1177/0011000007309858; Diemer, M. A., McWhirter, E. H., Ozer, E. J., & Rapa, L. J. (2015). Advances in the conceptualization and measurement of critical consciousness. *The Urban Review, 47,* 809–823; Freire, P. (1973). *Education for critical consciousness* (Vol. 1). New York: Bloomsbury; Freire, P. (2007). *Pedagogy of the oppressed* (3rd ed.). New York: Continuum International.

49. Freire, P. (1973). *Education for critical consciousness* (Vol. 1). New York: Bloomsbury; Freire, P. (2007). *Pedagogy of the oppressed* (3rd ed.). New York: Continuum International.

50. Diemer, M. A. (2009). Pathways to occupational attainment among poor youth of color the role of sociopolitical development. *The Counseling Psychologist, 37*, 6–35. doi:10.1177/0011000007309858.

51. Diemer, M. A., Rapa, L. J., Voight, A. M., & McWhirter, E. H. (2016). Critical consciousness: A developmental approach to addressing marginalization and oppression. *Child Development Perspectives, 10*, 216–221.

52. Diemer, M. A., Rapa, L. J., Voight, A. M., & McWhirter, E. H. (2016). Critical consciousness: A developmental approach to addressing marginalization and oppression. *Child Development Perspectives, 10*, 216–221. doi:10.1111/cdep.12193; Watts, R. J., Diemer, M. A., & Voight, A. M. (2011). Critical consciousness: Current status and future directions. *New Directions for Child and Adolescent Development, 134*, 43–57. doi:10.1002/cd.310

53. Freire, P. (1973). *Education for critical consciousness* (Vol. 1). New York: Bloomsbury; Watts, R. J., Diemer, M. A., & Voight, A. M. (2011). Critical consciousness: Current status and future directions. *New Directions for Child and Adolescent Development, 134*, 43–57. doi:10.1002/cd.310; Namulundah, F. (1998). *Bell hooks' engaged pedagogy: A transgressive education for critical consciousness.* Westport, CT: Bergin & Garvey; Watts, R. J., & Hipolito-Delgado, C. (2015). Thinking ourselves to liberation? Advancing sociopolitical action in critical consciousness. *Urban Review, 47*, 847–867. doi:10.1007/s11256-015-0341-x

54. Blustein, D. L. (2006). *The psychology of working: A new perspective for career development, counseling, and public policy.* New York: Routledge; Blustein, D. L., Kozan, S., Connors-Kellgren, A., & Rand, B. (2015). Social class and career intervention. In P. Hartung, M. L. Savickas, & W. B. Walsh (Eds.), *The APA handbook of career intervention* (pp. 242–257). Washington, DC: American Psychological Association.

55. Yu, N. (Ed.). (2018). *Consciousness-Raising.* London: Routledge; Watts, R. J., & Hipolito-Delgado, C. (2015). Thinking ourselves to liberation? Advancing sociopolitical action in critical consciousness. *Urban Review, 47*, 847–867. doi:10.1007/s11256-015-0341-x; El-Amin, A., Seider, S., Graves, D., Tamerat, J., Clark, S., Soutter, M., . . . Malhotra, S. (2017). Critical consciousness: A key to student achievement. *Phi Delta Kappan, 98*(5), 18–23. https://doi.org/10.1177/0031721717690360

Chapter 8

1. *The Institute for Career Transitions.* (2018, October 26). About. Retrieved from http://www.ictransitions.org/home-the-institute-for-career-transitions-ict/about-the-institute-for-career-transitions/

2. Lazear, E. P., & Spletzer, J. R. (2012). *Hiring, churn and the business cycle* (Report No. 17910). Cambridge, MA: National Bureau of Economic Research. Retrieved from

https://www.nber.org/papers/w17910.pdf; Chamberlain, A. (2016, December 10). *America's job churning machine.* Retrieved from https://medium.com/@andrew. chamberlain/americas-job-churning-53b0064ed44c

3. Krugman, P. (2012). *End this depression now!* New York: Norton; Piketty, T. (2014). *Capital in the twenty-first century.* Cambridge, MA: Belknap Press of Harvard University Press; Stiglitz, J. (2015). *The great divide: Unequal societies and what we can do about them.* New York: Norton.

4. Sharone, O. (2013). *Flawed system, flawed self: Job searching and unemployment experiences.* Chicago: University of Chicago Press.

5. Sharone, O. (2013). *Flawed system, flawed self: Job searching and unemployment experiences.* Chicago: University of Chicago Press.

6. Friedman, T. L. (2016). *Thank you for being late: An optimist's guide to thriving in the age of acceleration.* New York: Farrar, Straus and Giroux; Hyman, L. (2018). *TEMP: How American work, American business, and the American dream became temporary.* New York: Penguin-Random House; Kalleberg, A. L., & Vallas, S. P. (2017). Probing precarious work: Theory, research, and politics. In A. L. Kalleberg & S. P. Vallas (Eds.), *Precarious work* (pp. 1–30). Bingley, England: Emerald; Sharone, O. (2013). *Flawed system, flawed self: Job searching and unemployment experiences.* Chicago: University of Chicago Press; Stiglitz, J. (2015). *The great divide: Unequal societies and what we can do about them.* New York: Norton.

7. Brynjolfsson, E., & McAfee, A. (2014). *The second machine age: Work, progress, and prosperity in a time of brilliant technologies.* New York: Norton; Ford, M. (2015). *Rise of the robots: Technology and the threat of a jobless future.* New York: Basic Books; National Academy of Sciences. (2017). *Information technology and the US workforce: Where are we and where do we go from here?* Washington, DC: Author. doi:10.17226/24649

8. Hyman, L. (2018). *TEMP: How American work, American business, and the American dream became temporary.* New York: Penguin-Random House; Kalleberg, A. L., & Vallas, S. P. (2017). Probing precarious work: Theory, research, and politics. In A. L. Kalleberg & S. P. Vallas (Eds.), *Precarious work* (pp. 1–30). Bingley, England: Emerald; Blustein, D. L., Connors-Kellgren, A., Olle, C., & Diamonti, A. (2017). Promising career and workforce development practices in supporting the needs of unemployed populations. In V. S. Solberg & S. Ali (Eds.), *Handbook of career and workforce development: Practice and policy* (pp. 97–123). New York: Routledge.

9. Blustein, D. L., Kozan, S., & Connors-Kellgren, A. (2013). Unemployment and underemployment: A narrative analysis about loss. *Journal of Vocational Behavior, 82,* 256–265; Blustein, D. L., Connors-Kellgren, A., Olle, C., & Diamonti, A. (2017). Promising career and workforce development practices in supporting the needs of unemployed populations. In V. S. Solberg & S. Ali (Eds.), *Handbook of career and workforce development: Practice and policy* (pp. 97–123). New York: Routledge; Herbert, B. (2014). *Losing our way: An intimate portrait of a troubled America.* New York: Penguin-Random House.

10. Brynjolfsson, E., & McAfee, A. (2014). *The second machine age: Work, progress, and prosperity in a time of brilliant technologies.* New York: Norton; Ford, M. (2015).

Rise of the robots: Technology and the threat of a jobless future. New York: Basic Books; National Academy of Sciences. (2017). *Information technology and the US workforce: Where are we and where do we go from here?* Washington, DC: Author. doi:10.17226/24649

11. Goldberg, E. M., & Morrison, S. L. (1988). Schizophrenia and social class. In C. Buck, A. Llopis, E. Najera, & M. Terris (Eds.), *The challenge of epidemiology: Issues and selected readings* (pp. 368–383). Washington, DC: Pan American Health Organization.

12. Mossakowski, K. N. (2014). Social causation and social selection. In W. C. Cockerham, R. Dingwall, & S. Quah (Eds.), *The Wiley Blackwell encyclopedia of health, illness, behavior, and society* (pp. 2154–2160). New York: Wiley; Paul, K. I., & Moser, K. (2009). Unemployment impairs mental health: Meta-analyses. *Journal of Vocational Behavior, 74,* 264–282; Wanberg, C. R. (2012). The individual experience of unemployment. *Annual Review of Psychology, 63,* 369–396.

13. Jahoda, M. (1981). Work, employment, and unemployment: Values, theories, and approaches in social research. *American Psychologist, 36,* 184–191. doi.org/10.1037/0003-066X.36.2.184; Jahoda, M. (1982). *Employment and unemployment.* Cambridge, England: University Press.

14. Blustein, D. L. (Ed.). (2013). *The Oxford handbook of the psychology of working.* New York: Oxford University Press; Blustein, D. L., Connors-Kellgren, A., Olle, C., & Diamonti, A. (2017). Promising career and workforce development practices in supporting the needs of unemployed populations. In V. S. Solberg & S. Ali (Eds.), *Handbook of career and workforce development: Practice and policy* (pp. 97–123). New York: Routledge; O'Brien, G. E. (1986). *Psychology of work and unemployment.* New York: Wiley.

15. Autin, K. L., Duffy, R. D., Blustein, D. L., Gensmer, N. P., Douglass, R. P., England, J. W., & Allan, B. A. (2019). The development and initial validation of the Work Needs Satisfaction Scale: Measuring basic needs within the psychology of working theory. *Journal of Counseling Psychology, 66, 195-209;* ; Blustein, D. L. (2008). The role of work in psychological health and well-being: A conceptual, historical, and public policy perspective. *American Psychologist, 6,* 228–240; Wanberg, C. R. (2012). The individual experience of unemployment. *Annual Review of Psychology, 63,* 369–396.

16. Paul, K. I., & Moser, K. (2009). Unemployment impairs mental health: Meta-analyses. *Journal of Vocational Behavior, 74,* 264–282.

17. Blustein, D. L., Connors-Kellgren, A., Olle, C., & Diamonti, A. (2017). Promising career and workforce development practices in supporting the needs of unemployed populations. In V. S. Solberg & S. Ali (Eds.), *Handbook of career and workforce development: Practice and policy* (pp. 97–123). New York: Routledge; Wanberg, C. R. (2012). The individual experience of unemployment. *Annual Review of Psychology, 63,* 369–396.

18. Heppner, M. J. (2013). Women, men, and work: The long journey to gender equity. In S. D. Brown & R. W. Lent (Eds.), *Career development and counseling: Putting theory and research to work* (2nd ed., pp. 187–214). Hoboken, NJ: Wiley; Mahalik, J.

R., Good, G. E., Tager, D., Levant, R. F., & Mackowiak, C. (2012). Developing a taxonomy of helpful and harmful practices for clinical work with boys and men. *Journal
of Counseling Psychology, 59,* 591–603; Addis, M. E., & James R Mahalik, J. R. (2003).
Men, masculinity, and the contexts of help seeking. *American Psychologist, 58,* 5–14.
doi:/10.1037/0003-066X.58.1.5

19. Sharone, O., Blustein, D. L., & Van Horn, C. E. (2018). Long-term unemployment
     in the United States. In J. Trevino (Ed.), *Cambridge handbook of social problems* (pp.
     551–566). New York: Cambridge University Press; Wanberg, C. R. (2012). The indi-
     vidual experience of unemployment. *Annual Review of Psychology, 63,* 369–396.

20. Bartley, M. (2018). Unemployment and mental health. In D. Bhugra, K. Bhui, S.
     Y. Shan Wong, & S. E. Gilman (Eds.), *Oxford textbook of public mental health* (pp.
     144–50). Oxford, England: Oxford University Press; Strandh, M., Winefield, A.,
     Nilsson, K., & Hammarström, A. (2014). Unemployment and mental health scarring
     during the life course. *European Journal of Public Health, 24,* 440–5. doi.org/10.1093/
     eurpub/cku005; McKee-Ryan, F., Song, Z., Wanberg, R. C., & Kinicki, A. J. (2005).
     Psychological and physical well-being during unemployment: A meta-analytic
     study. *Journal of Applied Psychology, 90,* 53–76.

21. Bentley, J. (1984). *Martin Niemöller: 1892–1984.* New York: Macmillan Free Press.

22. Bolles, R. N. (2018). *What color is your parachute?* Emeryville, CA: Ten Speed
     Press.

23. Bourdieu, P. (1984). *Distinction: A social critique of the judgment of taste.*
     New York: Routledge Classics; Sharone, O. (2013). *Flawed system, flawed self: Job
     searching and unemployment experiences.* Chicago: University of Chicago Press.

24. Blustein, D. L., Kozan, S., & Connors-Kellgren, A. (2013). Unemployment and un-
     deremployment: A narrative analysis about loss. *Journal of Vocational Behavior, 82,*
     256–265; Gabriel, Y., Gray, D. E., & Goregaokar, H. (2010). Temporary derailment
     or the end of the line? Managers coping with unemployment at 50. *Organization
     Studies, 21,* 1687–1712.

25. Hyman, L. (2018). *TEMP: How American work, American business, and the
     American dream became temporary.* New York: Penguin-Random House; Kalleberg,
     A. L., & Vallas, S. P. (2017). Probing precarious work: Theory, research, and pol-
     itics. In A. L. Kalleberg & S. P. Vallas (Eds.), *Precarious work* (pp. 1–30). Bingley,
     England: Emerald.

26. Kalleberg, A. L., & Vallas, S. P. (2017). Probing precarious work: Theory, research,
     and politics. In A. L. Kalleberg & S. P. Vallas (Eds.), *Precarious work* (pp. 1–30).
     Bingley, England: Emerald; Standing, G. (2014). *A precariat charter: From denizens
     to citizens.* New York: Bloomsbury.

27. Bowlby, J. (1988). *A secure base: Parent-child attachment and healthy human develop-
     ment.* New York: Basic Books; Hurvich, M. (2003). The place of annihilation anxieties
     in psychoanalytic theory. *Journal of the American Psychoanalytic Association, 51*(2),
     579–616; Maslow, A. (1968). *Toward a psychology of being* (2nd ed.). New York: Van
     Nostrand Reinhold.

28. Paul, K. I., & Moser, K. (2009). Unemployment impairs mental health: Meta-
     analyses. *Journal of Vocational Behavior, 74,* 264–282.

Chapter 9

1. Blustein, D. L. (Ed.). (2013). *The Oxford handbook of the psychology of working.* New York: Oxford University Press; Di Fabio, A., Blustein, D. L. (Eds.). (2016). *From meaning of working to meaningful lives: The challenges of expanding decent work.* Lausanne, Switzerland: Frontiers Media. doi:10.3389/978-2-88919-970-9; International Labor Organization. (2018). *World employment social outlook: Trends 2018.* Geneva, Switzerland: Author; Organization for Economic Cooperation and Development. (2015). *Securing livelihoods for all: Foresight for action.* Development Centre Studies. Paris: Author. doi:10.1787/9789264231894-en

2. International Labor Organization. (1999). *Report of the director-general: Decent work. International Labour Conference, 87° Session.* Geneva, Switzerland: Author; International Labor Organization. (2008). *ILO declaration on social justice for a fair globalization.* Retrieved from http://www.ilo.org/wcmsp5/groups/public/ ---dgreports/---cabinet/documents/genericdocument/wcms_371208.pdf; International Labor Organization (2018). *World employment social outlook: Trends 2018.* Geneva, Switzerland: Author.

3. Blustein, D. L. (2006). *The psychology of working: A new perspective for career development, counseling and public policy.* New York: Routledge; Duffy, R. D., Blustein, D. L., Diemer, M. A., & Autin, K. L. (2016). The psychology of working theory. *Journal of Counseling Psychology, 63,* 127–148. doi:10.1037/cou0000140; Linley, P. A., Harrington, S., & Garcea, N. (Eds.). (2013). *The Oxford handbook of positive psychology and work.* New York: Oxford University Press.

4. Guichard, J. (2009). Self-constructing. *Journal of Vocational Behavior, 75,* 251–8; Savickas, M. L. (2011). The self in vocational psychology: Object, subject, and project. In P. J. Hartung & L. M. Subich (Eds.), *Developing self in work and career: Concepts, cases, and contexts* (pp. 17–33). Washington, DC: American Psychological Association.

5. Flum, H. (2015). Relationships and career development: An integrative approach. In P. J. Hartung, M. L. Savickas, & B. W. Walsh (Eds.), *APA handbook of career intervention, Volume 1: Foundations* (pp. 145–58). Washington, DC: American Psychological Association. doi:10.1037/14438-009

6. Blustein, D. L., Masdonati, J., & Rossier, J. (2017). *Psychology and the International Labor Organization: The role of psychology in the Decent Work Agenda* [White Paper]. Retrieved from https://www.ilo.org/global/research/publications/WCMS_561013/ lang--en/index.htm; Praskova, A., Creed, P. A., & Hood, M. (2015). Career identity and the complex mediating relationships between career preparatory actions and career progress markers. *Journal of Vocational Behavior, 87,* 145–153. https://doi.org/ 10.1016/j.jvb.2015.01.001

7. International Labor Organization. (2018). *World employment social outlook: Trends 2018.* Geneva, Switzerland: Author; Organization for Economic Cooperation and Development. (2015). *Securing livelihoods for all: Foresight for action.* Development Centre Studies. Paris: Author. doi:10.1787/9789264231894-en

8. Folbre, N. (Ed.). (2012). *For love and money: Care provision in the United States.* New York: Russell Sage Foundation; Richardson, M. S., & Schaefer, C. (2013). From work and family to a dual model of working. In D. L. Blustein (Ed.), *The Oxford handbook of the psychology of working* (pp. 141–59). New York: Oxford University Press.

9. Miller, A. (1976). *Death of a salesman.* London: Penguin Books; Springsteen, B. (2001). *Bruce Springsteen songs.* New York: Harper Entertainment; Steinbeck, J. (1939). *The grapes of wrath.* New York: Viking; Ward, D. C. (2017). *The sweat of their face: Portraying American workers.* Washington, DC: Smithsonian Books.

10. National Academy of Sciences. (2017). *Information technology and the US workforce: Where are we and where do we go from here?* Washington, DC: Author. doi:10.17226/24649; Organization for Economic Cooperation and Development. (2015). *Securing livelihoods for all: Foresight for action.* Development Centre Studies. Paris: Author. doi:10.1787/9789264231894-en

11. Blustein, D. L., Chaves, A. P. Diemer, M. A., Gallagher, L. A., Marshall, K. G., Sirin, S., & Bhati, K. S. (2002). Voices of the "forgotten half": The role of social class in the school-to-work transition. *Journal of Counseling Psychology, 49,* 311–323; Diemer, M. A. (2009). Pathways to occupational attainment among poor youth of color the role of sociopolitical development. *The Counseling Psychologist, 37,* 6–35. doi:10.1177/0011000007309858; Marfleet, P., & Blustein, D. L. (2011). "Needed not wanted": Irregular migrants and the world of work. *Journal of Vocational Behavior, 78,* 381–389; Ribeiro, M. A. (2015). Contemporary patterns of career construction of a group of urban workers in São Paulo (Brazil). *Journal of Vocational Behavior, 88,* 19–27.

12. Kalleberg, A. L., & Vallas, S. P. (2017). Probing precarious work: Theory, research, and politics. In A. L. Kalleberg & S. P. Vallas (Eds.), *Precarious work* (pp. 1–30). Bingley, England: Emerald; Standing, G. (2014). *A precariat charter: From denizens to citizens.* New York: Bloomsbury.

13. Donkin, R. (2010). *The history of work.* New York: Springer.

14. Kalleberg, A. L., & Vallas, S. P. (2017). Probing precarious work: Theory, research, and politics. In A. L. Kalleberg & S. P. Vallas (Eds.), *Precarious work* (pp. 1–30). Bingley, England: Emerald; Standing, G. (2014). *A precariat charter: From denizens to citizens.* New York: Bloomsbury.

15. Blustein, D. L., Kozan, S., & Connors-Kellgren, A. (2013). Unemployment and underemployment: A narrative analysis about loss. *Journal of Vocational Behavior, 82,* 256–265.

16. Fouad, N. A., Singh, R., Cappaert, K., Chang, W. H., & Wan, M. (2016). Comparison of women engineers who persist in or depart from engineering. *Journal of Vocational Behavior, 92,* 79–93. doi:10.1016/j.jvb.2015.11.002; Burke, R. J., & Page, K. M. (Eds.). (2017). *Research handbook on work and well being.* Northampton, MA: Elgar. doi:10.4337/9781785363269; Wilson, W. J. (1996). *When work disappears: The world of the new urban poor.* New York: Knopf.

17. Herbert, B. (2014). *Losing our way: An intimate portrait of a troubled America.* New York: Penguin-Random House; Putnam, R. D. (2016). *Our kids: The American Dream in crisis.* New York: Simon & Schuster.

18. Sen, A. (1999). *Development as freedom*. New York: Knopf.
19. Duffy, R. D., Blustein, D. L., Diemer, M. A., & Autin, K. L. (2016). The psychology of working theory. *Journal of Counseling Psychology, 63*, 127–148; Fouad, N. A., & Bynner, J. (2008). Work transitions. *American Psychologist, 63*, 241–251. doi:10.1037/0003-006X.63.4.241; Lent, R. W., Brown, S. D., & Hackett, G. (1994). Toward a unifying social cognitive theory of career and academic interest, choice, and performance. *Journal of Vocational Behavior, 45*, 79–122. doi: 10.1006/jvbe.1994.1027
20. Sen, A. (1999). *Development as freedom*. New York: Knopf.
21. Lent, R. W., Brown, S. D., & Hackett, G. (1994). Toward a unifying social cognitive theory of career and academic interest, choice, and performance. *Journal of Vocational Behavior, 45*, 79–122; Lent, R. W., & Brown, S. D. (2013). Social cognitive model of career self-management: Toward a unifying view of adaptive career behavior across the life span. *Journal of Counseling Psychology, 60*, 557–568. doi:/10.1037/a0033446; Richardson, M. S. (2012). Counseling for work and relationships. *The Counseling Psychologist, 40*, 190–242. doi:10.1177/0011000011406452
22. Heckman, J. J. (2006). Skill formation and the economics of investing in disadvantaged children. *Science, 312*(5782), 1900–1902. doi:10.1126/science.1128898; Lerner, R. M. (2018). *Concepts and theories of human development* (3rd ed.). New York: Routledge.
23. Paul, K. I., & Moser, K. (2009). Unemployment impairs mental health: Meta-analyses. *Journal of Vocational Behavior, 74*, 264–282. doi:10.1016/j.jvb.2009.01.001; Wanberg, C. R. (2012). The individual experience of unemployment. *Annual Review of Psychology, 63*, 369–396. doi:/10.1146/annurev-psych-120710-100500
24. Kalleberg, A. (2009). Precarious work, insecure workers: Employment relations in transition. *American Sociological Review, 74*, 1–22. doi:10.1177/000312240907400101; Kalleberg, A. L., & Vallas, S. P. (2017). Probing precarious work: Theory, research, and politics. In A. L. Kalleberg & S. P. Vallas (Eds.), *Precarious work* (pp. 1–30). Bingley, England: Emerald; Smith, L. (2015). Reforming the minimum wage: Toward a psychological perspective. *American Psychologist, 70*, 557–565. doi:10.1037/a0039579; Stiglitz, J. (2015). *The great divide: Unequal societies and what we can do about them*. New York: Norton. doi:/10.1037/a0039579; Van Horn, C. E. (2014). *Working scared (or not at all): The lost decade, the Great Recession, and restoring the shattered American dream*. Lanham, MD: Rowman & Littlefield. doi:/10.5860/choice.50-6864; Wanberg, C. R. (2012). The individual experience of unemployment. *Annual Review of Psychology, 63*, 369–396. doi:/10.1146/annurev-psych-120710-100500
25. Kalleberg, A. L., & Vallas, S. P. (2017). Probing precarious work: Theory, research, and politics. In A. L. Kalleberg & S. P. Vallas (Eds.), *Precarious work* (pp. 1–30). Bingley, England: Emerald; Stiglitz, J. (2015). *The great divide: Unequal societies and what we can do about them*. New York: Norton. doi:/10.1037/a0039579
26. Sharone, O. (2013). *Flawed system, flawed self: Job searching and unemployment experiences*. Chicago: University of Chicago Press.
27. Herbert, B. (2014). *Losing our way: An intimate portrait of a troubled America*. New York: Penguin-Random House; Putnam, R. D. (2016). *Our kids: The American*

dream in crisis. New York: Simon & Schuster; Vance, J. D. (2018). *Hillbilly elegy: A memoir of a family and culture in crisis.* Farmington Hills, MI: Large Print Press.

28. Bolles, R. N. (2018). *What color is your parachute? 2018: A practical manual for job-hunters and career-changers.* Emeryville, CA: Ten Speed Press; Gottman, J. M., & Silver, N. (2018). *The seven principles for making marriage work: A practical guide from the country's foremost relationship expert.* New York: Harmony Books; Orsillo, S. M., & Roemer, L. (2011). *The mindful way through anxiety: Break free from chronic worry and reclaim your life.* New York: Guilford Press; Williams, J. M., & Kabat-Zinn, J. (2007). *The mindful way through depression: Freeing yourself from chronic unhappiness.* New York: Guilford Press.

29. Orsillo, S. M., & Roemer, L. (2011). *The mindful way through anxiety: Break free from chronic worry and reclaim your life.* New York: Guilford Press; Williams, J. M., & Kabat-Zinn, J. (2007). *The mindful way through depression: Freeing yourself from chronic unhappiness.* New York: Guilford Press.

30. Sharone, O. (2013). *Flawed system, flawed self: Job searching and unemployment experiences.* Chicago: University of Chicago Press.

31. Diemer, M. A., Rapa, L. J., Voight, A. M., & McWhirter, E. H. (2016). Critical consciousness: A developmental approach to addressing marginalization and oppression. *Child Development Perspectives, 10,* 216–221.

32. Herbert, B. (2014). *Losing our way: An intimate portrait of a troubled America.* New York: Penguin-Random House; Putnam, R. D. (2016). *Our kids: The American dream in crisis.* New York: Simon & Schuster; Wilson, W. J. (1996). *When work disappears: The world of the new urban poor.* New York: Knopf.

33. Blustein, D. L., Connors-Kellgren, A., Olle, C., & Diamonti, A. (2017). Promising career and workforce development practices in supporting the needs of unemployed populations. In V. S. Solberg & S. Ali (Eds.), *Handbook of career and workforce development: Practice and policy* (pp. 97–123). New York: Routledge.

34. Brown, S. D., Ryan Krane, N. E., Brecheisen, J., Castelino, P., Budisin, I., Miller, M., & Edens, L. (2003). Critical ingredients of career choice interventions: More analyses and new hypotheses. *Journal of Vocational Behavior, 62,* 411–428; Whiston, S. C., Li, Y., Mitts, N. G., & Wright, L. (2017). Effectiveness of career choice interventions: A meta-analytic replication and extension. *Journal of Vocational Behavior, 100,* 175–184.

35. Brown, S. D., & Lent, R. W. (Eds.). (2013). *Career development and counselling: Putting theory and research to work.* Hoboken, NJ: Wiley; Savickas, M. L. (2012). Life design: A paradigm for career interventions in the 21st century. *Journal of Counseling and Development, 90,* 13–19; Savickas, M. L. (2013). Career construction theory and practice. In S. D. Brown & R. W. Lent (Eds.), *Career development and counseling: Putting theory and research to work* (2nd ed., pp. 42–70). Hoboken, NJ: Wiley. doi:/10.4135/9781412952675.n34

36. Blustein, D. L. (2006). *The psychology of working: A new perspective for career development, counseling, and public policy.* New York: Routledge; Friedman, T. L. (2016). *Thank you for being late: An optimist's guide to thriving in the age of accelerations.* New York: Picador.

37. Friedman, T. L. (2016). *Thank you for being late: An optimist's guide to thriving in the age of accelerations.* New York: Picador.

38. Mayseless, O. (2016). *The caring motivation: An integrated theory.* New York: Oxford University Press; Prilleltensky, I. (1997). Values, assumptions, and practices: Assessing the moral implications of psychological discourse and action. *American Psychologist, 52,* 517–535.

39. Blustein, D. L., Kenny, M. E., Di Fabio, A., & Guichard, J. (2018). Expanding the impact of the psychology of working: Engaging psychology in the struggle for decent work and human rights. *Journal of Career Assessment, 27,* 3–28. https://doi.org/10.1177/1069072718774002

40. McArthur, J., & Rasmussen, K. (2017). *How successful were the Millennium Development Goals?* Washington, DC: Brookings. Retrieved from https://www.brookings.edu/blog/future-development/2017/01/11/how-successful-were-the-millennium-development-goals/; United Nations. (2015). *The Millennium Development Goals report.* New York: Author. Retrieved from http://www.un.org/millenniumgoals/2015_MDG_Report/pdf/MDG%202015%20rev%20(July%201).pdf

41. Hooley, T., Sultana, R. G., & Thomsen, R. (Eds.). (2018). *Career guidance for social justice: Contesting Neoliberalism.* New York: Routledge; Kalleberg, A. L., & Vallas, S. P. (2017). Probing precarious work: Theory, research, and politics. In A. L. Kalleberg & S. P. Vallas (Eds.), *Precarious work* (pp. 1–30). Bingley, England: Emerald; Piketty, T. (2014). *Capital in the 21st century.* Cambridge, MA: Harvard University Press; Stiglitz, J. (2015). *The great divide: Unequal societies and what we can do about them.* New York: Norton.

42. Hooley, T., Sultana, R. G., & Thomsen, R. (Eds.). (2018). *Career guidance for social justice: Contesting Neoliberalism.* New York: Routledge; Kalleberg, A. L., & Vallas, S. P. (2017). Probing precarious work: Theory, research, and politics. In A. L. Kalleberg & S. P. Vallas (Eds.), *Precarious work* (pp. 1–30). Bingley, England: Emerald.

43. Hooley, T., Sultana, R. G., & Thomsen, R. (Eds.). (2018). *Career guidance for social justice: Contesting neoliberalism.* New York: Routledge; Kalleberg, A. L., & Vallas, S. P. (2017). Probing precarious work: Theory, research, and politics. In A. L. Kalleberg & S. P. Vallas (Eds.), *Precarious work* (pp. 1–30). Bingley, England: Emerald; Prilletensky, I., & Stead, G. (2012). Critical psychology, well-being, and work. In D. L. Blustein (Ed.), *The Oxford handbook of the psychology of working* (pp. 19–36). New York: Oxford University Press; Smith, L. (2010). *Psychology, poverty, and the end of social exclusion: Putting our practice to work* (Vol. 7). New York: Teachers College Press.

44. Frey, C. B., & Osbourne, M. A. (2013). *The future of employment: How susceptible are jobs to computerisation.* Working paper, Oxford Martin Progamme on the Impacts of Future Technology. Retrieved from http://www.oxfordmartin.ox.ac.uk/downloads/academic/The_Future_of_Employment.pdf; National Academy of Sciences. (2017). *Information technology and the US workforce: Where are we and where do we go from here?* Washington, DC: Author. doi:10.17226/24649; Organization for Economic

Cooperation and Development. (2015). *Securing livelihoods for all: Foresight for action*. Development Centre Studies. Paris: Author. doi:10.1787/9789264231894-en

45. National Academy of Sciences. (2017). *Information technology and the US Workforce: Where are we and where do we go from here?* Washington, DC: Author. doi:10.17226/24649

46. Parijs, P. V., & Vanderborght, Y. (2017). *Basic income: A radical proposal for a free society and a sane economy*. Cambridge, MA: Harvard University Press; Widerquist, K. (2019). *A critical analysis of basic income experiments for researchers, policymakers, and citizens (exploring the basic income guarantee)*. London: Palgrave Pivot.

47. Bosch, G. (2017). *Can a universal basic income resolve future income security challenges?* [Powerpoint slides]. Retrieved from https://www.ilo.org/wcmsp5/groups/public/---dgreports/---inst/documents/presentation/wcms_562866.pdf; European Social Survey, ESS. (n.d.). *The future of welfare: Basic income?* Retrieved from http://www.europeansocialsurvey.org/about/news/essnews0037.html

48. Brand, J. E. (2015). The far-reaching impact of job loss and unemployment. *Annual Review of Sociology, 41*, 359–375. doi:10.1146/071913-043237; Rodgers, G., Swepston, L., Lee, E., & Van Daele, J. (2009). *The International Labour Organization and the quest for social justice, 1919–2009*, Geneva, Switzerland: International Labour Office. Retrieved from https://www.ilo.org/wcmsp5/groups/public/---dgreports/---dcomm/---publ/documents/publication/wcms_104643.pdf; International Labor Organization. (2018). *World employment social outlook: Trends 2018*. Geneva, Switzerland: Author; Wilson, W. J. (1996). *When work disappears: The world of the new urban poor*. New York: Knopf.

49. Blustein, D. L. (2008). The role of work in psychological health and well-being. *American Psychologist, 63*, 228–240. doi:10.1037/0003-066X.63.4.228; Lent, R. W., & Brown, S. D. (2008). Social cognitive career theory and subjective well-being in the context of work. *Journal of Career Assessment, 16*, 6–21; Swanson, J. L. (2012). Work and psychological health. In N. A. Fouad, J. A. Carter, & L. M. Subich (Eds.), *APA handbook of counseling psychology, Vol. 2: Practice, interventions, and applications* (pp. 3–27). Washington, DC: American Psychological Association.

50. Kenny, M. E. (2013). The promise of work as a component of educational reform. In D. L. Blustein (Ed.), *The Oxford handbook of the psychology of working* (pp. 273–291). New York: Oxford University Press. doi:10.1093/oxfordhb/9780199758791.013.0016; Patrinos, H. A. (2018). *Education and economic development: Five reforms that have worked*. Retrieved from http://blogs.worldbank.org/education/education-and-economic-development-five-reforms-have-worked;, Education Development Center. (2017). *Building the foundational skills needed for success in work at the human-technology frontier* [White paper]. Waltham, MA: EDC. Retrieved from https://www.edc.org/sites/default/files/uploads/HumanTechnology FrontierWhitePaper.pdf

51. Organization for Economic Cooperation and Development. (2015). *Securing livelihoods for all: Foresight for action*. Development Centre Studies. Paris: Author. doi:10.1787/9789264231894-en

52. Brynjolfsson, E., & McAfee, A. (2014). *The second machine age: Work, progress, and prosperity in a time of brilliant technologies.* New York: Norton; Pink, D. H. (2012). *A whole new mind: Why right-brainers will rule the future.* New York: Riverhead Books; Friedman, T. L. (2016). *Thank you for being late: An optimist's guide to thriving in the age of accelerations.* New York: Picador.

53. Folbre, N. (Ed.). (2012). *For love and money: Care provision in the United States.* New York: Russell Sage Foundation; Osterman, P. (2017). *Who will care for us: Long-term care and the long-term workforce.* New York: Russell Sage Foundation.

Index

Note: Figures are indicated by an italic *f* following the page number.